A PLUME BOOK

THE NEATEST LITTLE GUIDE TO STOCK MARKET INVESTING

JASON KELLY graduated in 1993 from the University of Colorado at Boulder with a bachelor of arts in English. He worked for several years at IBM's Silicon Valley Laboratory, where he wrote articles and books that won him the Society for Technical Communications Merit Award. He moved from writing about computers to writing about finance, and found his niche in the stock market. Having realized his dream of being able to live and work anywhere in the world, Jason moved to Japan in 2002 and works from his office in the countryside about two hours from Tokyo. After the March 2011 earthquake and tsunami, he founded Socks for Japan, a volunteer organization that hand-delivered 160,000 care packages from around the world to survivors. He keeps busy writing new books and *The Kelly Letter*, and exploring Japan. With his sister and business partner, Emily, he co-owns Red Frog Coffee in Longmont, Colorado. Visit his website at www.jasonkelly.com.

"*The Neatest Little Guide* stands alone. There is no other book on the market like this one."

—Michael H. Sherman, chairman,
Sierra Global Management LLC,
on *The Neatest Little Guide to Mutual Fund Investing*

D0954519

THE
Neatest Little
Guide to
Stock Market
Investing

2013 EDITION

JASON KELLY

A PLUME BOOK

PLUME
Published by the Penguin Group
Penguin Group (USA) Inc., 375 Hudson Street, New York, New York 10014, U.S.A. • Penguin Group (Canada), 90 Eglinton Avenue East, Suite 700, Toronto, Ontario, Canada M4P 2Y3 (a division of Pearson Penguin Canada Inc.) • Penguin Books Ltd., 80 Strand, London WC2R 0RL, England • Penguin Ireland, 25 St. Stephen's Green, Dublin 2, Ireland (a division of Penguin Books Ltd.) • Penguin Group (Australia), 707 Collins Street, Melbourne, Victoria 3008, Australia (a division of Pearson Australia Group Pty. Ltd.) • Penguin Books India Pvt. Ltd., 11 Community Centre, Panchsheel Park, New Delhi – 110 017, India • Penguin Group (NZ), 67 Apollo Drive, Rosedale, Auckland 0632, New Zealand (a division of Pearson New Zealand Ltd.) • Penguin Books, Rosebank Office Park, 181 Jan Smuts Avenue, Parktown North 2193, South Africa • Penguin China, B7 Jaiming Center, 27 East Third Ring Road North, Chaoyang District, Beijing 100020, China

Penguin Books Ltd., Registered Offices: 80 Strand, London WC2R 0RL, England

First published by Plume, a member of Penguin Group (USA) Inc.

First Printing, January 1998
First printing (revised edition), January 2004
First printing (second revised edition), January 2008
First printing (third revised edition), January 2010
First printing (fourth revised edition), January 2013
10 9 8 7 6 5 4 3 2

LIBRARY OF CONGRESS CATALOGING-IN-PUBLICATION DATA

CIP data is available.
ISBN 978-0-452-29862-0

Printed in the United States of America

Ten Steps to Investing in Stocks

Contents

Acknowledgments

I'm fortunate to work with a wonderful team of people.

Doris Michaels remains the only agent I've ever had, and it's a joy to still work with her after all these years.

I'm not the only one who took a liking to Doris. Charlie Michaels met her first and married her. He is president of Sierra Global Management, LLC, a hedge fund company in New York City. Charlie's thorough understanding of the stock market helped with the first edition of this book, and his comments have provided the last word in each subsequent edition.

This book is packed full of content from many fine people and organizations. Thanks to Bill Miller, one of the best mutual fund managers in the business who took time to speak with me over the phone and review the material I wrote about him, and answer questions from subscribers to *The Kelly Letter*. Thanks to Morningstar, Standard & Poor's, Value Line, and Yahoo! Finance for supplying me with all the data I requested, and to OnlineTradingConcepts.com and StockCharts.com for supplying the charts I requested.

Finally, a nod of gratitude to the swell folks at Plume. My editor, Kate Napolitano, understood the spirit of past editions and helped me make this one a fine mixture of fresh material in a familiar voice. The people who've cared for this title through the years have been a pleasure to know, and I'm happy to count Kate among them. She's a delightful partner.

Foreword:
This Book Always Works

The advice in this book works. It keeps you out of dangerous stocks and shows you how to find good stocks that make money over time.

I wrote the first edition in 1996 and 1997, just before the market began its steep ascent into the bubble of the century. Back then, Enron and WorldCom were talked about as must-own companies and the Internet was expected to put so-called old economy companies like Wal-Mart out of business. Who would walk the aisles of a store when they could shop online in their pajamas?

Plenty of us, evidently. In the years following this book's first publication to early 2012, Wal-Mart stock tripled while most Internet start-ups disappeared and Enron and WorldCom declared bankruptcy. In 2011, Wal-Mart's annual sales were $450 billion. The two leading Internet merchants at that time, Amazon.com and eBay, had annual sales of only $48 billion and $12 billion, respectively.

The subprime crash of 2008 destroyed famous companies like AIG (-97 percent), Bear Stearns (-100 percent), Lehman Brothers (-100 percent), and General Motors (-100 percent). Wal-Mart stock, however, *gained* 20 percent in 2008. It increased sales and cash flow per share in every one of the previous 10 years, and did so again in 2008, 2009, 2010, and 2011. Had you invested $10,000 in Wal-Mart at the beginning of 1975, it would have been worth $60 million at the end of 2011 thanks to the company's steady growth and nine 2-for-1 stock splits.

This book would have kept you out of Enron, WorldCom, the dot-com disasters, and the likes of Lehman Brothers. It would not have kept you out of the market's volatility, and no approach to stocks will. The market *is* volatile in the short term and rises over the long term.

On that path, you want companies like Wal-Mart working for your money. This book shows you how to find them. Its methods win in flat markets, rising markets, and falling markets because superior companies always come out on top.

Invest in them and you'll come out on top, too.

I also present a value-averaging technique that produces steady 3 percent quarterly growth, and bold index strategies for beating the market over time. The Dow dividend strategies and my doubling strategies for the Dow and S&P MidCap 400 offer excellent profit potential. When combined with methods to limit market weakness, they work wonders on your wealth.

This book is packed with advice that you can use right away. Read it, follow it, and watch your net worth grow.

THE

Neatest Little
Guide to
Stock Market
Investing

1
Speak the Language of Stocks

Anybody can make money in the stock market. By picking up the phone or turning on the computer, you can own a piece of a company—and all of its fortune or folly—without ever attending a board meeting, developing a product, or devising a marketing strategy. When I was eleven years old, my grandfather explained to me in less than ten seconds why he invested in stocks. We sat by his pool in Arcadia, California, and he read the stock tables. I asked why he looked at all that fine print on such a beautiful day. He said, "Because it takes only $10,000 and two tenbaggers to become a millionaire." That didn't mean much to me at the time, but it does now. A tenbagger is a stock that grows tenfold. Invest $10,000 in your first tenbagger and you have $100,000. Invest that $100,000 in your second tenbagger and you have $1 million. That, in less than ten seconds, is why everybody should invest in stocks.

This chapter further explains why investing in stocks is a good idea, then covers some basic information you'll use in the rest of the book when you begin investing.

Why Stocks Are Good Investments

You should know why stocks are good investments before you start investing in them. There are two reasons to own stocks. First, because they allow you to own successful companies and, second, because they've been the best investments over time.

Stocks Allow You to Own Successful Companies

Stocks are good investments because they allow you to own successful companies. Just like you can have equity in your home, you can have equity in a company by owning its stock. That's why stocks are sometimes called *equities*.

Think of all the rich people you've read about. How did they get rich? Was it by lending money to relatives who never repay? No. Was it by winning the lottery? Not very often. Was it by inheriting money? In some cases, but it's irrelevant because nobody has control over this factor. In most cases, rich people got rich by owning something.

That something might have been real estate. You learned the first time you watched *Gone with the Wind* that land has value and that owning some is a good idea. In most cases, though, people get rich by owning a business. Schoolchildren learn about John D. Rockefeller, Andrew Carnegie, and J.P. Morgan. They all owned businesses. Henry Ford sold cars, Ray Kroc sold hamburgers from McDonald's, Thomas Watson sold business machines from IBM, Steve Jobs sold iPhones from Apple, Scott Cook and Tom Proulx sold financial software from Intuit, Howard Schultz sold coffee from Il Giornale. What's that, you never heard of Il Giornale? Oh, but you have, just not by that name. Schultz rebranded it Starbucks after buying the company from its original owners in 1987. All these people owned their companies. I sold magazine subscriptions door-to-door in school to raise money for the student council. I didn't get rich because I didn't own the subscription company. See the difference?

I could have taken some of that money I earned pawning off another copy of *Reader's Digest* on Mrs. Klein and bought shares of the subscription company. Suddenly, I would have been a business owner encouraging my classmates to "sell, sell, sell!" even if it meant they would win the portable radio instead of me winning it. The business they generated would have improved the subscription company's bottom line and, as a shareholder, I would have profited. If all went as planned, I could have bought a dozen portable radios.

That's why owning stocks is a good idea. They make you an owner of a company. Not an employee or a lender—an owner. When a company prospers, so do its owners.

Barnes & Noble Booksellers #2909
5353 Almaden Expressway Bldg. B
San Jose, CA 95118
408-979-061

STR:2909 REG:002 TRN:6021 CSHR:Bobby Y

Neatest Little Guide to Stock Market Inv
  9780452298620   T1
  (1 @ 16.00)   16.00

Subtotal   16.00
Sales Tax T1 (8.750%)   1.40
TOTAL   17.40
CASH   20.00
CASH CHANGE   2.60-

A MEMBER WOULD HAVE SAVED   1.60

            Thanks for shopping at
               Barnes & Noble

101.32A   11/15/2013 08:22PM

                CUSTOMER COPY

Booksellers inventory management system.

Opened music CDs/DVDs/audio books may not be returned, and can be exchanged only for the same title and only if defective. NOOKs purchased from other retailers or sellers are returnable only to the retailer or seller from which they are purchased, pursuant to such retailer's or seller's return policy. Magazines, newspapers, eBooks, digital downloads, and used books are not returnable or exchangeable. Defective NOOKs may be exchanged at the store in accordance with the applicable warranty.

Returns or exchanges will not be permitted (i) after 14 days or without receipt or (ii) for product not carried by Barnes & Noble or Barnes & Noble.com.

Policy on receipt may appear in two sections.

Return Policy

With a sales receipt or Barnes & Noble.com packing slip, a full refund in the original form of payment will be issued from any Barnes & Noble Booksellers store for returns of undamaged NOOKs, new and unread books, and unopened and undamaged music CDs, DVDs, and audio books made within 14 days of purchase from a Barnes & Noble Booksellers store or Barnes & Noble.com with the below exceptions:

A store credit for the purchase price will be issued (i) for purchases made by check less than 7 days prior to the date of return, (ii) when a gift receipt is presented within 60 days of purchase, (iii) for textbooks, or (iv) for products purchased at Barnes & Noble College bookstores that are listed for sale in the Barnes & Noble Booksellers inventory management system.

Opened music CDs/DVDs/audio books may not be returned, and can be exchanged only for the same title and only if defective. NOOKs purchased from

Stocks Have Been the Best Investments over Time

That's cute, you're thinking, but does it really work that way? Let's take a look at history and a few hard numbers.

The stock market has returned about 10.5 percent a year for the past 75 years or so. Corporate bonds returned 4.5 percent, U.S. Treasuries returned 3.3 percent, and inflation grew at 3.3 percent. Notice that Treasuries and inflation ran neck and neck? That means your investment in Treasuries returned nothing to you after inflation. When you include the drain of taxes, you lost money by investing in Treasuries. You need stocks. Everybody who intends to be around longer than ten years needs to invest in stocks. That's where the money is.

Investing in stocks helps both the investor and the company. Take McDonald's, for instance. It went public in 1965 at $22.50 per share. If you bought 100 shares, the company would have had an extra $2,250 to put toward new restaurants and better hamburgers. Maybe your money would have funded the research and development of the Big Mac, one of America's great inventions. Forty-seven years and twelve stock splits later, your 100 shares of McDonald's would have become 74,360 shares worth more than $7.4 million. Both you and McDonald's prospered, thanks to the stock market.

How Stocks Trade

When stocks are bought and sold, it's called *trading*. So a person might say "IBM is trading at $140." That means if you wanted to buy IBM stock, you'd pay $140 for one share.

Every company has a *ticker symbol*, which is the unique code used to identify its stock. In articles and reports, the ticker symbol is usually shown in parentheses after the first instance of the company name, for example, Facebook (FB), Google (GOOG), Harley-Davidson (HOG), IBM (IBM), and Toyota (TM).

A $1 move in stock price is called a *point*. If IBM goes from $140 to $143, you'd say that it rose three points. In the real world, IBM doesn't usually trade in such clean increments as $140 and $143. Instead, it would trade for, say, $143.38.

Some investors purchase shares of stock in blocks of 100. A block of 100 shares is called a *round lot*. Round lots provide a convenient way to track your stock investments because for every round lot you own, a one-point move up or down adds or subtracts $100 from the value of your investment. If you own 100 shares of IBM at $143, it's worth $14,300. If it rises two points to $145, your investment is worth $200 more, for a total of $14,500. Simple, eh?

Preferred Stock vs. Common Stock

There are two types of stock, preferred and common. Both represent ownership in a company. Preferred stock has a set dividend that does not fluctuate based on how well the company is performing. Preferred stockholders receive their dividends before common stockholders. Finally, preferred stockholders are paid first if the company fails and is liquidated.

Common stock is what most of us own. That's what you get when you place a standard order for some number of shares. Common stock entitles you to voting rights and any dividends that the company decides to pay. The dividends will fluctuate with the company's success or failure.

How You Make Money Owning Stocks

This is really the bottom line to investors. The only reason you own a business is to profit from it. The way you profit by owning stocks is through capital appreciation and dividends.

Through Capital Appreciation

Sometimes called capital gains, *capital appreciation* is the profit you keep after you buy a stock and sell it at a higher price. Buy low, sell high is a common investment aphorism but it is just as legitimate to buy high, sell higher.

Expressed as a percentage, the difference between your purchase price and your sell price is your return. For example, if you buy a stock at $30 and sell it later for $60, your return is 100 percent. Sell it later for $90 and your return is 200 percent. If you bought Cisco in 1990 at 10 cents and sold it in 2000 at $70, your return was 69,900 percent. If you bought Hansen Natural in February 2003 at 40 cents and sold it in July 2006 at $50, your return was 12,400 percent. If you bought Green Mountain Coffee Roasters in October 2008 at $6 and sold it in August 2011 at $100, your return was 1,567 percent.

The goal is *ap*preciation, but sometimes investors end up with *de*preciation by mistake. If you bought Citigroup in November 2007 at $35 and sold it in November 2008 at $6, your return was -83 percent.

Through Dividends

As an owner of a company, you might share in the company's profits in the form of a stock *dividend* taken from company earnings. Companies report earnings every quarter and determine whether to pay a dividend. If earnings are low or the company loses money, dividends are usually the first thing to get cut. On a *declaration date* in each quarter, the company decides what the dividend payout will be.

To receive a dividend, you must own the stock by the *ex-dividend date*, which is four business days before the company looks at the list of shareholders to see who gets the dividend. The day the company actually looks at the list of shareholders is called the *record date*.

If you own the stock by the ex-dividend date, and are therefore on the list of shareholders by the record date, you get a dividend check. The company decides how much the dividend will be per share, multiplies the number of shares you own by the dividend, and deposits the total amount into your brokerage account. If you own 10,000 shares and the dividend is $.35, the company will deposit $3,500 on the *payment date*. It's that simple.

Most publications report a company's annual dividend, not the quarterly. The company that just paid you a $.35 per share quarterly dividend would be listed in most publications as having a dividend of $1.40. That's just the $.35 quarterly dividend multiplied by the four quarters in the year.

Total Return

The money you make from a stock's capital appreciation combined with the money you make from the stock's dividend is your total return. Just add the rise in the stock price to the dividends you received, then divide by the stock's purchase price.

For instance, let's say you bought IBM at $45 and sold it two years later at $110. IBM paid an annual dividend of $1 the first year and $1.40 the second year. The rise in the stock's price was $65, and the total dividend paid per share was $2.40. Add those to get $67.40. Divide that by the stock's purchase price of $45 and you get 1.5, or 150 percent total return.

All About Stock Splits

A stock split occurs when a company increases the number of its stock shares outstanding without increasing shareholders' equity. To you as an investor, that means you'll own a different number of shares but they'll add up to the same amount of money. A common stock split is 2-for-1. Say you own 100 shares of a stock trading at $180. Your account is worth $18,000. If the stock splits 2-for-1 you will own 200 shares that trade at $90. Your account is still worth $18,000. What's the point? The point is that you now have something to do with your spare time: Adjust your financial statements to account for the split.

Not really. Companies split their stock to make it affordable to more investors. Many people would shy away from a $180 stock, but would consider a $90 one. Perhaps that's still too expensive. The company could approve a 4-for-1 split and take the $180 stock down to $45. Your 100 shares would become 400 shares, but would still be worth $18,000. People considering the stock might be more likely to buy at $45 than at $180, even though they're getting the same amount of ownership in the company for each dollar they invest. It's a psychological thing, and who are we to question it?

Mathematically, stock splits are completely irrelevant to investors but they are often a sign of good things to come. A company usually won't split its stock unless it's optimistic about the future. Think about it. Would you cut your stock price in half or more if the market was about to do the same? Of course not.

Headlines would declare the end of your fortunes and lawsuits might pile up. Stock splits tend to happen when a company has done well, driven up the price of its stock, expects to continue doing well, drops the price of its stock through a split, and expects to keep driving up the stock price after the split.

Stock splits were everyday occurrences in the 1990s bull market. IBM split twice, Oracle split five times, Microsoft split seven times, and Cisco split eight times. A $10,000 investment in Microsoft in January 1990 was worth about $900,000 in January 2000. The stock didn't just run straight up 90-fold, however. It made five 2-for-1 splits and two 3-for-2 splits along the way. It rose and split, rose and split, rose and split, rose and split, rose and split, rose and split, and rose and split until voilà! $10 grand turned into $900 grand. You can be sure that Microsoft wouldn't have been splitting its stock if it wasn't excited about its future.

Remember that a stock split drops the price of the stock. Lower prices tend to move quicker than higher prices. Also, the fluctuations of a lower-priced stock have a greater percentage impact on return than they do against higher-priced stocks. A $2 increase is a 4 percent gain for a $50 stock, but only a 2 percent gain for a $100 stock.

More important than all this, however, is that splits are downright fun. You'll love it when your 100 shares become 200 and every $1 gain in price puts $200 in your pocket instead of the previous $100. You'll feel like a real pro when revealing your performance to friends and need to toss in the phrase *split-adjusted* at the end. I recommend raising one eyebrow and lowering your voice for effect.

Why and How a Company Sells Stock

Companies want you to buy their stock so they can use your money to get new equipment, develop better products, and expand their operations. Your investment money strengthens the company. But first the company needs to make its stock available. This section describes how.

The magazine subscription selling job I held in school made me think a lot about becoming a business owner. I imagined teaching all the other kids how to sell subscriptions, collecting their money at the end of the day, using some of it to buy a prize for the top seller, sending a small amount to the magazines, and depositing the rest into my bank account. Pretty simple business model, right? Pretend for a minute that I did it. I called my business Mister Magazine.

I realized early on that Mister Magazine needed office space. A treehouse would do. I needed lumber to build it, and I needed to get electricity and phones installed. That takes money that I didn't have. After all, that's why I went into business: to make money. If I already had it, I wouldn't have needed to go into business! There are two ways I could have raised money for Mister Magazine.

First, I could have drawn up a business plan and pleaded with my local bank. When I showed the officer the sketches of corporate headquarters in a tree, my guess is that our interview would have been quite short. A lot of fledgling businesses face just that problem. They aren't established enough to get a loan, or if they do get one it comes with such a high interest rate to offset the risk that it ends up strangling the business anyway. Nope, a loan wouldn't do it for Mister Magazine.

Selling Stock Is a Great Way to Raise Money

My second option was to sell shares of Mister Magazine to investors who wanted a piece of the upcoming profits. By selling shares I would raise money, I wouldn't owe anybody anything, and I would acquire a bunch of people who *really* wanted Mister Magazine to succeed. They would own part of it after all! I chose this second option to raise money, and I decided that 10 shares comprised Mister Magazine's entire operation. I could have chosen 100 shares or 100,000 shares. The amount doesn't matter. The only thing investors care about is what percentage of Mister Magazine they'll own. I decided to keep 6 shares for myself to retain majority ownership and sell 4 shares to parents in my community for $100 each. The parents were my *venture capitalists* in this case. After the sale, I owned 60 percent of Mister Magazine and four parents in the community owned 40 percent. It was a private deal, though. You couldn't find Mister Magazine listed in the paper yet.

The first year of operation at Mister Magazine went great. I hired 20 kids to sell magazines door-to-door, I negotiated a cheap deal with the magazines, and I found a wholesale prize distributor who sold gadgets for half their usual price. My employees were happy and Mister Magazine grew to be worth $5,000. How did my investors fare? Quite well. Those initial $100 shares became $500 shares in one year. That's a 400 percent annual return!

Clearly there was only one thing for me to do. I needed to immediately drop out of school and expand Mister Magazine to outlying communities, and then the entire United States. It was time to come down out of the treehouse and establish a ground-based headquarters, evolving as a business just as humanity evolved as a species. To fund this ambitious expansion, I decided to take Mister Magazine public.

Going Public Raises Even More Money

Instead of selling shares to just four parents in my community, my next step was to sell Mister Magazine to millions of investors by getting listed on a stock exchange. Stock exchanges provide a place for investors to trade stock. The most famous from U.S. history are the New York Stock Exchange (NYSE, founded 1792), the American Stock Exchange (Amex, founded 1842), and the National Association of Securities Dealers Automated Quotations (NASDAQ, founded 1971).

In 2007, the NYSE Group bought Paris-based Euronext to become the first global equities exchange, called NYSE Euronext. The new entity then went on to acquire the American Stock Exchange in 2008, combine it with the Alternext European small-company exchange, rename it NYSE Alternext US with a focus on small companies, and move all of its trading floor operations to the NYSE's Wall Street trading floor. Yet another merger was in the works as this edition went to press: Germany's Deutsche Borse attempted a $10 billion acquisition of NYSE Euronext to create the world's biggest stock exchange operator. The U.S. Securities and Exchange Commission approved the deal, but European Union officials hesitated to do so for fear of quashing competition.

Let's see our chances of getting Mister Magazine listed on the New York Stock Exchange, the NASDAQ, and the NYSE Alternext US:

New York Stock Exchange

This is the biggest and oldest of America's exchanges. Its famous floor is located along Wall Street in Manhattan. It caters to well-established companies like IBM, Ford, and McDonald's. To be listed, a company must have at least 400 U.S. shareholders and at least 1.1 million shares of stock outstanding, and then pass an earnings or valuation test with criteria such as pretax income of $10 million or more over the past three years, and a global market capitalization of at least $750 million. As you can see, it's a big deal to be listed on the NYSE. *Outstanding*, by the way, refers to stock owned by shareholders.

NASDAQ

The NASDAQ rose to prominence by trading cool high-tech companies like Microsoft, Intuit, and Dell. It's sometimes called the over the counter (OTC) market because there's no floor to see on Wall Street or any other street. Instead, the NASDAQ comprises brokers networked together around the country who trade stocks back and forth with computers. Some of the brokers are known as *market makers* because they supply the stock when you want to buy it. You'll never know which broker supplied the stock you're buying, and you won't care. To be listed on the NASDAQ Global Market, a company must have at least 400 shareholders, at least 1.1 million shares of outstanding stock worth $8 million or more, and pretax income of $1 million or more in the latest fiscal year or in two of the past three fiscal years.

NYSE Alternext US

With its focus on emerging companies that want simplified market access, NYSE Alternext US offers the most lenient listing requirements. A company must have pretax income of at least $750,000 over the past fiscal year or two of the three most recent fiscal years; publicly held shares valued at $3 million or more; shareholders' equity of at least $4 million; and either 800 shareholders with 500,000 shares outstanding or 400 shareholders with 1,000,000 shares outstanding.

Working with an Investment Banker

Obviously, Mister Magazine didn't have a prayer of making any of the three primary exchanges. But let's say a colossal exception was made and I worked with the investment banking side of a large firm like Bank of America, Citigroup, Goldman Sachs, JPMorgan Chase, or Wells Fargo to make an *initial public offering*, or *IPO*. That's what a company's first offering of stock to the public is called. I told the investment banker how much money I wanted to raise and the banker determined how many shares to sell at what price. I wanted to raise $10 million. The banker could have sold 5 million shares at $2 each, 10 million at $1 each, or 2 million at $5 each. As long as the combination produced the target amount, it didn't matter.

The investment banker committed to buy the shares if nobody else did and got to keep a small amount of profit per share for this risk. The banker initially sold shares of Mister Magazine to the *primary market*, which consists of the banker's preferred private accounts. After the primary market had dibs on the tantalizing new shares of Mister Magazine, the investment banker offered the remaining shares to the *secondary market*, which consists of everyday shmoes like you and me who read a stock's price in the paper or online and buy it.

Making a Secondary Offering

Once the banker made the initial public offering, I had my money and a bunch of new investors in the company. When it came time to raise more money, I sold additional shares of stock in what's called a *secondary offering*. No matter how many additional times I sell more stock, it's always called a secondary offering. I would also have the option of selling bonds to investors. When an investor buys a corporate bond, he or she is lending money to the corporation and will be paid back with interest. That means bonds have the same drawbacks that bank loans do. Mister Magazine would be forced to pay interest on the money it borrowed from investors instead of just selling them a share of stock in the company through a secondary offering.

Secondary offerings are sometimes necessary because companies don't receive a dime in profit from shares once they're being traded on the open market. After a company issues and sells a share of stock, all profits and losses generated by that stock belong to the investors trading it. Even if the price of the stock quadruples in value and it's bought and sold 10 times in a day, the issuing company doesn't make any money off it. The reason is simple: the investor who buys a share of stock owns it. He or she can sell that share for whatever price the market will pay. The company isn't entitled to any of the profits from the sale because the investor is the sole owner of that share of stock until it's sold to a buyer who then becomes the new owner. Unless the company buys back its own stock, it won't own the shares again.

It's no different than you selling your car. Do you owe Ford a share of the sale price when you finally get rid of that old Pinto in your garage? Of course not. You place an ad in the paper, deposit the buyer's check, and go on your way. It's the same situation if you own shares of Ford Motor Company. You place the sell order, take the buyer's money, pay a brokerage commission, and go on your way. Ford doesn't even know it happened.

Now, the shrewder among you might be wondering why companies care what happens to their stock price once they've got their dough. After all, they don't see any profit from you selling to me and me selling to another guy. That's true, but remember that companies might want to make another secondary offering later, and another, and another, and another. If a company issues 1,000,000 new shares at $40 it makes $40 million. If it issues 1,000,000 new shares at $10 it makes $10 million. Do you suppose most companies would rather make $40 million than $10 million? Of course they would, and that's why companies like to see their stock prices high. Not to mention that a falling stock price breeds ugly headlines.

What People Mean by "The Market"

You hear every day that the market is up or down. Have you ever paused to wonder what *the market* is? Usually, that phrase refers to the U.S. stock market as measured by the Dow Jones Industrial Average, often abbreviated DJIA or called simply the Dow. The Dow is not the entire market at all, but rather an average of 30 well-known companies such as Coca-Cola, Exxon Mobil, McDonald's, Microsoft, and Wal-Mart. The companies tracked by the Dow are chosen by the editors of *The Wall Street Journal.* The list changes occasionally as companies merge, lose prominence, or rise to the top of their industry.

The Dow is an *average.* Averages and *indexes* are just ways for us to judge the trend of the overall market by looking at a piece of it. The Dow is the most widely cited measurement, but not the only gauge of the market. A more popular index among investors is the Standard & Poor's 500, or just the S&P 500. It tracks 500 large companies that together account for some 75 percent of the entire U.S. stock market. The S&P MidCap 400 tracks 400 medium-sized companies while the S&P SmallCap 600 tracks 600 small companies. The NASDAQ 100 follows 100 top stocks from the NASDAQ such as Adobe, Amazon.com, Apple, Costco, eBay, Intel, Netflix, Oracle, Starbucks, Urban Outfitters, and Whole Foods Market. It's one of the hippest indexes around, although, with its focus on tech and biotech, also one of the most volatile. Here's the total return of these five indexes as of December 31, 2008:

Index	Tracks	3-Year	5-Year	10-Year
Dow Jones	30 Large Companies	-15%	-13%	-2%
S&P 500	500 Large Companies	-25%	-16%	-24%
S&P MidCap 400	400 Medium Companies	-25%	-4%	41%
S&P SmallCap 600	600 Small Companies	-23%	0%	54%
NASDAQ 100	100 Leading NASDAQ Companies	-23%	-14%	-31%

Fun decade, eh?

What a difference a bear market makes. The subprime crash

of 2008 did all the damage above. For proof, look at the total return of those same five indexes just two years prior, as of December 29, 2006:

Index	Tracks	3-Year	5-Year	10-Year
Dow Jones	30 Large Companies	19%	24%	93%
S&P 500	500 Large Companies	28%	24%	88%
S&P MidCap 400	400 Medium Companies	40%	58%	214%
S&P SmallCap 600	600 Small Companies	48%	72%	176%
NASDAQ 100	100 Leading NASDAQ Companies	20%	11%	114%

Then three years after, as of December 30, 2011:

Index	Tracks	3-Year	5-Year	10-Year
Dow Jones	30 Large Companies	39%	-2%	22%
S&P 500	500 Large Companies	39%	-11%	10%
S&P MidCap 400	400 Medium Companies	63%	9%	73%
S&P SmallCap 600	600 Small Companies	54%	4%	79%
NASDAQ 100	100 Leading NASDAQ Companies	88%	30%	44%

I want to draw your attention to the medium and small companies. Notice how much stronger than the others they were over the 5- and 10-year periods. They're good places to focus, and in Chapter 4 I'll show you how to use them to your long-term advantage.

There are dozens of other indexes that you will encounter as you dig deeper into the world of investing. Each is an attempt to monitor the progress of a market by looking at a sliver of that market.

You probably already use indexes in other parts of your life, although you might not know it. We create them all the time to help ourselves compare different values. For example, let's say you are interested in buying a new Toyota Camry. If one of your main selection criteria is fuel economy, how do you know if the Camry performs well in that area? You compare its miles-per-gallon number with the average miles-per-gallon number of other midsize passenger cars, such as the Ford Fusion and the Honda Accord. After several comparisons, you know what is a good number, what is average, and what is below average. Notice that you don't compare the Camry with a Hyundai Accent or a Chevy Suburban. Those vehicles are in different classes and are irrelevant to your comparison. Thus, in this case, midsize passenger cars comprise your index.

As you encounter different market indexes, just remember that each looks at a piece of the market to monitor how that part of the market is performing.

How to Choose a Broker to Buy Stocks

You buy stocks through a brokerage firm. A brokerage firm is a business licensed by the government to trade *securities* for investors. Brokerage firms join different stock exchanges and abide by their rules as well as the rules laid down by the *Securities and Exchange Commission*, or *SEC*.

Two Types of Brokerage Firms

There are full-service brokerage firms and discount brokerage firms. Here's a description of each:

Full-Service Brokerage Firms

These are the largest, best-known brokerage firms in the world, who spend millions of dollars a year advertising their names. You've probably heard of Bank of America, Goldman Sachs, Morgan Stanley, Smith Barney, UBS, and others of their ilk. They're all the same. Regardless of their advertising slogans, the two words that should immediately come to mind when you hear the names of full-service brokerage firms are *expensive* and *misleading*. Other than that, they're great. Most full-service brokerage firms are divided into an investment banking division, a research division, and a retail division.

The investment banking division is what helps young companies make their initial public offering of stock and sell additional shares in secondary offerings. The brokerage firm keeps a profit on each share of stock sold. This is where the firm makes most of its money. Therefore, every one of the full-service brokerages wants to keep solid investment banking relationships with their public companies. Never forget that full-service brokerage firms make their money by selling shares of stock for the companies they take public. They make their money whether investors purchasing those shares get a good deal or a bad deal. In other words, it doesn't make a bit of difference to the full-service broker whether investors make or lose money. The firm always makes money. To be fair, most brokers do want to find winning investments for their clients if for no other reason than future business.

The research division of a full-service brokerage firm analyzes and writes evaluations, fact sheets, and periodic reports on publicly traded companies. Supposedly this information is provided to you, an individual investor, to help you make educated decisions. However, remember from the previous paragraph that the brokerage firm makes its money by maintaining solid relationships with companies. There are millions of investors, but only a few thousand companies. Whom do you think the broker wants to keep happy? The companies, of course. So, you'll rarely see a recommendation to "sell" a stock. Instead, a broker will recommend that you "hold" it. No company wants to see a firm telling investors to sell its stock. The brokerage's solution is to just never issue that ugly word. *The Wall Street Journal* revealed how blatant this directive is when it discovered a memo from Morgan Stanley's director of new stock issues stating that the company's policy was "no negative comments about our clients." The memo also instructed analysts to clear their stock ratings and opinions "which might be viewed negatively" with the company's corporate finance department.

The retail division is what you and I deal with. It's comprised of brokers, who are really just sales reps, who call their clients and urge them to trade certain stocks. They charge large commissions that they split with the brokerage firm. The justification for the large commissions is that you're paying for all the research the company does on your behalf. But as you now know, that research is misleading anyway. It exists simply to urge you to trade the companies that the firm represents. So, you are paying to receive a type of advertising! The only reason full-service brokerage firms have a retail division is so that they have a sales channel for the companies they represent.

When the investment banking division takes a new company like Mister Magazine public, the research division puts the stock on a buy list, and the retail division brokers start making their phone calls. When you answer the phone and buy the stock, the broker and firm make money. It's an interesting twist on *full service*, don't you think?

Discount Brokerage Firms

Discount brokerage firms do not conduct initial public offerings or secondary offerings. Most don't have in-house research divisions, either. They just handle your buy and sell orders and charge a low commission to do so. The commissions are discounted because the firms don't shoulder the expense of a full-service research department and a legion of sales reps in a retail sales department.

Compare Commissions

If you bought 500 shares of a $40 stock off the NYSE, here's the commission you should expect to pay at the different types of brokerage firms:

Full Service $100–$200
Discount $5–$20

Most discount brokers offer research in the form of company reports, charting tools, newsletters, news summaries, and other helpful material. But they don't have anybody call you to urge a buy or sell. The decisions are your decisions and the discount brokerage firm simply carries out your orders. Because they don't maintain investment banking relationships with companies and because they make the same commission off any stock you trade, discount brokers don't have an interest in selling you the stock of any specific company.

Discount brokers used to be famous for offering online and telephone trading as innovative ways to further reduce costs. Now, online trading is the norm. A broker bragging about its online trading these days is like a movie theater bragging about its air-conditioning.

By the way, there used to be a third category of broker called a *deep-discount broker* that offered nothing more than cheap trading. Over the years, discount brokers lowered their prices and deep-discount brokers added research and tools, so the distinction between the two categories disappeared. Now, lots of good research and fine online interfaces are available for low trading fees at companies from both former categories. So, I put them in the same category: discount brokers.

Discount brokers are very popular, and you've probably heard of a couple. Charles Schwab, E*Trade, Fidelity, Scottrade, and TD Ameritrade are all discount brokerage firms.

The Case for Discounters

In this book I'll show you how to rely on discounters to place your trades. Here's why:

Technology Has Made Full-Service Brokers Obsolete

Full-service brokerage firms are anachronisms. They're left over from the days when individual investors didn't have access to the trading mechanisms that brokers use. To place a trade on an exchange floor in the old days, investors needed brokers and runners and agents to carry out that order. Investors were accustomed to paying a commission for all that trouble.

But all that trouble doesn't exist anymore. The NYSE got rid of the hitching posts on Wall Street, and floor specialists receive most orders via Super DOT, a computerized order-routing and reporting system that completes the trading loop in seconds. The NASDAQ doesn't even have an exchange floor! It's just a network of computers and brokers.

Think about that. If you know what stock you want to buy, shouldn't you just type it into a computer or punch it into a touch-tone phone yourself? Of course you should! It doesn't make any sense to call a full-service broker—or in many cases, they'll call you—and pay him or her a commission to type your stock trade into a computer. The full-service firms know this, of course, but they prefer to have you invest the way you would have in 1897 because they can get a lot of commission money out of you in the process.

You Need to Double-Check Full-Service Information

Some would argue that the extensive research and hand-holding you get from a full-service brokerage firm make it worth the extra commission money. But the only thing you'll hear from analysts in the research division of a full-service firm is what the marketing department encourages them to tell you. In other words, the stocks they want to sell in order to further their relationship with a public company will be pitched as good stocks for you to buy. Don't assume that cold call from your brother-in-law the full-service broker has your interests foremost in mind. The advice might be good, but it might not.

Zacks Investment Research tracked the stocks recommended by eight full-service brokers over a three-year period and found that five failed to beat the S&P 500. That's a 63 percent failure rate *before* commissions! Even if you weren't a statistics major, you know that a 63 percent chance of failure makes those high commissions hard to justify.

SmartMoney profiled an investor who paid $11,000 in fees and commissions to Salomon Smith Barney (now Morgan Stanley Smith Barney, but 49 percent owned by Citigroup), with his average stock trade costing $300. He realized he was doing all of his own research anyway and finally switched to Charles Schwab, where the research tools were better than those offered by Smith Barney and the average stock trade cost only $15.

Because you can't just accept that a broker's advice is good, you need to do your own research. So, why not just place the trade yourself, too? You'll save a bundle.

You Should Monitor Your Own Investments

Not only do you need to double-check everything full-service brokers tell you, the unsolicited phone calls you receive from them can be confusing. If you are a truly individual investor conducting your own research and placing trades with a discounter, you limit yourself to only what you need to know.

For example, say you researched a stock and decided on a suitable purchase price and a target sell price. You told your discount broker what price to buy at. Two weeks later, the stock hit that price and you automatically picked up 100 shares. Then you told your discounter the price you wanted to sell at, say, 30 percent more than your purchase price. That's it. You went about your life and let the stock run its course. Six months later, it hit your sell price and you automatically sold all 100 shares and made 30 percent minus commissions.

Notice that you—and you alone—decided what happened in the course of that stock ownership. Unbeknownst to you, your stock dropped 30 percent in value before it made a roaring comeback to your sell price. If you'd gone through a full-service broker, there's a good chance he or she would have called you when it was down and provided every negative headline regarding the company's future. Maybe he or she would have caught you at a vulnerable time and you would have sold at a loss, all because you couldn't choose your own information level. And, of course, the broker would make a commission on your sale at a loss and your subsequent purchase of a new stock.

When you take care of your own investments, you choose what to monitor. Maybe you want to know every uptick and downtick of your stocks and every bit of news affecting them. But it might be that you just want the big picture by checking prices once a month, perusing top stories on the Internet, and keeping an eye on a few related stocks in the same industry. The point is that it should be up to you, not up to a broker who stands to profit off your frequent buying and selling. Keep the background noise low.

How to Evaluate Stocks

Evaluating stocks is actually quite easy. Once you've done it a few times you'll develop a pattern of research that you can repeat with every new stock that interests you. But first, you need to understand the difference between growth and value investing, fundamental and technical analysis, know some basic stock measurements, and understand how to read the stock pages.

Growth Investing vs. Value Investing

This is the most basic division between investors, akin to North and South. But, like North and South, there's a lot of area between each extreme that's hard to classify. Think of growth and value as being on a continuum. Most investors fall somewhere in the middle, and combining the two styles has proven to be a great investment approach.

Growth Investing

Growth investors look for companies that are sales and earnings machines. Such companies have a lot of potential, and growth investors are willing to pay handsomely for them. A growth company's potential might stem from a new product, a breakthrough patent, overseas expansion, or excellent management.

Key company measurements that growth investors examine are earnings and recent stock price strength. A growth company without strong earnings is like an Indy 500 race car without an engine. Dividends aren't very important to growth investors because many growth companies pay small or no dividends. Instead, they reinvest profits to expand and improve their business. Hopefully, the reinvestments produce even more growth in the future. Growing companies post bigger earnings each year, and the amount of those earnings increases should be getting bigger, too. Most growth investors set minimum criteria for investing in a company. Perhaps it should be growing at least 20 percent a year and pushing new highs in stock price.

Growth companies you're probably familiar with are Applied Materials, Boston Beer Company (Samuel Adams brand), Chipotle Mexican Grill, Google, and Vera Bradley. Now you know what people mean when they drive past yet another Chipotle and say, "That place is growing like a weed."

Growth investors are searching for hot hands, not great bargains. They'll pay more for good companies. As a result, many growth investors don't even look at a stock's price in relation to its earnings or its book value because they know a lot of growth stocks are expensive and they don't care. They just look at a stock's potential and go for it, hoping that current successes continue and get even better. They buy momentum, inertia, steamrolling forward movement. That's the nature of growth investing.

William O'Neil, a top growth investor whose strategy you'll learn on page 71, says in his seminar that growth investors are like baseball teams that pay huge salaries to top-ranked batters. They come at a high price, but if they keep batting .300 and winning games, then it's worth it. Likewise, you won't find many bargains among growth stocks. But if they keep growing it's worth it.

Because a growth stock depends on its earnings and the acceleration of those earnings, the expectations of analysts and investors are high. That creates a risky situation. If a growth company fails to deliver the earnings that everybody expects, all hell breaks loose. Red flags fly left and right, phones vibrate madly, the stock price falls, reports shoot from fax machines and fill up email in-boxes, and nobody's dinner tastes quite as good as it did the night of last quarter's earnings report.

Value Investing

Value investors look for stocks on the cheap. They compare stock prices with different measures of a company's business, such as its earnings, assets, cash flow, and sales volume. The idea is that if you don't pay too much for what you get, there's less chance of losing money.

Value stocks have low P/E ratios and low price-to-book ratios. They are companies that have been overlooked on their journey to success, have fallen on hard times after more successful years, or are in a slump for any number of reasons. Hopefully they're on a comeback and the value investor purchases shares at the bottom of an uphill climb. Here's where value and growth are tied together. In both cases, investors want to buy companies with a bright future. The difference is that growth investors usually buy those companies when they're already steamrolling ahead to that bright future, while value investors usually buy those companies when they're still getting ready to start or are recovering from a tumble.

Using O'Neil's baseball analogy, value investors comb the locker rooms for bandaged players trying to rehabilitate. They don't cost much, and you might uncover a future star. Of course, you might get exactly what you paid for: a broken player, or a broken company.

The value investor is a bargain hunter extraordinaire. From my interviews with professionals and novices alike, I gather that value investing is closer to what we've been taught from the time we were kids. What did you look at when buying candy? Probably which kind you could get the most of for your pocketful of allowance money. In school, you probably bought the package of notebook paper with the most sheets for your dollar. When relatives came by for the holidays they might have swapped stories of the great bargains or "steals" they purchased recently. We're used to examining price with an eye toward value. It's no different in the world of investing.

Value investors pay particular attention to dividends. A company that pays dividends contributes to an investor's profit even if the stock price does not rise. That's comforting. Also, among big companies, the dividend yield is a great indicator of how bargain priced a company is.

Combining Growth and Value

Growth investing and value investing are not mutually exclusive. Many growth investors use some measure of value to time their purchase of growth stocks. Most value investors use some measure of growth potential to evaluate a troubled company's chances of recovery.

Growth investors tend to get in when things are heating up and bail out at the first sign of slowing growth. Value investors tend to be very careful about where their money goes and let it ride out fluctuations once they decide where to invest. The contrast in these two styles is why I think value investing is more suitable to the average individual investor. Most individuals do not have the time or resources to monitor split-second changes in their stocks to act accordingly. It seems that conducting thorough research periodically and letting the chosen stocks do their thing is the best approach for most individual investors. That being the case, why go through the hassle of all the trading that accompanies pure growth portfolios?

These are my thoughts only, and throughout this book I try to provide equal space to each style. I think most of us end up combining the styles in our personal portfolios, but with a tendency one way or the other. I've enjoyed excellent results from both growth and value investments, although I tend toward value.

Fundamental Analysis vs. Technical Analysis

There are two ways to evaluate a stock. The first way is using *fundamental analysis*, which examines information about the company's health and potential to succeed. You use fundamental information to learn about a company. The second way is using *technical analysis*, which examines the past behavior of the stock price in different market conditions and attempts to predict the stock's future price based on current and projected market conditions and trading volume. You use technical information to learn about a company's stock.

In this guide, you'll learn to use fundamental analysis and technical analysis together.

Fundamental Analysis

For individual investors, fundamental analysis should form the core of their evaluations. Choosing good companies is what I consider the foundation of successful investing. Also, healthy companies make the best long-term investments and I advocate a long-term investment strategy. By looking at a company's management, its rate of growth, how much it earns, and how much it pays to keep the lights on and the cash register ringing are easy things for you and me to understand. After all, we constantly balance the same things in our own lives. You earn a certain amount of money, budget how to spend it, and keep an eye on your habits. If you consistently run low on funds, you pull out the stack of bills and figure out how you can change that. It's very similar to running a business.

Once you have a picture of a company's fundamentals, you can determine its intrinsic value. *Intrinsic value* is the price a stock should sell at under normal market conditions. The most important fundamental measure in determining a company's intrinsic value is earnings: what the company is earning now and what you expect it to earn in the future. After that, you'll want to know what the company's assets are, if it's in debt, and the history of its management. Once you have a clear picture of the company's intrinsic value, you examine its price to see if it's selling above or below its value. If it's selling below its value, it's a good buy. If it's selling above its value, it's overpriced. Of course there's more to it than that, but for now let's leave it black and white.

Technical Analysis

Technical analysis, on the other hand, is a little harder to understand. Its premise is that supply and demand drive all stock prices. Fundamental information doesn't matter until it affects demand, and usually shows up on the stock chart before it becomes news. Chartists believe the price chart tells you what news is coming, not that the news tells you what will happen to the stock price. The main measurement technical analysts use to gauge demand is trading volume. After that, they look at chart trends to forecast future direction, and place their money to benefit from the price movement in that direction.

Technical analysis is useful, but takes more than a nodding

acquaintance to use correctly. This little guide will not provide you with a complete look at the intricacies of technical analysis.

However, there are a few simple technical measures that you'll find helpful as you embark on your stock-picking adventure. You'll use them to gauge where the overall market is trending and where stocks of interest to you are trending against that backdrop. You'll find those stocks by conducting fundamental research. See how the two relate? You evaluate the company behind the stock with fundamental analysis, then you evaluate the trend of the stock with technical analysis. The idea is to buy the stock of a strong company as that stock is trending up.

The bottom line is that most investors use a combination of both fundamental and technical analysis.

Some Fundamental Stock Measurements

The annoying thing about stock measurements is that even if every one of them gives a green light to a stock you're considering, it might still end up being a bad investment. It's not like measuring your inseam. Once you know that number, you know the length of pants to buy, and if they're that length, they fit. Period. It's not that simple with stocks.

Nonetheless, knowing how your stocks measure up is important. Knowing something that might make a difference is better than knowing nothing at all. In most cases, the measurements do reveal valuable information. In this section, I explain the most common stock measurements and also a few you won't find listed in many other places. They're my favorites.

Important Note: This section gives you an up-front, nodding acquaintance with these measurements. I just explain them here. Later in the book, I show where to find them and how to use them on your Stocks to Watch worksheet. Also, you don't need to calculate most of the measurements on your own. They're already calculated for you in newspapers, reference volumes, the Internet, and other places.

Cash Flow per Share

Cash flow is the stream of cash through a business. You want it to be positive and you'd love it to be big. Sometimes even profitable businesses don't have strong cash flows because they sell their goods on credit.

You know all those ads you see to buy now with no payments until next year? Those are just the kind of business activities that boost profits without increasing cash flow. It's true that somebody buys the couch or dishwasher or weed zapper and the sale goes on the books, but the business doesn't see any money until next year. That can be a problem if there isn't enough money around to keep the lights on and the water running. Bills need to be paid on time no matter what a customer's payment schedule is.

A well-managed business can do fine with buy now, pay later plans. With enough cash in the bank, the bills are covered. In the meantime, special promos do sell a lot of product that will eventually be paid for. Also, the profits that are finally realized might be higher than the advertised prices due to accrued interest and other fine print.

Cash flow per share—what we're examining—is simply a company's cash flow divided by the number of shares outstanding. That lets you see what price you're paying for a share of the company's cash flow.

Current Ratio

The *current ratio* is the most popular gauge of a company's ability to pay its short-term bills. It's measured by dividing current assets by current liabilities. The ratio reveals how easily a company can deal with unexpected expenses or opportunities. It's usually expressed in the number of times, such as "current assets are three times current liabilities." That might be a company with current assets of $300,000 and current liabilities of $100,000. Another way to state the current ratio would be 3-to-1.

A company's assets are everything it owns: cars, machines, patents, computers, and so on. Its *current* assets are things that are used up and replenished frequently such as cash, inventory, and accounts receivable. A company's liabilities are everything it owes: loans, bills, and such. Its *current* liabilities are the ones usually due within one year.

As you can see, comparing current assets with current liabilities shows you if the company is prepared for short-term obligations and able to take advantage of short-term opportunities.

That's what you want. Look for companies with a current ratio of at least 2-to-1.

Dividend Yield

A stock's *dividend yield* is its annual cash dividend divided by its current price. If Mister Magazine paid a quarterly dividend of $.15, you assume that its annual dividend is $.60—15 cents per quarter times four quarters in a year gives you 60 cents. Let's say its current stock price is $15. Divide .60 by 15 to get a yield of .04 or 4 percent. It's simple to figure a stock's dividend yield, but you won't need to do it. It's printed for you in the newspaper every day, and displayed constantly online.

At first, dividend yield probably looks pretty boring. A lot of stocks don't pay dividends anyway, and who really cares what a stock yields in dividends? If you want steady payouts, you'll go to your local bank.

But alas, amigo, the dividend yield reveals plenty about a stock's price. It tells you more about a stock's price than it does about a stock's dividend. Why? Because there are only two numbers involved in the dividend yield. If one number remains constant, then the other number drives any changes. With most companies, the dividend payout remains fairly constant. That leaves you with only one other number to influence dividend yield: stock price. It changes daily and its relationship to the dividend is immediately reflected in the dividend yield.

Look what happens. If Mister Magazine's price rises from $15 to $30 but it maintains a constant dividend of $.60, its dividend yield drops to 2 percent. If the price then rises to $60, the dividend yield drops to 1 percent. If the dividend remains constant and the yield changes, you know the price is moving. In this case, Mister Magazine's decreasing yield tells you that the stock price is rising and might be overvalued.

What's a Quarter?

A quarter is simply a three-month time period. Calendar quarters are January to March, April to June, July to September, and October to December.

Many companies define their own business year, which might not be the same as a calendar year. Company-defined years are called *fiscal years*. A fiscal quarter is still three months, but won't necessarily be a calendar quarter. For instance, a fiscal quarter might be August to October.

Being the astute person that you are, as evidenced by the fact that you chose this book from a crowded shelf, you might be thinking that you could find some bargain stocks by looking for high dividend yields. You are correct. Large companies that maintain steady dividends are judged all the time by their dividend yields. You'll learn in Chapter 3 that history proves that high-yielding, market-leading companies can be selected by dividend yield alone. Then, in Chapter 4, you'll learn automated investment strategies that use high dividend yield to select winners from the 30 stocks in the Dow Jones Industrial Average.

Earnings per Share (EPS)

This is the king of growth measures. *Earnings per share*, sometimes called *EPS*, takes what a company earned and divides it by the number of stock shares outstanding. It's the last thing listed on a company's income statement, the famous bottom line that everybody lives and dies for. Earnings per share is usually reported for either last quarter or last year. Analysts project future earnings, too.

Say Mister Magazine's earnings were $4,500 last quarter and there were 10 shares of stock outstanding. Mister Magazine's earnings per share would be $450. That's quite high. In real life, earnings per share tend to fall between $1 and $5 with occasional spikes to $10 or $20. But they can be anything, and they go negative when the company loses money.

For example, the economic downturn of 2008 hit company earnings hard. Aluminum giant Alcoa reported that it lost $1.2 billion in the fourth quarter, which came to -1.49 per share, or -0.28 excluding onetime items. The company cut 13 percent of its workforce, which came to 13,500 people, and put a freeze on hiring and salaries.

The problem with earnings per share is that it's subject to manipulation and market pressure. Notice in the preceding paragraph that Alcoa provided two ways to calculate its earnings in the fourth quarter of 2008 (4Q08). That happens a lot. Every company knows that investors examine earnings. Every company wants to report the biggest earnings number possible. So different companies use different accounting methods. Some deduct the dividends paid to preferred stock holders while others

don't issue preferred stock; some need to worry about investments that can be converted to common stock while others
don't; and every company chooses its own pace to depreciate
equipment. Sometimes earnings are affected by market conditions beyond a company's control. For instance, the cost of
goods sold fluctuates as market conditions change. A computer
company might sell the same computer model all year long. But
if the price of memory goes up, so does the company's cost of
building computers. One reason Alcoa cited for its earnings
decline was a 35 percent drop in aluminum prices during the
quarter. You don't need to know the details of how every company determines its earnings, but you should at least be aware
that this is not a cut-and-dried number. It's subject to manipulation and market pressure.

This oft-forgotten tidbit about earnings became headline
news back in 2001 and 2002. Enron and WorldCom misstated
earnings and declared bankruptcy when reporters uncovered the
fraud. Salomon Smith Barney telecom analyst Jack Grubman
had frequently described WorldCom in his research reports as a
"must own" stock, providing another example of full-service
brokerage advice you can live without. Enron and WorldCom
became delisted penny stocks.

Earnings per share remains a useful measurement. The bigger
the number, the better. It doesn't take a mental giant to see why.
The more a company earns, the more successful it is and the more
desirable it becomes to investors. That should make the stock
price rise. If the company's earnings per share increases quarter
after quarter at a faster rate, that's called *earnings momentum* or
earnings acceleration and is a popular way of identifying solid
growth companies. Some of the best performing mutual fund
managers use momentum investing to choose their stocks. I've
heard investors say they're searching for "the big mo," referring
to a hidden company with incredible earnings momentum.

Quarterly reports from a company showing either higher or
lower earnings per share than expected are called *earnings surprises*. They often cause a stock to rise or fall sharply. Analysts
study surprises carefully, hoping to spot a trend early.

Net Profit Margin

A company's *net profit margin* is determined by dividing the money left over after paying all its expenses by the amount of money it had before paying expenses. So, if a company makes $1 million and pays $900,000 in expenses, its net profit margin is 10 percent ($100,000 divided by $1,000,000). If a competing company also makes $1 million but pays only $700,000 in expenses, its net profit margin is 30 percent ($300,000 divided by $1,000,000). All other things being equal, which company's stock would you rather own? The company with a 30 percent profit margin, of course. It makes the same amount of money as its competitor but keeps more. Put differently, it spends less to earn the same income. A high profit margin tells you that the company's management is good at controlling costs. That's great news because every dollar frittered away unnecessarily is one less dollar of profit for shareholders.

High net profit margins are the hallmarks of companies that dominate their industries. When any industry is thriving, people notice and start new companies to compete against the existing ones. All the companies need to buy similar equipment, similar supplies, hire employees with similar skills, market to the same customers, and research similar improvements. Notice how similar the companies in an industry become? They can't all survive forever. When the shakeout comes, companies that are able to maintain a high net profit margin will make the most money and will survive. They've somehow figured a way to squeeze more profit from sales, a clear sign of superior management. Not only does the high net profit margin itself translate immediately into higher profits and a stronger bottom line, it also reveals to you a management team that is probably ahead of competitors in many areas of running a company in their industry.

Price/Book Ratio

Price/book compares a stock's price with how much the stock is worth right now if somebody liquidated the company.

In other words, if I took all of Mister Magazine's office space, magazine inventory, telephones, computers, and delivery bicycles to the local business auction, I'd get a sum of money for it. Let's say I could get $5,000. If there are currently 10 shares of Mister

Magazine stock outstanding, each one would be entitled to $500 of the company's sale price. Thus, Mister Magazine stock has a *book value per share* of $500. That's the "book" part of the price/book ratio. Explained in official terms, book value per share is common stockholders' equity divided by outstanding shares. You'll find both figures on the company's balance sheet.

Next, divide the current price by the book value to get the price/book ratio. If Mister Magazine currently sells for $400 a share, its price/book is .80 ($400 divided by $500). If the ratio is less than 1, that means you're paying less for the stock than its liquidation value. That's good. If the company goes bankrupt, you should still get your money back. If the ratio is more than 1, you're paying more than the stock's liquidation value.

Of course, a lot of crucial information about a company isn't reflected in its book value. Who cares about the fax machines and desks when you've got a business that earns money and a popular brand name? The value of McDonald's goes way beyond french fry machines and drive-through microphones. I can buy my own french fry machines, but can I serve billions and billions of people with them? Heck no, so I'm willing to pay more than book value for McDonald's.

Price/Earnings Ratio (P/E or Multiple)

This is the king of value measures. The price of a stock divided by its earnings per share is called its *price/earnings ratio*, or *P/E*, or *multiple*. At cocktail parties, just say "P and E." Every stock has a trailing P/E and a forward P/E. The trailing P/E uses earnings from the past 12 months while the forward P/E uses next year's projected earnings from an analyst. A stock's P/E ratio fluctuates all the time from changes in its price, which happen every day, and changes in its earnings, which happen every quarter.

A stock selling for $40 a share that earned $2 last year and is projected to earn $4 next year has a trailing P/E of 20 and a forward P/E of 10.

A stock's price by itself is meaningless. If one stock sells for $100 and another for $20, which would you rather buy? You have no idea unless you can put those two prices in context with company earnings. Once you know the P/E for each stock, then you can see if the stock is selling for a good price or not. Suppose the $100 stock earned $10 last year and the $20 stock earned $1. The $100 stock has a trailing P/E of 10. The $20 stock has a trailing P/E of 20. The $100 stock is a better value because you're buying more earnings power with your money.

Use a stock's P/E to determine how much you're paying for a company's earning power. If the P/E is high, you should expect to get high earnings growth for the extra money you paid for the stock. It's riskier to invest in a high P/E stock than a low P/E because it's more difficult for the high P/E to meet the high earnings expectations of its shareholders and analysts. Many of today's newest technology companies trade with high P/E ratios, generally over 20. Companies with low P/E ratios usually operate in slow-growth industries. Also, mature companies with low P/E ratios often pay dividends while new companies with high P/E ratios usually do not.

Price/Sales Ratio (P/S or PSR)

This is one of my favorites. P/E compares price with earnings, price/book compares price with liquidation value, and *price/sales* or *PSR* compares price with sales revenue. To determine a stock's PSR, simply take the company's total market value and divide it by the most recent four quarters of sales revenue. Sometimes you'll know the price per share and the sales per share. In fact, we use both on this book's Stocks to Watch worksheet. In that case, simply divide the price per share by the sales per share to get PSR.

For instance, if there are 10 shares of Mister Magazine stock outstanding and the current price is $400, Mister Magazine has a *total market value* of $4,000. If Mister Magazine has sales of $10,000 in the past four quarters, its PSR is .40. Running the numbers per share gives us the same result. Mister Magazine's stock price is $400 and its sales are $1,000 per share. Four hundred dollars divided by $1,000 is .40.

In winter 2012, Coca-Cola had a market value of $153 billion and sales of $46 billion. That produced a 3.3 PSR. PepsiCo had a market value of $103 billion and sales of $65 billion, for a 1.6 PSR. These numbers revealed something important to investors considering both stocks. People were paying $3.30 for each dollar of Coke's sales, but only $1.60 for each dollar of Pepsi's sales.

"So what?" you might say. "It's profits I care about, not sales." That's a common objection to using PSR. But remember from the explanation of earnings on page 28 that companies can manipulate earnings all sorts of ways. They use accounting rules that are flexible to interpret how much it costs them to do business and then subtract that number from revenue to get earnings. The flexible accounting can spit out small or big numbers as needed. But with sales revenue, there's not a lot to adjust. It's just what you sold—end of story.

Of course, it never hurts to see big sales *and* big earnings. The two aren't mutually exclusive.

Price/Cash-Flow Ratio (P/CF)

This is a very effective measurement of a company's valuation, as you'll hear from master investors in the next chapter. The steady stream of cash that's left over from profits after paying expenses is the heart of business success.

Like sales, cash flow avoids accounting tricks that can be used to boost earnings, and many investors find it even more illuminating than sales because it reveals what's left of sales after they've run through a company's expense structure. Projecting a company's ability to generate cash in the future, then looking at how much you're paying now for a share of that future cash flow with the price/cash-flow ratio is a good way to know whether you're getting a bargain or not.

If Mister Magazine's operations kicked off $80 of cash flow and the current price is $400, its price/cash-flow ratio is 5. If the price rises to $800 but the cash flow stays constant at $80, then price/cash-flow rises to 10. You're now paying twice as much for its cash flow as you were paying before, indicating that the stock is less of a bargain now.

Cash flow is sometimes further refined to free cash flow. The difference is that free cash flow is the cash left after operating cash flow pays for capital assets, which are things such as land, buildings, machines, equipment, and so on.

One of the master investors you'll meet in the next chapter, Bill Miller, found that "free cash flow yield is the single best predictor of excess return." That's just price/cash-flow turned around as cash-flow/price expressed as a percentage. In the Mister Magazine example above with $80 of cash flow and a $400 price, the price/cash-flow is 5 (400 divided by 80) and the cash-flow yield is .20 or 20 percent (80 divided by 400). A high cash-flow yield, which is to say a low price/cash-flow ratio, is a good indicator of low valuation and positive returns ahead.

Return on Equity (ROE)

Some people consider this the ultimate measure of a stock's success. *Return on equity* shows you the rate of return to shareholders by dividing net income by total shareholders' equity. Bigger is always better with this number because it means the company is making a lot of money off the investments that shareholders have made. A good return on equity is anything above 20 percent.

Let's see how this number changes as fortunes fluctuate. In 1995, Apple Computer (now just Apple) reported net income of $424 million and total shareholders' equity of $2.901 billion. Dividing 424 by 2,901 gave a return on equity of only 15 percent. Adding to the trouble, income dropped to a negative $816 million in 1996 with total shareholders' equity of $2.058 billion. That was a return on equity of -40 percent. Generally speaking, folks, minus signs in front of investment numbers are bad.

Apple's iPod-inspired turnaround worked wonders on the company's finances. Its 2006 return on equity of 23 percent was impressive. The release of the iPhone kept the momentum going. In 2008, Apple's return on equity reached 27 percent on net income of $2.947 billion. Its 2008 net income was bigger than its 1995 shareholders' equity. The release of the iPad extended this positive momentum even further. In 2011, Apple's return on equity weighed in at 42 percent on net income of $25.9 billion. In August of that year, it edged out Exxon Mobil to become the biggest company in the world by market cap, which you get by multiplying the number of outstanding shares of stock by the current market price per share. Apple's weighed in at $337 billion that August. In January 2012, it reached $400 billion. By then, however, Exxon's had climbed to $420 billion, as you'll read in a closer look at market cap on page 40.

Some Technical Stock Measurements

As I mentioned earlier, this book doesn't teach exhaustive technical analysis. We'll use just five technical measurements to help us time our purchase of stocks. The idea is that we want to buy companies with solid fundamentals per the previous section, just as their stock prices show confirming signals per the tools in this section.

SMA

This is a *simple moving average* of the stock's price and smooths out the bounciness of the raw price so you can better detect its trend. The position of the current price in relation to the SMA provides hints on where the price is heading next.

MACD

The letters stand for *moving average convergence divergence*, which sounds like a marital relations map but is a stock indicator created by Gerald Appel in the 1960s. It compares the exponential moving average of a stock's price from two time periods, usually 12 and 26 days or weeks or months, and then plots that difference to show a trend.

MACD is easier to understand when looking at a chart, so we'll look at one together later in the book.

Relative Strength Index

RSI alerts you to when a stock's price has stretched too far in one direction or the other and is due for a snap back toward the middle. When it stretches too far up, it's called *overbought*. When it stretches too far down, it's called *oversold*.

RSI fluctuates between 0 and 100. Most commonly, anything higher than 70 is considered overbought and due for a pullback, and anything lower than 30 oversold and due for a bounce.

Relative Price Strength

Relative price strength shows you how a stock's price has performed compared with the prices of all other stocks. In this book, you'll learn to use relative price strength as it's presented in *Investor's Business Daily*, a national newspaper that ranks the relative price strength of all stocks from 1 to 99. Stocks that rank

90 have outperformed 90 percent of all other stocks. Stocks that rank 20 have underperformed 80 percent of all other stocks. Pretty simple.

Volume

This is an easy one. *Volume* is simply the amount of a stock that's traded on any given day, week, or any other time period. A stock's volume is a good indicator of how much interest people have in the stock. That's important to know because the stock market is greatly affected by supply and demand. If everybody wants to buy a certain stock, its price will rise. If nobody wants it, the price will fall. Some investors like to buy stocks with low volume, hoping that major institutions will discover them and begin trading heavily. Demand soars and so do prices. Lots of investors watch stock volume in an attempt to catch trends early. As with surfing, you want to be in front of the wave.

Volume is measured in either the number of shares traded or the dollar amount that is moved as a result of that trading. If 1,000,000 shares of Mister Magazine changed hands on Tuesday at a price of $8, the share volume was 1,000,000 and the dollar volume was $8,000,000.

The strongest signal from volume occurs when it surges higher as the stock price moves. Rising volume on a rising stock price shows something good going on at the company. Rising volume on a falling stock price shows something bad. The stronger the volume, the more persistent the stock's price trend.

How to Read the Stock Pages

The Internet is the most popular place to get stock information these days, but some people still prefer a newspaper. Your local paper probably has a listing, and you can always access one of the national investment papers such as *Investor's Business Daily* or *The Wall Street Journal.*

The format of stock pages changes slightly from paper to paper, but if you can read one you can wing it through any other. Also, most papers include a box that explains their format. In fact, why are you reading about it here? Just turn to your paper's stock pages and read how to use them right there. On the off chance that you don't have a paper handy, I'll explain how to read the stock pages. On the following page, there is an excerpt from the January 28, 2007, *Los Angeles Times* that includes information for Disney.

As you can see, there are eight columns of information. The first two columns show the stock's *52-week High and Low* prices. Like the names imply, these are just the highest price and lowest price the stock traded for over the past 52 weeks. These figures are adjusted to reflect any stock splits. The 52-week high and low are handy because they show the range a stock has traded in. It's helpful to know if the stock is currently selling near the highest price anybody has paid for it in the past year, or if it's cheaper than anybody's seen in a year. Also, you can see if there's a huge space between the high and low or if they're close together. Sometimes the figures are within a few dollars of each other. Such a narrow trading range might appeal to you if you prefer quiet stocks that pay steady dividends. On the other hand, if you're seeking major price appreciation, you might like to see a huge differential between the stock's high and low. Disney's 52-week high was 35.97 and its low was 24.90. Five years later, on January 27, 2012, they were 44.34 and 28.19.

The third column, called *YTD %chg*, shows the stock's percentage price change since the beginning of the year or its initial public offering. You'll see the abbreviation YTD a lot with investing. It means *year-to-date*. Disney had appreciated 0.8 percent since the beginning of 2007. On January 28, 2009, it had depreciated 1.8 percent YTD, and would, less than a week later, report a 32 percent quarterly earnings decline amid what chief executive Bob Iger described as likely "the weakest economy in our lifetime." Things perked up in later years, though. On January 27, 2012, Disney stock had appreciated 4.7 percent YTD, and reported better-than-expected earnings growth of 12 percent.

The fourth column, called *Stock-Div*, lists the name of the company followed immediately by the dividend. The dividend shown is an annual figure determined by the last quarterly or semiannual payout. Disney's dividend was 31 cents. Divide by 4 and you know that the last quarterly dividend Disney paid was 7.75 cents. If you'd owned a single share you could have almost paid for one photocopy with your dividend check. The

LOS ANGELES TIMES

52-week high . low		YTD %chg.	Stock-Div	Yld	P/E	Close	$ chg
19.21	13.58	+1.0	DeutTel .87e	4.7		18.38	-.59
66.36	47.40	+4.6	DevDv 2.36	3.6	39	65.83	+1.28
74.75	48.94	+1.5	DevonE .45	.7	9	68.08	+.42
80.20	58.64	-1.0	Diageo 2.29e	2.9		78.48	+.16
97.90	62.26	+1.4	DiaOffs .50a	.6	19	81.04	+1.83
18.46	12.26	+1.6	DiamRk .72	3.9	32	18.30	-.09
17.00	9.50	+.9	DianaShip 1.50e	9.4	21	15.96	-.77
56.29	34.90	+2.4	DicksSprt		28	50.19	-.79
47.13	36.40	-4.5	Diebold .86	1.9	40	44.48	-.69
37.31	22.66	+3.9	DigitalRlt 1.15f	3.2	81	35.57	+.02
36.47	23.94	-5.1	Dillards .16	.5	14	33.18	-1.10
26.17	23.28	-1.1	Dillard38 1.88	7.6		24.67	+.08
25.57	13.28	-3.4	DirecTV		26	24.09	+.10
35.97	24.90	+.8	Disney .31f	.9	21	34.55	-.95
21.80	14.65	+1.0	Dist&Srv .45e	2.2		20.78	+.54
16.40	12.44	+1.1	DivCapRl 1.26	7.7	q	16.42	+.24
19.06	11.33	-5.0	DrReddy s .06e	.3		17.29	-1.29
35.00	17.83	+5.2	DolbyLab		41	32.63	+2.14
18.32	12.10	+4.8	DollarG .20	1.2	30	16.73	-.74
50.09	37.35	+1.4	DollarTh		19	46.27	+1.20
25.79	24.99	-1.3	DmCNG pf 1.95	7.8		25.04	+.02
84.44	68.72	-2.1	DomRes 2.84f	3.5	18	82.07	+1.31
49.95	**22.50**	**-3.5**	**DmRsBW 3.88e**	**15.2**	**q**	**25.50**	**+2.42**
29.10	21.01	+2.2	Dominos .48	1.7	16	28.61	-.09
8.72	4.75	-5.5	Domtar g			7.98	-.53
38.97	30.16	-1.9	Donldson .36	1.1	21	34.05	-.22
37.48	28.50	+3.8	DonlleyRR 1.04	2.8	34	36.89	+.53
12.07	1.98	-13.9	DoralFin			2.47	+.03
16.44	12.10	-6.9	DoubleHull 1.74e	11.5		15.07	-.93
27.93	22.99	+2.1	DEmmett n .12p			27.15	-.50
51.92	42.83	-3.2	Dover .74	1.6	17	47.47	-1.41
20.60	9.33	+6.1	DoverDG s .18	1.3	18	14.18	-.17
6.50	4.68	+1.1	DoverMot .06	1.1	36	5.37	+.15
21.48	18.25	-3.0	Dow30Pr 1.80	8.8	q	20.36	-.44
44.30	33.00	+4.5	DowChm 1.50	3.6	11	41.70	-.38
41.39	32.16	+.2	DowJns 1.00	2.6	8	38.09	-.96
77.30	59.08	-3.2	DowneyFn .48f	.7	10	70.27	+1.64
30.50	20.05	-3.8	DrmwksA		29	28.38	-1.28
22.99	18.28	-4.4	DreClyDiv 1.30	5.9	q	21.96	-.15
28.45	18.03	+3.5	DresserR		34	25.33	+.03
38.90	22.26	+4.9	Drew Inds		16	27.29	+1.27
4.53	3.90	+3.3	DryHYSt .39	8.9	q	4.36	+.02

small *f* after Disney's dividend means that it increased on the last declaration. By the way, in the five years following this excerpt, Disney boosted its dividend from 31 cents to 60. The company hiked its dividend from 40 to 60 cents in December 2011. Iger said Disney "had a great creative, strategic and financial year.

We are pleased to be able to raise our shareholder dividend by 50 percent while continuing to invest for future growth."

The fifth column provides the stock's *yield*. It's shown as an annualized percentage return provided by the dividend. You can use the figure to compare the stock's dividend performance with your savings account or CD. More importantly, you can use it to find undervalued large companies as you'll learn in Chapter 2 and Chapter 3. Disney's yield was 0.9 percent. Five years later, it was 1.5 percent.

The sixth column shows the stock's *price-earnings ratio* or *P/E*. The P/E is figured by dividing the closing price of the stock by the company's total earnings per share for the latest four quarters. It's the most common measure of whether a stock is a good deal. All else being equal, you'd prefer to buy a stock with a low P/E because it means you're paying a relatively small amount to own a share in the earnings. Disney's P/E was 21. Two years later, in the midst of the subprime mortgage crisis, it was 10. Three years after that, it was 16.

The seventh and eighth columns show the *closing price* and *dollar change* for the previous day. Disney closed at $34.55, down 95 cents. Five years later, it closed at $39.25, down 10 cents.

There are footnotes sprinkled throughout stock tables that identify things like preferred stock shares, ex-dividend dates, and new stocks. These differ from paper to paper but should be defined in your paper's explanatory notes.

Three Stock Classifications You Should Know

People always try to categorize objects in their lives to make them easier to deal with. If you hear the model name of a new car your first question is probably "What type of car is it?" You know that sports cars are fast, minivans haul a lot of people, and trucks carry cargo. Stocks are categorized hundreds of different ways. In fact, from my interviews with brokers, planners, investment clubs, and people on the street, I'm convinced that there is a classification system for each investor. Our view of the world is shaped by our experiences and personalities, which is why no two people view the same stock in the same way.

Perception Is Everything

A long time ago, I stopped by a local computer store to see the new IBM Aptiva. While I tested it out, two men joined me at the keyboard.

One said, "I used to work for IBM and I'd never own anything from the company. It's the fattest, most bureaucratic business I've ever seen." The other said, "I still work for IBM and I'd never survive without our products. We have the best technology and it's reliable."

Interestingly, the first man bought IBM stock when it traded around $170 and watched it drop to $45. The second man bought it at $45 and watched it rise to $130.

Same company, different employees. Same computers, different experiences. Same stock, different prices.

Surprise! You need to know only three widely accepted classifications: the size of the company, its industry classification, and whether it's growth or value. I hate complexity as much as you do and I think these three classifications provide all the information we need.

Company Size

A company is either big or small. Next topic.

Although it's not that simple, company size is pretty straightforward. To investors, company size is called *market capitalization* or just *market cap*. Market cap is determined by multiplying the number of outstanding shares of stock by the current market price per share. So if Mister Magazine has grown like Jack's beanstalk and there are 4 million shares of its stock outstanding and they trade for $10 per share, Mister Magazine's market cap is $40 million.

Is that big or small? Compared with the treehouse operation it started as, that's huge! From its $1,000 initial sale to venture capitalists, Mister Magazine has grown 3,999,900 percent. So from an initial investor and company founder perspective, Mister Magazine is enormous.

But compared with Exxon Mobil it's a drop of oil in a tanker. Exxon's market cap was about $420 billion in January 2012. That's 10,500 times bigger than Mister Magazine. As you can imagine, owning shares of Exxon and owning shares of Mister Magazine would probably be very different investment experiences.

The notion of how to divide companies along market cap lines has changed over the years. Take a look at the five market cap ranges used in the mid-1990s by Morningstar, the most popular fund rating service, to classify the holdings of stock mutual funds:

Giant	>$25 Bil
Large	$5 Bil–$25 Bil
Medium	$1 Bil–$5 Bil
Small	$250 Mil–$1 Bil
Micro	<$250 Mil

In mid-1996, Morningstar looked at the 50 mutual funds in each category with the highest concentration in stocks of that market cap range, then measured their combined performance. Here's how the groups compared:

Market Cap	3-Year	5-Year	10-Year
Giant	14.72%	12.77%	10.39%
Large	14.17%	14.44%	11.78%
Medium	16.09%	16.09%	11.99%
Small	15.19%	16.83%	8.70%
Micro	16.45%	16.56%	11.45%

The problem with viewing market cap in absolute terms is that market caps change every day. Prices fluctuate and companies issue more stock or buy back outstanding shares. More important than a company's absolute market cap is its relative market cap, that is, how big it is compared with other companies.

For that very reason, Morningstar replaced its rigid market cap table with a system of only three relative sizes:

Large Companies	comprising the top 70 percent of U.S. market value
Medium Companies	comprising the next 20 percent of U.S. market value
Small Companies	comprising the next 10 percent of U.S. market value

In early 2009, large companies weighed in at an average market cap of $52 billion, medium companies at $4 billion, and small companies at $940 million. The groups posted the following average annual returns:

Market Cap	1-Year	3-Year	5-Year
Large	-31.0%	-7.7%	-1.8%
Medium	-35.2%	-13.2%	-2.9%
Small	-33.9%	-14.2%	-3.3%

In early 2012, large companies weighed in at an average market cap of $65 billion, medium companies at $5.6 billion, and small companies at $1.5 billion. They posted the following average annual returns:

Market Cap	1-Year	3-Year	5-Year
Large	+5.2%	+6.1%	+0.1%
Medium	+3.5%	+8.1%	+0.5%
Small	+2.4%	+8.4%	+0.6%

Industry Classification

You need to know what a company does to make money, otherwise you don't know which other companies to compare it with. Also, if you know what industry a company operates in, you can keep an eye on that industry for trends.

In many cases, you'll know off the top of your head what a company does to earn a buck. You're probably aware that Boeing makes airplanes, Harley Davidson makes motorcycles, Coke makes soft drinks, AT&T provides phone service, and Dell sells computers. A lot of bigger companies make money in several ways, however, and you should know all of them. Altria makes Marlboro and other cigarette brands, but also owns Chateau Ste. Michelle winery, the leading single producer of Riesling wine in the U.S., and owns part of SABMiller, brewer of Miller Genuine Draft beer.

You'll become aware of a company's business simply by getting interested enough to invest. If somebody mentions to you that Allamuck Corporation is going gangbusters and tripled in size over the past year, you'll probably look it up. Once there, you'll either rule it out based on a few key measures or get excited and want to learn more. If you call Allamuck for an annual report, search the Internet for Allamuck info, or make a trip to your local library, you're going to know what Allamuck does for a living.

You'll learn specific places to find company profiles in Chapter 6.

Growth or Value

The last label you want to place on your stocks is whether they're growth or value. You read all about growth investing versus value investing on page 20. When you're examining a potential company, know whether it's increasing sales and earnings and is expected to continue doing so. That's a growth company.

Maybe, instead, the company has had a rough couple of years and its stock price is at an all-time low. After reviewing everything you know about the company, you might decide that it's not as bad off as everybody thinks. That's a value company.

Growth companies and value companies behave differently. Make sure you know which type you're buying.

2
How the Masters Tell Us to Invest

Now that you speak the language of stocks and should be able to follow a discussion about them, let's talk strategy! When I decided to enter the stock market, I was nervous. Just about everybody is. At first glance, it looks like there are a few people making lots of money and a lot of people making little money. Come to think of it, things look pretty much that same way at second, third, and fourth glance.

But as long as you follow an informed path and conduct your own research, you'll be fine. Buying what headlines tell you to buy doesn't work. Buying what your neighbor, friend, or relative tells you to buy doesn't work. But buying what seems best to you after thorough research can work.

This chapter and the next two contain the most important information in the book. The rest of the book deals with the mechanics of investing: learning the basics, choosing a broker, placing an order, and so on. But these three chapters help you form a strategy.

In this chapter, you'll learn how the best investors make money and how you can, too. Investing is full of legends. Some of their stories involve overnight profits, a lot of luck, or complex theories. Those legends don't help you and me when we're sitting at the kitchen table with a newspaper trying to figure out a good way to retire. What helped me and will help you is studying the masters who use an approach that has proven itself over time and is feasible for individual investors to adopt.

Meet the Masters

Benjamin Graham—Ben to those who've read a lot of his stuff—is one of the most influential investment writers ever. His hallmark achievement is a book called _The Intelligent Investor_, which presents a rational value-oriented way to invest in stocks. It is to investing what _Moby-Dick_ is to American literature: an absolute must-read for anybody studying the topic. Graham is the grandfather of value investing.

Philip Fisher is one of the first people to reveal growth-investing strategies. His book, _Common Stocks and Uncommon Profits_, discusses the characteristics of superior companies and how anybody can identify them. I suppose it is to investing what _Huckleberry Finn_ is to American literature: the second must-read for serious students of the topic. Fisher is the grandfather of growth investing.

Then comes Warren Buffett, considered by many to be the world's greatest investor. Buffett is still active today, running his company from Omaha and continuing to rack up impressive performance. Through his capital allocation skills alone, Buffett amassed a fortune greater than $50 billion by achieving an average annual book value gain of 21 percent for more than 40 years. He studied and admired both Graham and Fisher, then combined their teachings in his own style.

Next is Peter Lynch. He managed the Fidelity Magellan Fund for 13 years and took it from assets of only $20 million to more than $14 billion. He turned a $10,000 investment into $190,000 in 10 years. He is considered by many to be the best mutual fund manager in history.

William O'Neil is the founder of _Investor's Business Daily_, a newspaper that a lot of investors prefer over _The Wall Street Journal_. Before founding _IBD_, he enjoyed a successful stock-investing career that allowed him to purchase a seat on the New York Stock Exchange when he was only 30 years old. He is a committed growth investor and a great lecturer.

Bill Miller is our last master and one of my personal favorites. For thirty years, he managed Legg Mason Value Trust, famous for beating the S&P 500 15 years in a row from 1990 to 2005. Miller did it by discarding traditional growth and value filters to seek bargains of either stripe based on future free cash flows. That built an eclectic portfolio of both expensive and cheap stocks by traditional measures. He's a contrarian, unafraid to stand alone when he believes he's right, which is most of the time.

That's our lineup. These six masters cover the spectrum of large companies to small companies, and growth style to value style. Kick back and spend a little time learning what the masters have to tell. Don't worry about knowing every piece of their advice by heart. I close out the chapter with a section pulling all their opinions together.

Benjamin Graham

Benjamin Graham wrote *The Intelligent Investor*, probably the most widely recognized investment book in the world, and *Security Analysis*, coauthored with David Dodd. Graham mentored Warren Buffett, and in a preface to *The Intelligent Investor* Buffett wrote, "I read the first edition of this book early in 1950, when I was nineteen. I thought then that it was by far the best book about investing ever written. I still think it is." I didn't read it until I was twenty, which explains why Buffett is still slightly wealthier than I am.

Market Fluctuation and Emotion

Graham teaches that nobody ever knows what the market will do. I want to emphasize this innocent-looking observation. *Nobody ever knows what the market will do.* That includes analysts, your wealthy aunt, every newsletter writer, and every stockbroker. Graham isn't the only successful investor to point this fact out. When J.P. Morgan was asked what the market would do, he replied, "It will fluctuate." The nice thing about nobody knowing what the market will do is that you can profit by reacting intelligently to what it does do.

Viewing a stock as ownership in a business instead of as an electronic symbol to be traded helps keep perspective in volatile times. Graham offered a famous way of understanding the stock market, saying it behaves like a voting machine in the short term but like a weighing machine in the long term. As investors "vote" on a stock by buying and selling it in reaction to ephemeral news events and other emotional inputs, its price rises and falls. Over time, however, the performance of businesses moves the aggregate of investors to behave accordingly by buying winning companies and selling losing ones. The market eventually moves past voting on noise to weighing business results and assigning higher stock prices to more valuable companies in the long term.

We are all part of the general public and the general public is usually wrong. To counteract our inherent emotional weakness, Graham says we should automate parts of our investment strategy. By that he means use a set formula to find good stocks. Not a formula like you used in algebra, but a set of measurements that aren't subject to emotion. You don't want to fall victim to just "feeling good" about a company's future. Human emotions are frail beasts. Nobody's wealth should ride on them.

Automated, measurable criteria give us something stable to fall back on when we get confused by bold headlines and great stories. Nobody is immune to such pressures. If your whole office is talking about a new toy for the Christmas season that's already breaking retail sales records in Florida, Maine, and New Hampshire, who wants to point out that the manufacturer lost money the past two years? After your office mates buy the stock, they're going to start pinning newspaper stories about the company on their corkboards, displaying the shiny toy in their offices, and maybe hanging postcards of the exotic travel destinations they'll be visiting with their profits. It's a party! We all want to go to a party. But by developing an automatic filter that we can view such parties through, intelligent investors won't suffer lost money when the party's over.

Stock Valuations

Every stock has both a business valuation and a market valuation. The *business valuation* is simply the stock's book value and its earnings. Remember from page 30 that book value is determined by dividing all the company's assets by the number of stock shares outstanding. In other words, it's the amount you could get if you liquidated the company—sold everything the company owns, like the delivery trucks, fax machines, and conference tables. However, and this is important, investors need to factor in earnings with book value to fully appreciate a company's business valuation. It's not enough for us to know what we could sell the place for; we must also know what potential profit the place holds. We get that by looking at earnings per share, which you read about on page 28.

The *market valuation* is what the stock trades for. It might be higher or lower than the stock's business valuation. You'd much rather buy stocks at prices lower than their business valuations, of course, because they're on sale.

Just like you can buy your favorite sweatshirt for $10 less during a clearance sale, you can sometimes buy stock in your favorite companies for $10 per share less than they're actually worth. In Graham's language, such a stock's market valuation would be $10 less than its business valuation.

Graham recommends that investors buy stocks at prices near their business valuations. That means you'd like price/book ratios to be around 1 and you would also like P/E ratios low, preferably below 15.

Don't worry about the specific measures Graham uses to evaluate stocks. Instead, concentrate on the nature of those measures. He suggests measures that show a stock's value: price/book and P/E. He also suggests measures that show a stock's growth potential: financial position and earnings growth. Notice how Graham blends value and growth measures because it's going to form the foundation of this book's strategy.

When you buy stocks that are cheap compared with their worth, you can ignore market fluctuations. Sometimes the market will drop the price of a stock for no apparent reason. So our job as investors is to identify stocks with strong potential and watch the market for buying opportunities. In Graham's own words, we should "use these vagaries to play the master game of buying low and selling high."

Margin of Safety

Graham's greatest gift to investors was his concept of a *margin of safety*, which is the difference between a company's business valuation and its market valuation. That definition is sometimes too vague to be meaningful. Don't think of this as a hard number. A better way to think of it is as a spectrum, so that a stock either has a big margin of safety or it has a small one. A stock with a big margin of safety can go way down in price and still be a good investment; a stock with a small margin of safety can only drop a little in price and still be considered a good investment.

Graham was deliberately vague in describing a stock's margin of safety. He said that investment analysis is not an exact science. There are hard factors like book value, financial statements, and debt, but there are subjective factors like quality of management and nature of the business. He preferred to examine measurable qualities of a business because, well, they're measurable. If you're paying less for a company than it would sell for piece by piece, there's a good margin of safety there. If you're paying a lot more for a company than it would sell for and a lot more than what it's earning just because the papers say the new team of people taking over are brilliant, there's little margin of safety. What if, just what if, those brilliant folks make a mistake? Your losses could be extreme. But if hard numbers limit those losses when the brilliant managers mess up, you're still relatively safe. There's a lot of room for management to make mistakes because there's value underlying the company they're running. That's the margin of safety. It's not reducible to a single number, but the notion makes sense.

Graham emphasized the financial health of companies when discussing margin of safety. Long-term debt is very bad because it reduces the company's business valuation. The bills need to be paid even when brilliant managers make mistakes.

The one hard figure Graham assigned to margin of safety was that investors should buy a stock for no more than two-thirds of its book value. Another way of stating that is that a stock's price/book ratio should be no more than .66. So if a company has a book value of $50 per share, you should pay no more than $33 for it. Even at that low price, Graham wanted to see a low P/E ratio, which usually accompanies a low price/book ratio.

What You Should Retain from Graham

Graham was a great investor who insisted on paying a fair price for a stock no matter how bright its prospects were. That's a value approach to investing. However, he recognized the importance of a company's ability to grow earnings. This combination of value and growth is the foundation of good investing that I recommend in this book's strategy. Other key points:

✔ Nobody ever knows what the market will do, but we can profit by reacting intelligently to what it does do. It's a voting machine in the short term, but a weighing machine in the long term.

✔ Because we are all members of the general public and the public is usually wrong, we should rely on hard measurements to counteract our emotions and give ourselves something to feel secure about.

✔ Stocks have business valuations and market valuations. The first is what the company would be worth if it was liquidated, the second is the price the market has placed on the stock.

✔ We should know a stock's margin of safety, which is a general feel for how much that stock can drop in price and still be a good investment. Central to determining a stock's margin of safety is knowing the difference between its business valuation and market valuation.

Philip Fisher

Philip Fisher wrote *Common Stocks and Uncommon Profits*. Warren Buffet was so impressed with the book that he met with Fisher personally to learn more about his strategies. In 1969, Buffet told *Forbes*, "I'm 15 percent Fisher and 85 percent Benjamin Graham."

Characteristics of Superior Companies

Fisher wrote that investors should buy businesses with the ability to grow sales and profits over the years at rates greater than their industry average. Such companies are either "fortunate and able" or "fortunate because they are able." These seem like very similar things at first blush, but Fisher distinguished them with examples. A company that is fortunate and able has a good product right from the start, solid management, and it benefits from factors beyond the company's control such as an unforeseen use of its product. A company that is fortunate because it is able might have a mediocre product to begin with, but the management team is so clever that they adapt the product to the marketplace and diversify into other areas that offer opportunity. Thus, "fortunate because they are able" refers to shrewd management more than anything.

Shrewd management is hard to define. To me it's a bit like indecency: I know it when I see it but can't say in advance what it is. To Fisher, shrewd management always looks past the current set of products to new items that will grow sales in the future. That sometimes requires trading immediate profits for long-term gains, something that's unpopular on Wall Street. Because investors scrutinize earnings regularly, it's imperative that management communicate honestly with shareholders in good times and bad. Management's integrity was vitally important to Fisher, as it is to most good investors.

Sales are the key to prosperity. A company's extensive research and development of a superior product is irrelevant if it doesn't sell. Investors should examine the capability of a company's sales organization, paying particular attention to the extent of its customer research.

Of course, profits must follow sales. Enormous sales growth is irrelevant if it doesn't produce corresponding profits. To make sure a company is profitable, look at its profit margins. This stuff isn't as mysterious as you thought, is it? A company's profit margins coupled with its ability to maintain and improve them will tell you everything you need to know about its earning power. You'll learn later how to check a company's profit margins.

Profits must be realized soon enough to be useful. This means keeping a positive cash flow. Bad companies sell a million widgets on credit and then resort to borrowing money or issuing more stock to keep alive while the check is in the mail. Good companies get their money soon enough to live off it. That means when it's time to expand into new markets, build new factories, hire more people, or market to a wider audience, a good company taps its bank account.

The last characteristic of a superior company is its status as the lowest-cost producer of its products or services and dedication to remaining such. Companies with low break-even points and high profit margins can survive hard times. Almost any company looks good when the economy is soaring. But only the leanest operations look good when the going gets tough. This is related in spirit to Graham's margin of safety. Low cost, high profit operations are the safest around because they have an edge in all phases of the economy.

Characteristics of Superior Investors

To succeed at investing, Fisher thought most people should concentrate on industries they already know. He called this your circle of competence.

Within that circle of competence, investors should conduct thorough and unconventional research to understand the superiority of a company over its competitors. The best source of information is the individuals who know the company. Customers, suppliers, former and current employees, competitors, and industry associations all have tidbits of information that are useful to investors. Fisher called this information scuttlebutt, a navy term describing gossip around a ship's drinking fountain. Instead of gossiping about your mate's late-night escapades, Fisher thought you should go out and gossip about the prospects of potential investments.

Scuttlebutt and other research are time-consuming. You can thoroughly understand only so many companies. Therefore, Fisher recommended a focused portfolio. He rarely placed more than ten companies in a portfolio, and even at that, most of the money was usually concentrated in three or four stocks. A few superior companies are better than a slew of mediocre ones.

What You Should Retain from Fisher

Fisher recommends investing in companies with the power to earn a profit and outpace their competition. That's a growth approach to investing. To find superior companies, he was willing to look beyond hard numbers to factors that are not measurable, such as capabilities of management and the perception of those who know the company. Other key points:

✔ Buy businesses with the ability to grow sales and profits over the years at rates greater than their industry average.

✔ Look for capable management. The best management is willing to sacrifice immediate profits for long-term gains and maintains integrity and honesty with shareholders.

✔ Sales are key to everything. You should examine the capabilities of a company's sales organization, paying particular attention to its customer research.

✔ Profits must follow sales. Sales are irrelevant if they don't produce profit. You should know a company's profit margins.

✔ Profits must be realized soon enough to be useful. You should look for positive cash flow and a healthy cash reserve so the company can meet obligations without borrowing.

✔ Lowest-cost producers have an edge in all phases of the economy. Combined with a high profit margin, low-cost production is Fisher's version of Graham's margin of safety.

✔ You should invest in areas you're already familiar with: your circle of competence.

✔ You should conduct thorough, unconventional research by interviewing people who know the company best, such as employees, competitors, and suppliers.

✔ Because of the extensive research needed to uncover superior companies, you should own just a handful at any given time. A few superior companies beats a slew of mediocre ones.

Warren Buffett

You wouldn't be thrown out of an investment club for saying Warren Buffett is the world's greatest investor. Some have made money faster, others have made it in flashier ways, but few can match Buffett's methodical investment methods or his long-term record.

First, some background. In 1956, Buffett began a limited investment partnership with $100,000 raised from family and friends. The partnership remained in existence for 13 years, during which time Buffett produced an average annual return of 29 percent. As his reputation grew, Buffett accepted more investors into the fold and moved his offices from home to Kiewit Plaza in Omaha. In 1969, Buffett disbanded the partnership, sent his investors' money to safe places, and took control of a textile company called Berkshire Hathaway. Berkshire became Buffett's holding company to own businesses like Dairy Queen, See's Candy, The Pampered Chef, Clayton Homes, NetJets, and World Book Encyclopedias.

Berkshire also bought insurance companies, which became the cornerstone of Buffett's success. Why insurance companies? Because premium-paying policyholders provide a constant stream of cash. Buffett invested this cash, called "float," until claims needed to be paid. Because Berkshire Hathaway is located in Nebraska, a state with loose insurance regulations, Buffett invested a lot of the float in stocks. Most insurance companies choose safe bonds for their investments, usually allocating no more than 20 percent to stocks. But Buffett chose stocks—sometimes allocating over 95 percent of the float to them—and both he and Berkshire grew wealthy because of his picks. Buffett amassed a personal fortune of $50 billion, give or take a few billion.

Your situation is probably not like Warren Buffett's. You probably don't enjoy a steady stream of insurance premiums to invest as you see fit. You probably can't acquire companies as permanent holdings in your spare time. If you can, you don't need this book! But if you're like the vast majority of us and are investing limited personal resources in the stock market, read this section for pieces of Buffett's strategy that you can apply to your own program. I'll pull them together into this book's strategy later.

One other point before we dive in. A look at Buffett's stock techniques is a look back in time. Although he's still active today, his approach to capital allocation has gradually changed focus from stocks to whole companies as Berkshire succeeded and its cash flow ramped up. Buffett wrote in the 2006 annual report that he and his partner Charlie Munger continue "to need 'elephants' in order for us to use Berkshire's flood of incoming cash. Charlie and I must therefore ignore the pursuit of mice and focus our acquisition efforts on much bigger game."

Tough problem to have, eh?

The Stock Market

In the old days when investors checked stock prices on quote machines instead of the Internet, Warren Buffett was famous for not having one in his office. The world's greatest investor doesn't check stock prices because they're unreliable indicators of a company's worth. Some days they're up, others they're down. Sometimes Wall Street thinks the market looks good, other times it thinks it looks bad. It's willy-nilly, unreasonable, and unnecessary to know. Remember that Graham felt the same way: Nobody ever knows what the market will do.

At some point every investor needs to know what the stock of a company he or she is interested in sells for. That part's a given. What Buffett's habits show us is the fruitlessness of knowing minute movements, hourly changes, and daily aberrations. In the 1993 Berkshire Hathaway annual report, Buffett wrote, "After we buy a stock, consequently, we would not be disturbed if markets closed for a year or two. We don't need a daily quote on our 100 percent position in See's or H.H. Brown to validate our well being. Why, then, should we need a quote on our 7 percent interest in Coke?"

He still feels that way. In his February 2012 letter to shareholders, he wrote about Berkshire's stock in American Express, Bank of America, Coca-Cola, IBM, and Wells Fargo: "We view these holdings as partnership interests in wonderful businesses, not as marketable securities to be bought or sold based on their near-term prospects." He actually prefers falling stock prices and pointed out the following in the letter:

> The logic is simple: If you are going to be a net buyer of stocks in the future, either directly with your own money or indirectly (through your ownership of a company that is repurchasing shares), you are hurt when stocks rise. You benefit when stocks swoon. Emotions, however, too often complicate the matter: Most people, including those who will be net buyers in the future, take comfort in seeing stock prices advance. These shareholders resemble a commuter who rejoices after the price of gas increases, simply because his tank contains a day's supply.
>
> Charlie and I don't expect to win many of you over to our way of thinking—we've observed enough human behavior to know the futility of that—but we do want you to be aware of our personal calculus. And here a confession is in order: In my early days I, too, rejoiced when the market rose. Then I read Chapter Eight of Ben Graham's *The Intelligent Investor*,

the chapter dealing with how investors should view fluctuations in stock prices. Immediately the scales fell from my eyes, and low prices became my friend. Picking up that book was one of the luckiest moments in my life.

In an October 16, 2008, op-ed in *The New York Times*, in the heat of the subprime mortgage crash, Buffett educated investors on the need to reverse their emotions in the stock market:

> The financial world is a mess, both in the United States and abroad. Its problems, moreover, have been leaking into the general economy, and the leaks are now turning into a gusher. In the near term, unemployment will rise, business activity will falter and headlines will continue to be scary. So . . . I've been buying American stocks. . . . Why?
>
> A simple rule dictates my buying: Be fearful when others are greedy, and be greedy when others are fearful. And most certainly, fear is now widespread, gripping even seasoned investors. . . .
>
> Let me be clear on one point: I can't predict the short-term movements of the stock market. I haven't the faintest idea as to whether stocks will be higher or lower a month—or a year—from now. What is likely, however, is that the market will move higher, perhaps substantially so, well before either sentiment or the economy turns up. So if you wait for the robins, spring will be over.

Two years later, the S&P 500 had gained 25 percent from its close at 946 on the day of Buffett's op-ed.

Buying Quality Companies at Bargain Prices

Buffett emphasizes buying quality companies rather than speculating about the direction of a stock price. Good companies are still good companies when times are bad. If you buy a good company and the price of its stock drops, that doesn't signal anything more than a chance to pick up additional shares at a discount. Buffett says you should always understand the businesses in which you invest. The simpler, the better. Once you understand a business, you can make a judgment on the company's quality.

You should exercise the same scrutiny when buying shares in a company as you'd exercise when buying the company itself. In advice reminiscent of Fisher, Buffett told investors in a 1993 *Fortune* interview to "invest within your circle of competence. It's not how big the circle is that counts, it's how well you define the parameters."

Buying a quality business is vital to Buffett, far more vital even than buying at a discount. After all, what's the point of buying something on sale if you're getting junk? It won't perform well in the long term, which leaves you one option: Get lucky on a price run-up and sell in the short term. Time helps wonderful businesses but destroys mediocre ones, which means you should be comfortable standing by your companies over time. Investors must evaluate companies on their individual merits before looking at stock prices.

For example, Buffett bought GEICO stock after it declined from $60 to $2. The company faced a possible bankruptcy and a growing number of class-action lawsuits from shareholders. The world thought the stock would end up worthless, but Buffett loaded up on it anyway, eventually owning half of the company. Buying a stock that's declined 96.5 percent is clearly a value move because by just about any measure it's discounted. In GEICO's case, Buffett found a great company at a colossal bargain.

But then there's Coca-Cola. Buffett loved the soft drink from the time he bought and sold individual cans of it when he was five years old. He watched the company's phenomenal growth over three decades and in 1986 made Cherry Coke the official beverage of Berkshire's annual meetings. Yet he didn't invest in Coca-Cola until 1988. The stock had risen over five-hundredfold since 1928 and over fivefold since 1982. To many it looked overpriced, but Buffett invested more than $1 billion. Buying a stock that's risen fivefold in six years appears to be a growth move. In Buffett's case, however, he saw Coca-Cola selling for well under its intrinsic value, so to him it was still a great company at bargain prices.

In each of these two investment decisions, Buffett wasn't thinking value or growth. He wasn't pondering hot tips on the street because in both situations he acted against common consensus. He bought what he perceived to be quality businesses: GEICO when everybody thought it was dead, and Coca-Cola when everybody thought the opportunity had passed. The lesson we can take from this is that it is more important to buy solid, quality companies than it is to buy stocks at certain price levels. This is Buffett's use of Graham's margin of safety. You should examine a business to determine its value, then look at the stock price to see if it makes sense to buy now. It might, in which case you should. The price might decline after you buy, but that doesn't matter. The fact remains that you bought a solid business at a fair price. After that, Buffett advises you to watch what's on the playing field, not what's on the scoreboard. A price decline is the market's frenetic, short-term interpretation of the stock's worth. Ignore it.

By now it should be clear that Buffett advocates buying quality companies at bargain prices, which is a blend of Graham and Fisher. Now, let's delve deeper into Buffett's definition of a quality company and a bargain price.

Attributes of a Quality Company

First, a company's management must be honest with shareholders and always act in their interest. Integrity precedes everything in business because there's no point proceeding with a business evaluation if you don't trust the people running the place! Buffett himself is famous for his candid assessment of Berkshire in the company's annual reports. You should look for clear explanations of a company's successes and, more importantly, its failures in reports to shareholders. This is vital to your continued understanding of the businesses in which you invest.

Second, a company should earn more cash than is necessary to stay in business and direct that cash wisely. To Buffett this means either investing in activities that earn more than they cost, or returning the cash to shareholders in the form of increased dividends or stock buybacks. The measurement we'll use in this book's strategy to determine if management is investing excess cash wisely is return on equity. To Buffett, a company's earnings are no more important than its return on equity because they don't take into account the accumulation of previous earnings. In other words, I can take what I earned last year and make my company bigger and better. You would expect a bigger and better company to be able to earn more, right? Of course. And if it does, everybody's happy. Everybody but Buffett, that is. He's more concerned with whether or not that company's earnings grew enough to justify the cost of reinvesting the previous year's earnings, and the ones before that, and so on. That's why he looks at return on equity instead of plain earnings. It's just as important to know what a company does with what it earns as it is to know what it earns.

Third, a company should have a high net profit margin. Remember from page 30 that a company's net profit margin is determined by dividing the money left over after paying all its expenses by the amount of money it had before paying expenses. So, if a company makes $1 million and pays $900,000 in expenses, its net profit margin is 10 percent ($100,000 divided by $1,000,000).

Determining a Bargain Price

Buffett determines the value of a company by projecting its future cash flows and discounting them back to the present with the rate of long-term U.S. government bonds. I'm sure that sounds about as much fun as extracting termites from your home with chopsticks, but that's how he does it.

After determining a company's value, Buffett then looks at its stock price. It's one of the few times he pays attention to stock price. He compares the value with the price and determines the margin of safety. In other words, if the stock is selling for just under what the company is worth, there is a small margin of safety and he doesn't buy. If it sells for well under the company's worth, there is a large margin of safety and he buys. The reasoning is simple. If he made a small error in determining the value of the company, then the true value might prove to be below the stock price. But if the stock price is well below what he estimates the company to be worth, the chances of falling below it are less. It's a straightforward use of Graham's margin of safety.

Now, a few caveats and adjustments. Describing Buffett's way of determining a bargain price in two steps and characterizing it as simple is a bit misleading. It's accurate, but it's not easy to copy. I can also describe Tiger Woods's way of hitting a long drive in two steps: Keep legs loosely in place, swing club swiftly toward ball. There, now do you suppose you can golf like he does? Of course you can't, and it's no different with Buffett's determination of a bargain price. He's gifted and if you're as gifted as he is you probably don't need this book.

Arriving at an accurate assessment using Buffett's method requires an accurate forecast of future cash flow. Buffett's good at it, most of us aren't. Even within your circle of competence, you probably don't feel comfortable culling the factors of a company's success, estimating their future success, and translating it into today's dollars.

So, in this book we're going to focus on the intent of Buffett's method instead of the technique. We want to buy quality companies at bargain stock prices.

Managing Investments

Like Fisher, Buffett believes in a focused portfolio. Because he buys businesses instead of trading stocks, Buffett insists that he understands those businesses thoroughly. That means owning just a few companies at a time. In 1985, half of Berkshire's common stock portfolio was in GEICO. In 1987, Berkshire owned just three stocks and 49 percent of its portfolio was in Capital Cities/ABC. In 1990, 40 percent of Berkshire's portfolio was in Coca-Cola. In 2001, 33 percent was in Coke and 19 percent was in American Express. In 2011, 57 percent was divided among Coke, IBM, Wells Fargo, and American Express. Focused investments in areas you understand are superior to blanket investments across dozens of stocks in the name of diversification. If you research 30 companies and find 2 that are clearly better than the rest, why place your money in the top 5 or 10? For diversification, you might say. But diversifying across mediocre companies is riskier than focusing on good ones.

Buffett also discourages the common practice among investors of selling their top performers. If a stock runs up 100 percent, many sell it and take the profits. But Buffett believes in managing his portfolio the same way he manages his business. How would you react if a division of your business consistently showed a profit? You wouldn't sell it off. You would probably invest more in it. In the 1993 Berkshire Hathaway annual report, Buffett wrote, "An investor should ordinarily hold a small piece of an outstanding business with the same tenacity that an owner would exhibit if he owned all of that business."

Finally, Buffett disregards the opinions of others once he's made up his mind. Groupthink is what kills institutional investors because they'd rather make average, safe decisions than what Buffett identified in Berkshire's 1984 annual report as "intelligent-but-with-some-chance-of-looking-like-an-idiot" decisions. Do your own research, do it well, and stand by your decisions.

What You Should Retain from Buffett

Above all else, Warren Buffett believes in examining businesses, not stock prices. Once he finds a quality business, he buys it at a bargain price. His investment style combines the best of Graham and Fisher because he buys thriving companies at a discount. That's a combination of value and growth investing. Other key points:

✔ Ignore the stock market because it's fickle. Never speculate about the direction of prices. Look instead at individual companies and what makes them superb.

✔ Reverse your emotions. Be fearful when others are greedy, and be greedy when others are fearful.

✔ Buy stock in a company with the same scrutiny you'd exercise when buying the business itself. Buy within your circle of competence and thoroughly understand your investments.

✔ After choosing your investments well, you should stand by them through thick and thin. Time helps wonderful businesses but destroys mediocre ones.

✔ Buy quality companies at bargain prices.

✔ Quality companies:

  • *Have honest management teams that communicate with shareholders in a candid fashion and always act with the interests of shareholders in mind.*

- *Earn more cash than is necessary to stay in business and direct that cash wisely. They either invest in activities that earn more than they cost, or return the cash to shareholders in the form of increased dividends or stock buybacks. To determine how wisely a company has directed its cash, look at its return on equity.*

- *Have high net profit margins.*

- *Increase their market value by more than the value of earnings they retain.*

✔ Determine bargain prices by comparing a company's value to its stock price. Buy when the stock is considerably lower than the company's value. This is a straightforward use of Graham's margin of safety.

✔ Focus your portfolio on a few good companies. Concentrating on good stocks is safer than diversifying across mediocre ones.

✔ Just as a business puts more money into its most successful ventures, you should invest more money in your stocks that are performing well.

✔ Do your research, do it well, and disregard the opinions of others.

Peter Lynch

Peter Lynch managed the Fidelity Magellan Fund from 1977 to 1990. The fund held only $20 million when Lynch took over and grew to $14 billion during his tenure. In the last 5 years of Lynch's management, Magellan was the world's largest mutual fund and still outperformed 99 percent of all stock funds. If you had invested $10,000 in Magellan when Lynch took over, 10 years later you would have had $190,000.

After retiring, Lynch wrote *Beating the Street* and *One Up on Wall Street*. These two books explain his approach to investing. *One Up on Wall Street* targets individual investors and is the title I condense in this section. Lynch, like my grandfather, refers to winning stocks as "tenbaggers," ones that return 10 times your money.

Use What You Already Know

Using what you already know is the cornerstone of Lynch's advice. This should be familiar to you by now. Fisher advised us to invest within our circle of competence and Buffett seconded that notion, adding that we must thoroughly understand our investments. Now Lynch adds his support to the idea. I think we have enough reason to pay attention.

From your position as an employee or competitor in a field, you're conducting the best research on good investments. Professional money managers fly tens of thousands of miles to talk with people you interact with every day. Your manager, your supplier, your customers, your coworkers—and you yourself— have information that's worth a lot to other investors. Here's a shocking revelation: It's worth just as much to you!

Also, as a consumer you're conducting research all the time. You know what products you're buying and probably have a pretty good idea of what your neighbors are buying. Is there a trend afoot? Possibly, and you might see it long before Wall Street does.

It has always amazed Lynch that people who work in the aerospace industry invest in the auto industry; people who work in the auto industry invest in the computer industry; people who work in the computer industry invest in the entertainment industry; people who work in the entertainment industry don't have any money to invest. Well okay, the top .25 percent have a little. The point is that this grass-is-always-greener approach is ludicrous. Invest where you already spend most of your time.

Lynch recalls several good investments he discovered by just living his life. He found Taco Bell by eating a burrito on a trip to California. He found La Quinta by talking to people at the rival Holiday Inn. He found Apple Computer when his children insisted on owning one and the systems manager at Fidelity bought a bunch for the office. His wife liked L'eggs pantyhose from Hanes. L'eggs was convenient to purchase right at the checkout counter of most grocery stores. They resisted tearing and developing runs. They fit well. What more research was needed to conclude that this was a superior product? None, in Lynch's estimation. He bought Hanes and it grew sixfold before being bought out by Sara Lee.

Look where you work, pay attention to what you buy, and observe the buying habits of those around you.

Know Your Companies

Like Graham, Fisher, and Buffett, Lynch says to thoroughly understand the companies you're considering. He recommends looking at company size first. Big companies make small stock moves, small companies make big stock moves. It's important to know the size of companies you're considering.

Categorize Your Companies

Once you know the size of your companies, Lynch says to divide them into six categories: slow growers, stalwarts, cyclicals, fast growers, turnarounds, and asset plays. Slow growers are usually large, old companies that used to be small, young companies. Electric utilities are typical slow growers. Expect them to barely outpace inflation but to pay a good dividend. Stalwarts are large and old, too, but they're still growing strong. Coca-Cola is an example of a stalwart company. Cyclicals are companies whose fortunes rise and fall along with the economy. Airlines and steel companies are cyclical. Fast growers are small, young companies that grow at 20 percent or more a year. This is the land of tenbaggers to 200-baggers. Lynch identified Taco Bell, Wal-Mart, and The Gap as fast growers. More recently we've seen Cablevision and Google. Turnarounds are good companies that have been beaten down. Chrysler is Lynch's example and one of the best buys he made for Magellan in the early '80s. Those who bought Chrysler at $1.50 enjoyed a 32-bagger. Asset plays are companies with something valuable that Wall Street missed. Pebble Beach in California and Alico in Florida owned amazingly valuable real estate that nobody paid attention to. The telecommunications industry was an asset play 20 years ago.

Don't be concerned with the six categories per se. Don't set out to buy a stalwart company because it's stalwart. Instead, use selection criteria to turn up attractive companies and use these categories to know what you're buying. The intent of Lynch's categories is simply to know what kind of company you're investing in. Don't expect fast growth from a slow grower. If you're buying a stock that's down in price because you think it meets all of Buffett's criteria of a quality company, know if it's down in price because it's a cyclical in a down cycle, an overlooked asset play, or a turnaround. You'll know from the extensive research you've conducted on the companies you invest in, a wise approach taught by Graham, Fisher, Buffett, and Lynch.

Components of a Perfect Company

To Lynch the perfect company is simple to understand. That should be familiar to you by now. He writes, "The simpler it is, the better I like it. When somebody says, 'Any idiot could run this joint,' that's a plus as far as I'm concerned, because sooner or later any idiot probably is going to be running it."

If its name is boring or ugly and something about its business turns people off, so much the better. Lately there's been a move toward hip companies with names like TerraGyro Navigation and Internetica. Most investors steer clear of boring companies with boring names. Not Lynch. To him they're fortunes. He cites Seven Oaks International as a company that engages in a boring business. It processes grocery store coupons. Yippee! Put that Google search aside and let's take 10 cents off your next purchase of Grape Nuts. That'll get your blood pumping. The stock rose from $4 to $33. That really *will* get your blood pumping. Some companies engage in business that is disgusting, such as sewage and toxic waste. Lynch remembers the executives of Waste Management, Inc. who wore polo shirts that said "Solid Waste." Disgusting, right? The company became a 100-bagger.

The business should be ignored by institutions and analysts. Not surprisingly with businesses this unattractive, a lack of institutional ownership is almost a given. Lynch loves it when a company tells him the last analyst visited three years ago. Look where others refuse to look. It's not always just boring, unattractive businesses that are overlooked, either. Remember Chrysler? Nobody wanted that stock when it fell to $1.50. They all waited until it was priced at a respectable double-digit figure again. The smart money isn't always so smart.

Fast-growing businesses are best inside a slow-growth industry or, better still, a no-growth industry. It keeps competition away. Just think how many thousands of hotheaded business students want to conquer Silicon Valley. How many do you think want to conquer the funeral business? Not many. Burials aren't a growing industry, plus they're boring and depressing.

Companies that occupy a niche have a distinct advantage. Warren Buffett bought *The Washington Post* partly because it dominated its market. Most newspaper owners think they profit because of the quality of their paper. But Buffett pointed out that even a crummy paper can prosper if it's the only one in town. Lynch writes, "Thinking along the same lines, I bought as much stock as I could in Affiliated Publications, which owns the local *Boston Globe*. Since the *Globe* gets over 90 percent of the print ad revenues in Boston, how could the *Globe* lose?" Patents, trademarks, and strong brand loyalty all constitute a type of niche. Good luck starting a soft drink company and trying to get as many people to say the name of your product before they say Coke. Even Pepsi can't do it. Owning something unique is another type of niche. Lynch sums up this advantage perfectly: "Once I was standing at the edge of the Bingham Pit copper mine in Utah, and looking down into that impressive cavern, it occurred to me that nobody in Japan or Korea can invent a Bingham Pit."

Get yourself a double whammy by purchasing a company that has a niche and a product that people need to keep buying. Steady business is powerful stuff. What do you do when you percolate your last cup of coffee in the kitchen? Buy more. What do you do after smoking your last cigarette? Buy more. What do you do when your gas tank goes empty? Buy more. What do you do when you hit the plastic stopper at the bottom of your deodorant stick? Please, buy more. That phrase, "buy more," drives profits to the moon. It's the wind in the sales of Coca-Cola, McDonald's, Gillette (bought by Procter & Gamble in 2005), and Starbucks. Microsoft is a company with both a niche and repeat business. It owns the Windows operating system used on most personal computers and issues periodic upgrades that everybody needs to own. Also, guess what everybody needs after they own Windows? Applications to run. Microsoft just happens to make a lot of those, too.

Protect against trouble by investing in companies with a lot of cash and little debt. This can be seen as Lynch's margin of safety. If a company has accumulated cash, you can subtract the per

share amount from the stock's selling price to see the bargain
you're getting. Lynch did so with Ford in 1988. The stock sold
for $38 but the company had $16.30 per share in cash. "The
$16.30 bonus changed everything," Lynch remembers. "It meant
I was buying the auto company not for $38 a share, the stock
price at the time, but for $21.70 a share ($38 minus the $16.30 in
cash)." Debt works in the opposite direction. If a company owes
a ton of money, you're shouldering that burden when you buy
the stock. In a crisis situation, which comes everybody's way at
some point, companies with no debt can't go bankrupt. These
two components together—a lot of cash and little debt—mean
the same thing to a company that they mean to you. Would you
rather have a big bank statement or a big credit card bill? Duh,
think a second. The bank statement, of course. It's the same for
companies. Those with a lot of cash and little debt are secure.

Lynch advises paying attention to the stock price relative to
the company's value. You've read a lot on this already so I won't
rehash it except to point out that every one of the master investors in this section offers the same advice: Don't pay too much
for a stock. Check the P/E ratio and other measures of value. I
think we're onto something important. Lynch's rule of thumb
is that a company's P/E ratio should equal its earnings growth
rate. He writes, "If the P/E of Coca-Cola is 15, you'd expect the
company to be growing at about 15 percent a year. But if the P/E
is less than the growth rate, you may have found yourself a bargain."

The last two components of a perfect company involve the
handling of its stock. You want two things to be going on. First,
you want company insiders buying stock, and second, you want
the company itself buying back shares.

When employees and managers in a company buy the stock,
they become shareholders like anybody else. If managers are
shareholders, they're more likely to do good things for the stock.
If they just collect a paycheck, they're more likely to use profits to
increase salaries. Lynch writes, "When insiders are buying like
crazy, you can be certain that, at a minimum, the company will
not go bankrupt in the next six months." He's also careful to point
out that while insider buying is a good thing, insider selling is not
necessarily a bad thing. Remember, company insiders are people,
too. They need to buy new cars, send kids to college, and take

vacations. Selling stock is a quick way for them to raise money. There are all kinds of reasons to sell stock that have nothing to do with the seller's outlook on the stock's future. "But," Lynch writes, "there's only one reason that insiders buy: They think the stock price is undervalued and will eventually go up."

On an even bigger scale, you want the company itself buying back shares. If a company thinks it has a bright future, it makes sense to invest in itself. After a company buys its own stock, there are fewer shares circulating among the general public. Assuming everything remains healthy at the company, those fewer shares in circulation are more valuable than before the buyback. Earnings per share go up and the stock is more enticing to investors. If you own some of the shares still in circulation, you've got a hotter hand than you had before the buyback. Lynch explains, "If a company buys back half its shares and its overall earnings stay the same, the earnings per share have just doubled. Few companies could get that kind of result by cutting costs or selling more widgets."

Know Why to Buy

Lynch uses a nifty exercise to force himself to understand why he's investing in a stock. He calls it the two-minute drill. "Before buying a stock," he writes, "I like to be able to give a two-minute monologue that covers the reasons I'm interested in it, what has to happen for the company to succeed, and the pitfalls that stand in its path." The script should change for different types of companies because you'll want to emphasize different strengths. Lynch offers several examples, one of which I show here. It's for Coca-Cola, a stalwart company. Keep in mind that this situation might not exist when you read this:

> Coca-Cola is selling at the low end of its P/E range. The stock hasn't gone anywhere for two years. The company has improved itself in several ways. It sold half its interest in Columbia Pictures to the public. Diet drinks have sped up the growth rate dramatically. Last year the Japanese drank 36 percent more Cokes than they did the year before, and the Spanish upped their consumption by 26 percent. That's phenomenal progress. Foreign sales are excellent in general.

Through a separate stock offering, Coca-Cola Enterprises, the company has bought out many of its independent regional distributors. Now the company has better control over distribution and domestic sales. Because of these factors, Coca-Cola may do better than people think.

Isn't this a great technique? You become your own analyst when forced to provide a two-minute summary to yourself or an investment club. Of course, your knowledge runs far deeper than what's revealed in two minutes. All that knowledge is on your side when making good investment decisions.

Lynch explains that the real benefit of two-minute drills is that they make you know your companies. That's handy no matter which way the stock price moves because you can make your buy and sell decisions from information about the company instead of information from the market, the most fickle of all measurement tools. If you buy Coca-Cola because it's at the low end of its P/E range, is growing its business overseas, and has greater control over distribution, does any of that change if the stock drops 10 percent after you buy? Probably not. How about if the stock rises 20 percent after you buy? Still, probably not. Price itself should not be the only factor you look at when buying or selling. The company behind the stock should be your focus.

What You Should Retain from Lynch

Peter Lynch believes in using what you already know to find tenbaggers. Once you know why you're buying a company, you'll know how to behave as its stock price fluctuates. Given this approach, Lynch finds opportunities in both value and growth stocks. Other key points:

✔ Use what you already know to find stocks. As an employee, you know the details of your company and its industry better than most analysts. As a consumer, you're constantly researching the products and services of companies. Use that knowledge when investing.

✔ Categorize your companies. The exact categories you use aren't important, but know the types of companies you're investing in. Are you considering a fast grower, a stalwart, or a turn-around? Companies move from category to category over time.

✔ Perfect companies:

- *Are simple to understand. It's great to know that any idiot can run the place because sooner or later any idiot will run the place.*

- *Turn people off by being unattractive in some way. Maybe they're boring, ugly, or disgusting. More people want to invest in the latest Internet company than the latest grocery coupon company. Look where others won't.*

- *Are fast growers in slow-growth industries or, better still, no-growth industries. This keeps competition away. Every-body thinks they can make money in Silicon Valley; few think they can make money in the funeral business.*

- *Occupy a niche. If they own something unique or dom-inate a tiny market, it's hard for competition to muscle inside.*

- *Sell something that people need to keep buying. What do you do when you drink your last Coke? Buy more. Use your last disposable razor? Buy more. Steady business is powerful stuff.*

- *Have a lot of cash and little debt. Companies with no debt can't go bankrupt.*

- *Sell at a stock price that is a good value relative to the company's worth. This can be measured in several ways including P/E ratios and price-to-book ratios.*

- *Are run by managers and employees who invest in the company's stock. When personnel own a stake in the com-pany, they'll work harder to make it successful.*

- *Buy back shares of their own company stock. This is a show of faith in the company's future and it also decreases the number of shares in circulation, thereby increasing their worth.*

✔ Know why you buy. Deliver a two-minute monologue to yourself summarizing the reasons you're buying. This forces you to understand your companies and focus on their fundamental information as the stock market bats their prices around. When in doubt, refer to the reasons you bought in the first place.

William O'Neil

William O'Neil is best known as the founder of *Investor's Business Daily*, national competitor of *The Wall Street Journal*. When he was 30, O'Neil used profits he made trading stocks to purchase a seat on the New York Stock Exchange and to found his own investment research organization now based in Los Angeles.

In 1988, O'Neil wrote *How to Make Money in Stocks*, which presents everything he's learned about growth stock investing.

Use the CAN SLIM System to Find Growth Stocks

Not another diet plan, O'Neil's strange-sounding system for finding growth stocks is actually an acronym for the attributes of great companies. O'Neil stresses that every one of the attributes must apply to a company for him to invest in it. This is not an election where if a company boasts four of the seven attributes it wins. No, it must boast all seven attributes to be a winner. The seven attributes are:

C: Current quarterly earnings per share should be accelerating

O'Neil wants to see an increase in the current quarterly earnings per share when compared to the same quarter from the prior year. He writes plainly, "The percentage increase in earnings per share is the single most important element in stock selection today." Bigger increases are better than little ones, but investors should be careful not to be misled by huge increases over tiny ones from the previous year. "Ten cents per share versus one cent may be a 900 percent increase," he writes, "but it is definitely distorted and not as meaningful as $1 versus $.50. The 100 percent increase of $1 versus $.50 is not overstated by comparison to an unusually low number in the year ago quarter."

A: Annual earnings per share should be accelerating

Similar to the quarterly earnings increases, O'Neil wants to see each year's annual earnings per share for the past five years bigger than the prior year's earnings. A company should be growing at least 25 percent per year, preferably 50 percent or 100 percent. O'Neil gives this example: "A typical successful yearly earnings per share growth progression for a company's latest five-year period might look something like $.70, $1.15, $1.85, $2.80, $4." A nice bonus is an earnings estimate for next year predicting yet another increase.

N: New something or other should be driving the stock to new highs

On this attribute O'Neil is flexible but he wants to see something new that is positively affecting the company's future. In his firm's study of the greatest stocks from 1953 to 1993, O'Neil found that 95 percent of them had either a new product or service, new conditions in the company's industry, or a new management team. Most importantly, O'Neil likes to buy stocks pushing new highs. Cheap stocks are usually cheap for a reason.

S: Supply of stock should be small and demand should be high

Supply and demand affect the price of everything, including stocks. If two stocks are steaming upward at the same pace, the one with fewer shares outstanding will perform better. Why? Because there are fewer shares for the people who want to buy it. O'Neil provides the example of a company with 10 million shares outstanding and one with 60 million. All other factors being equal, the smaller company should be the "rip-roaring performer."

L: Leaders in an industry should be your target

When O'Neil talks about leaders in an industry, he means the stocks with the best relative price strengths. *Investor's Business Daily* shows the relative price strengths of stocks every day on a scale from 1 to 99, with 99 being the best. Using an interesting mnemonic device, O'Neil writes, "A potential winning stock's relative strength should be the same as a major league pitcher's fast ball. The average big league fast ball is clocked about 86 miles per hour and the outstanding pitchers throw 'heat' in the

90s." There you have it: Look for stocks with relative price strengths of 90 or better.

I: Institutional sponsorship should be moderate

Demand needs to be high to drive stock prices higher. Institutional buying is the best source of demand in the stock market. Mutual funds, pension plans, banks, government bodies, and insurance companies are all institutional investors. They buy millions of shares at once. O'Neil likes his stocks to be owned by a few institutions. Too many can mean that the stock is overowned. In that case, so many institutions own the stock that if they all react the same way to news, the stock might get dumped and its price will drop.

M: Market direction should be upward

O'Neil says that even if you get the first six factors of CAN SLIM right and choose a great portfolio of stocks but buy when the market as a whole is declining, 75 percent of your picks will sink with the market. To get a feel for the direction of the market, he suggests watching market averages every day. Keep an eye on daily price and volume charts of several different market averages such as the Dow, S&P 500, and NASDAQ composite. *Investor's Business Daily* publishes major market indicators on a single page every day.

Ignore Valuation

This is a radical departure from the previous four masters. O'Neil believes that you get what you pay for in the market. He's the quintessential growth investor, ignoring P/E ratios completely and focusing on earnings acceleration. He advises, "Don't buy a stock solely because the P/E ratio looks cheap. There usually are good reasons why it is cheap, and there is no golden rule in the marketplace that a stock which sells at eight or ten times earnings cannot eventually sell at four or five times earnings. . . . Everything sells for about what it is worth at the time."

The N in CAN SLIM specifies that a stock should be pushing new highs. That notion runs contrary to everything we've been taught as consumers. Most people don't want to buy a car selling for more than it ever has before, or a house, or a pair of shoes.

Yet O'Neil calls it the stock market's great paradox that "what seems too high and risky to the majority usually goes higher and what seems low and cheap usually goes lower." His firm studied stocks listed on either the new-high or new-low list in the newspaper and confirmed that stocks on the new-high list tend to go higher while stocks on the new-low list tend to go lower.

"Therefore," O'Neil summarizes, "your job is to buy when a stock looks high to the majority of conventional investors and to sell after it moves substantially higher and finally begins to look attractive to some of those same investors."

Beyond price acceleration, O'Neil looks at management stock ownership and a company's debt. He agrees with Lynch that it's a good sign for management to own a large percentage of stock and that great companies carry little debt. He writes, "A corporation that has been reducing its debt as a percent of equity over the last two or three years is well worth considering."

Managing a Portfolio

O'Neil says at his seminars to manage your portfolio like a retail business. Pretend you sell stuffed animals. As Christmas approaches, Babe the stuffed bull is outselling Smokey the stuffed bear 3-to-1. Which animal do you stock up on for the Christmas season? Babe the bull, of course, because he's given you the most profit and will probably do so in the future. According to O'Neil, it works the same way in your portfolio of stocks. "Sell your worst-performing stocks first and keep your best-acting investments a little longer." That means you shouldn't average down, a common practice of adding more money to your stocks that have fallen in price to buy additional shares at a discount.

Automate Buying and Selling

Like Graham, O'Neil likes automation. His CAN SLIM method is one way of automating your investments. Another is to set a place to stop losses. O'Neil stops his losses at 8 percent of new money placed in a stock. He's specific on the new money requirement. If you own a stock that's risen 50 percent and it slides back 10 percent, that's not necessarily a time to stop losses because overall you're ahead 40 percent. It's only with the addition of new money, when a loss means you're actually behind, that O'Neil advocates stopping losses. Even if it's money added to a rising position, O'Neil recommends stopping losses on that money if the stock slides back while keeping your initial investment money in the stock. It's wise to limit losses because it takes a greater percent gain to overcome any given percent loss. For instance, if you lose 33 percent, it takes a 50 percent gain to recover. O'Neil writes, "The whole secret to winning in the stock market is to lose the least amount possible when you're not right."

Stop Counting Turkeys

One of O'Neil's best examples shows the fallacy of hoping to recover losses from a falling stock. It's the story of an old man and his turkey trap.

There was an old man with a turkey trap that consisted of a box held up by a prop. Wild turkeys would follow a trail of corn under the box. When enough turkeys were inside, the old man would pull a string attached to the prop, thereby dropping the box over the turkeys inside. The goal was to trap as many turkeys as possible.

One day he had 12 turkeys in the box. One wandered out, leaving 11 behind. "Gosh, I wish I had pulled the string when all 12 were there," said the old man. "I'll wait a minute and maybe the other one will come back."

But while he waited for the 12th turkey to return, two more walked out. "I should have been satisfied with 11," the old man said. "As soon as I get one more back I'll pull the string." But the turkeys kept wandering out. The old man couldn't give up the idea that some of the original number would return. With a single turkey left, the old man said, "I'll wait until he walks out or another goes in, then I'll quit." The last turkey joined the others and the old man returned empty-handed.

O'Neil writes that the analogy to the psychology of the normal investor is amazingly close.

While he abhors averaging down, O'Neil advocates averaging up, also called pyramiding. This practice he learned from Jesse Livermore's *How to Trade in Stocks*. The plan is simply to move more money into your stocks that are increasing in value. This is the opposite of stopping losses when you're wrong. Pyramiding magnifies winnings when you're right, which is precisely what

Livermore teaches. O'Neil recalls, "From his book, I learned that your objective in the market was not to be right but to make big money when you were right." I suppose you could relate pyramiding to the turkey analogy in the above textbox by suggesting that the old man place additional turkey traps in the field where he's been most successful before.

After studying his successes and failures, O'Neil devised an automated profit and loss plan for prospering in the stock market:

- ✔ Buy exactly at the pivot point where a stock is moving to new highs after a flat area in an upward trend. O'Neil calls such flat areas consolidation periods.

- ✔ If the stock drops 8 percent from the buy point, sell.

- ✔ If the stock rises, pyramid more money into it up to 5 percent past the buy point. So if you bought a stock at $50 and it rose to $51, O'Neil would suggest adding more money. However, you shouldn't add more money after the stock reaches $52.50 because at that point it's risen 5 percent.

- ✔ Once a stock has risen 20 percent, sell.

- ✔ If a stock rises 20 percent in less than eight weeks, commit to holding at least eight weeks. After that time period, analyze the stock to see if you think it will rise even higher.

Focus, Make Gradual Moves, and Track Your Winners

Because he's found few people who do more than a few things well, O'Neil believes that a focused portfolio is better than a diversified one. He asks if you'd be comfortable visiting a dentist who's also a part-time engineer, music writer, and auto mechanic. O'Neil sees diversification as a dilution of your strengths. He writes, "The best results are achieved through concentration: putting all your eggs in just a few baskets that you know a great deal about and continuing to watch those baskets very carefully." He emphasizes that "the winning investor's objective should be to have one or two big winners rather than dozens of very small profits."

It's best to make gradual moves into and out of a stock. O'Neil says too many people are hesitant to move their money. To overcome this hesitation, he recommends buying and selling in parcels.

If you own a stock you love and it starts dropping in value, sell part of it as an insurance policy. If it rebounds, fine. You made back part of the loss with the money you kept in the stock. Like all insurance policies, you won't always need to use this one. O'Neil asks his seminar audiences, "Are you angry when you buy auto insurance and then go a year without wrecking your car? No!" He reasons that you shouldn't be angry to sell part of a losing position only to see the position fully recover. Ask yourself how much worse it would have been if you hadn't sold part of the position.

To help overcome the inherent tendency to buy more of the stocks in your portfolio that have gone down in price, O'Neil suggests keeping records in a different way. At the end of each time period, he says to rank your stocks by their performance from the previous evaluation period. "Let's say your Tektronix is down 8 percent, your Exxon is unchanged, and Polaroid is up 10 percent. Your list would start with Polaroid on top, then Exxon and Tektronix." After ranking your portfolio this way for several time periods, you'll see which stocks are lagging the group. O'Neil's intent is to force you to ignore the price you paid for each stock and concentrate instead on each stock's performance. He writes, "Eliminating the price-paid bias can be profitable and rewarding. If you base your sell decisions on your cost and hold stocks that are down in price because you do not want to accept the fact you have made an imprudent selection and lost money, you are making decisions exactly the opposite of those you would make if you were running your own business."

What You Should Retain from O'Neil

William O'Neil believes earnings acceleration is more important than buying stocks cheap. He advocates buying and selling in short time periods, stopping losses while they're small, and adding more money to winning stocks. He is an unmitigated growth investor. Other key points:

✔ Use the CAN SLIM system to find growth stocks. CAN SLIM is an acronym for the seven conditions that indicate an excellent investment:

- *C: current quarterly earnings per share should be accelerating*

- *A: annual earnings per share should be accelerating*

- *N: new something or other should be driving the stock to new highs*

- *S: supply of stock should be small and demand should be high*

- *L: leaders in an industry should be your target*

- *I: institutional sponsorship should be moderate*

- *M: market direction should be upward*

✔ Ignore valuation. Low P/E ratios often indicate stocks that are cheap for a reason. They can always get cheaper, too.

✔ Look for companies with a large percentage of management stock ownership and little debt.

✔ Contrary to what's taught to consumers, investors should buy stocks pushing new highs. What seems too high usually goes higher, what seems too low usually goes lower.

✔ Manage your portfolio like a retail business: get rid of unpopular products and acquire more of the popular ones. With stocks, sell your losers and keep your winners.

✔ Automate your investment strategy. Stop losses at 8 percent and add more money to winners up to 5 percent above the buy price.

✔ Focus on a few good stocks. Don't diversify across many mediocre ones.

✔ Make gradual moves into and out of a stock.

✔ To overcome the desire to buy more of the stocks that have declined in price, rank stocks by their performance over a time period. After a few tracking periods, sell the losers and add to the winners.

Bill Miller

Bill Miller managed Legg Mason Value Trust (LMVTX) from 1982 to 2012, acting as sole portfolio manager from the end of 1990, and became famous for beating the S&P 500 15 years in a row from 1990 to 2005. In that span, Value Trust averaged 16.4 percent a year compared with just 11.5 percent for the S&P 500. At the end of 2006, Value Trust had beaten the S&P 500 on a rolling 12-month basis 72 percent of the time. On a rolling 5-year basis, it did so 100 percent of the time.

From 2006 to 2012, however, the fund lost some 7.4 percent per year as the S&P 500 gained 2.2 percent. Miller's bold style ran headlong into the 2008 recession. From October 2007 to the November 2008 low, the S&P 500 fell 49 percent, but Value Trust fell 72 percent. Financial stocks were to blame. Value Trust held AIG, Bear Stearns, and Freddie Mac. In that infamous 13-month period, AIG declined 98 percent, Bear Stearns disappeared entirely when the Federal Reserve Bank of New York tried to save it with an emergency loan but ended up selling it to JPMorgan Chase for $10 per share, and Freddie Mac declined 99 percent.

Why, then, do I still include Miller as one of our master investors? Because everybody makes mistakes, and his long journey over peaks and through valleys can teach investors valuable lessons. Studying difficult periods often yields more insight than studying carefree ones. Miller shared some of the wisdom he gained in the subprime mortgage crash with me over the phone in February 2012, which I'll share with you later in this section. Finally, even after including poor returns from the crash, Value Trust outpaced the S&P 500 during Miller's tenure as sole portfolio manager from November 30, 1990, to October 31, 2010, by 1 percent annually, which adds up to a lot over 20 years.

Because Miller achieved fame at the helm of a fund called Value Trust, you might expect him to be a value investor on the hunt for low P/E ratios, low price-to-book ratios, and other mainstays of the typical value investor's toolbox. That he doesn't search only for such characteristics in his companies makes him fascinating, and worth studying.

Let's see how Bill Miller beat the market for 15 years in a row and how the recession of 2008 sharpened his methods.

Redefine Value by Looking Ahead

It should seem obvious that investing is an exercise in looking ahead, but not everybody approaches it that way. A lot of value investors check a stock's historical data to see if it's currently cheap by comparison.

For instance, if a stock's P/E ratio has averaged 20 for the last 10 years but it's now 15, it's historically cheap. Miller would say, so what? Unless it's cheap compared to what he expects from its future performance, he's not interested. Is there a reason to expect trouble? If so, maybe the lower P/E is justified. If there's a recovery ahead or a reason to believe that cash earnings will grow faster than the market thinks, then perhaps Miller will agree that the company is a bargain. The way he arrives there, however, is by looking ahead.

When you think about that, it helps to explain why Miller sometimes owns stocks that other value investors shun.

In the mid-1990s, most value investors were looking at beaten-down cyclical stocks of companies that make steel, cement, paper, or aluminum. Those were the classic low P/E, low price-to-book stocks of the time.

Miller, however, loaded up on technology companies like Amazon.com and Dell. He thought their prices were better values when viewed as a starting point to a future of strong growth and high returns on capital. He was right, and more so than even he expected when his tech bargains skyrocketed in the tech mania of the late 1990s. From June 1997 to April 1999, Amazon.com gained 6,600 percent. From early 1995 to early 2000, Dell gained 7,000 percent.

Years later, in an article on the history of value investing, *SmartMoney* described Miller's holding on to high-flying Dell in 1998 as "a betrayal equivalent to Bob Dylan's going electric."

In November 1999, *Barron's* ran an article by Miller called "Amazon's Allure: Why a Famed Value Investor Likes—Yipes!— a Stock Without Earnings." In it, Miller wrote, "It's true that some of the best technology companies have rarely looked attractive on traditional valuation methods, but that speaks more to the weakness of those methods than to the fundamental risk-reward relationships of those businesses. Had we understood valuation better, we would have owned Microsoft and Cisco Systems. Microsoft has gone up about 1 percent per week, on average, since it has been public. Companies don't outperform year in and year out for over a decade unless they were undervalued to begin with."

He then pointed out that you don't find undervaluation by comparing a stock's price with its trailing earnings, book value, or cash flow. Instead, you need to compare its price to the current value of the free cash that the business will create in the future. That's the same way Warren Buffett determines a bargain price.

This approach has remained a hallmark of Miller's style through the years. In a February 2003 interview with *Barron's*, he used the phrase "valuation illusion" to refer to stocks that look expensive by traditional measurements, but are actually bargains in light of their bright futures. He again spoke of Microsoft's 1 percent per week performance, and added the example of Wal-Mart. "From the day they came public, they looked expensive," he said. "Nonetheless, if you bought Wal-Mart when it went public at an expensive-looking 20 plus times earnings, you would have made returns of many thousand percent on that." Understanding the growth ahead of Microsoft and Wal-Mart would have made clear that they were bargains.

Miller wrote in his fourth-quarter 2006 shareholder letter, "We realized that real value investing means really asking what are the best values, and not assuming that because something looks expensive that it is, or assuming that because a stock is down in price and trades at low multiples that it is a bargain." He pointed out that "value funds tend to have almost all their money in low P/E, low price-to-book or cash flow, and growth funds have the opposite. . . . The question is not growth or value, but where is the best value?" Stocks with low P/E ratios and value stocks are not necessarily the same thing.

Don't think that his targeting technology was a fluke of the 1990s, either. At a Manhattan conference in May 2005, he told the audience that "the core part of all of those businesses—and by 'all of those,' I mean Google, Yahoo!, Amazon, eBay, and to a lesser extent, IAC/Interactive—is that they require very little marginal capital in order to generate huge amounts of free cash flow. And their ongoing business models can sustain, at the margin, returns on capital north of 100 percent."

When an attendee asked why he liked the very expensive Google in particular, Miller replied, "What's *not* to like? It's got huge profit margins. It grows very rapidly. The management has executed brilliantly. And it sits exactly in the nexus of where all of the long-term trends are going in media. . . . What Google is doing is using the old media network television model—which is, 'We will deliver content to you, the viewer, and because it's ad-supported, you don't have to pay for the content at all.' And what Google is doing is using that model to start to deliver actual content. . . . I mean actual products like Gmail—and maybe an operating system and maybe applications."

The key to getting bargains is looking ahead, not looking back. Miller participated in an event called Conversation with a Money Master at the 50th anniversary Financial Analysts Seminar hosted by the CFA Society of Chicago in July 2006, and the transcript appeared in the August 2006 edition of *Outstanding Investor Digest.*

About looking ahead instead of back, Miller told the moderator, "So they say, 'Oh, Toys "R" Us's historic multiple was X. And now it's .8X—and so there's an opportunity here.' Or, 'Look at what the pharmaceutical companies did for the last 50 years. And now they're cheap compared to that. So now they're a good value.' The problem is that in most value traps, the fundamental economics of the business have deteriorated, and the market's gradually marking down the valuation of those to reflect the fundamental economic deterioration. So what we've always tried to focus on is, in essence, what the *future* return on capital will be, not what the *past* return on capital has been. What's our best guess at the future return on capital and how the management can allocate that capital in a competitive situation that is dynamic so we can avoid, in essence, those value traps?"

He ends up owning some of this and some of that, with the only common theme being good value by his definition. His stocks look wildly different to onlookers because they sport measurements at opposite ends of the spectrum. Are they value stocks or growth stocks? It doesn't matter. They're stocks bought at bargain prices compared to what their futures hold.

Miller wrote in his fourth-quarter 2006 shareholder letter,

"When some look at our portfolio and see high-multiple names such as Google residing there with low-multiple names such as Citigroup, they sometimes ask what my definition of value is, as if multiples of earnings or book value were all that was involved in valuation. Valuation is inherently uncertain, since it involves the future. As I often remind our analysts, 100 percent of the information you have about a company represents the past, and 100 percent of the value depends on the future."

Future Free Cash Flow on Sale

If forced to distill his definition of a bargain stock down to a single measurement, Miller would likely choose a cheap present value of future free cash flow. To him, that factor has it all. It trumps low P/E ratios, low price-to-book ratios, low everything else. If you can buy future free cash flow at a cheap price, you found yourself a bargain.

Let's see if we can understand why he takes this approach.

Net income is the money left after a company pays its bills, taxes, interest expenses, and such. Free cash flow is the money left after a company uses its net income for capital expenditures, known as CAPEX, which is buying new equipment, buildings, or land to improve its business. So, free cash flow is what's left when there are no more expenses. Everything is paid and there's just a pile of cash in a bank account that's free for other uses. The regular stream of such cash into the account is the flow.

Miller told *Barron's* in February 2003, "One of the most important metrics we focus on is free cash flow—the ability to generate it and what it yields: that is, free cash flow per share divided by the stock price." For example, a stock with a price of $30 and an expected $3 of free cash flow this year is yielding 10 percent on free cash flow.

On the same amount of free cash flow, a cheap stock has a higher yield than an expensive stock. If the above stock had $3 of free cash flow per share but a share price of just $20, its free cash flow yield would be an even more impressive 15 percent. That's just 3 divided by 20 to get .15, or 15 percent. With a share price of $50, the stock's free cash flow yield would be a less attractive 6 percent.

Miller explained to *Barron's* in April 2001, "By the time a catalyst is evident, the stock price has already moved. For us, the main catalyst is a cheap stock price. The key to our process is trying to buy things at discounts to intrinsic business value, which, from a theoretical standpoint, is the present value of the future free cash flows. . . . We are looking for things that are statistically cheap. . . . Ideally, what we want is a company that is a leader in its industry, that has the capability of earning above-average returns on capital for the long term, a company that has tremendous long-term economics and those economics are either currently obscured by macroeconomic factors, industry factors, company-specific factors, or just the immaturity of the business."

Do What Is Unpopular

It should be clear by now that Miller has achieved his successes by doing things differently, going against the crowd. In investing, such a maverick is called contrarian. He invests in a way that's contrary to what most others do. He thinks differently, he looks different places, he reaches different conclusions, and he achieves better performance.

A True Contrarian

The funny thing about contrarianism is that so many people claim to embrace it. By definition, that can't be. Almost all value fund managers say they're looking for bargains "that others miss" as they merrily build a portfolio of the same stocks that others found.

Miller is not one of them. He's a true contrarian, to the extent that he sometimes finds himself disagreeing with the findings of his own analysis. He says that "most fund managers own what they *like* to own. We own what we *hate* to own."

Most investors focus too much on the short term, react to dramatic events, and overestimate the importance of widely covered news stories. Miller tries to take advantage of that by finding stocks that have been oversold by mistaken investors. That's why he frequently owns stocks that he and others both hate, like Amazon.com when people thought its low operating margins would last forever.

Miller wrote in his fourth-quarter 2006 shareholder letter, "It is trying to invest long-term in a short-term world, and being contrarian when conformity is more comfortable, and being willing to court controversy and be wrong, that has helped us outperform. 'Don't you read the papers?' one exasperated client asked us after we bought a stock that was embroiled in scandal. As I also like to remind our analysts, if it's in the papers, it's in the price."

He says that there are three types of competitive advantages: analytical, informational, and behavioral.

You have an analytical advantage when you take the same information that others have, but process it differently and reach different conclusions than they reach. With Miller, this is most evident in the way he redefines value, as shown above. He wrote in his third-quarter 2006 shareholder letter, "The most important question in markets is always, what is discounted? What does the market expect, as reflected in prices, and how do my expectations differ?"

You have an informational advantage when you know something important that others don't. Such information is hard to know because inside information is illegal and regulators are strict. There are, however, legal types of informational advantages such as what you can observe that others haven't, the time you take to contact people that others won't, and lucky breaks like overhearing the president of a pharmaceutical company make a cell phone call from an airport about receiving FDA approval on a new drug. Don't laugh. It happens. Stay alert.

Behavioral Finance

You have a behavioral advantage when you understand human behavior better than others and can use that understanding to exploit stock price movements. This advantage is the most interesting to Miller because it lasts. He told me in February 2012, "The findings of behavioral finance, decision theory, and cognitive psychology are among the most important tools available to the investor. They help one understand and interpret the behavior of markets and provide insight into recurring patterns that can be exploited for excess return. The trick is twofold: recognizing these biases in practice, and timing them for profit. Both are difficult, especially the latter. It is often quite clear what must happen, but if it takes far longer than you expected, you can suffer a lot of pain waiting."

He wrote in his September 2006 shareholder letter, "Until large numbers of people are able to alter their psychology (don't hold your breath), there is money to be made from prospect theory." This is not the place for an in-depth look at behavioral finance, but it's a good place for a glance at *prospect theory*. It shows that we hate losses twice as much as we love gains.

A 1979 study by Daniel Kahneman and Amos Tversky showed this in an interesting way when they set out to find why people are attracted to both insurance and gambling, two seemingly opposite financial ideas.

Subjects were told to choose between these two prospects:

Prospect 1: A 100 percent chance of losing $3,000

Prospect 2: An 80 percent chance of losing $4,000, but a 20 percent chance of losing nothing

Which would you choose? In the study, 92 percent of subjects chose prospect 2. The chance of losing nothing, even though it was improbable, was compelling enough to risk losing more. Prospect 1, however, is likely to lose less.

Next, subjects were told to choose between these two options:

Prospect 1: A 100 percent chance of gaining $3,000

Prospect 2: An 80 percent chance of gaining $4,000, but a 20 percent chance of gaining nothing

Which would you choose? In the study, 80 percent of subjects chose prospect 1. The guarantee of gaining something was more appealing than the probability of gaining more. Prospect 2, however, is likely to gain more.

People hate risk when it threatens gains, but they love risk when it could prevent losses. We're odd creatures, so intent on averting loss that we're willing to risk losing even more to do so. We are not bold enough when the odds favor gaining, and we are too timid around even small levels of risk. That, in abbreviated form, is what Kahneman and Tversky found and what is called prospect theory. It's one tenet of behavioral finance that Miller finds useful.

He wrote in his September 2006 shareholder letter that "people are too risk averse and therefore systematically misprice risky assets more often than not. . . . Loss is painful, on average twice as painful as gain is pleasurable in matters financial. That is, people on average need about a 2 to 1 payoff on an even odds bet to take the bet. But even a modest advantage yields big gains over time, which is why casinos make so much money. People get more bullish as prices go up, and more bearish as they go down. They overweight recent trends relative to their long-term significance, and their emotions give greater weight to events the more dramatic they are, often out of all proportion to the probability of their occurrence. All of these features of how our beliefs affect our behavior are actionable if they are systematically incorporated into an investment process."

Another of Miller's favorite ideas from behavioral finance is called *myopic loss aversion.* Richard Thaler at the University of Chicago used it to explain the equity premium puzzle. Stocks have returned about 7 percent per year after inflation while bonds have returned less than 1 percent. The puzzle's question is, if stocks return more than bonds over the long term, why would any long-term investor choose to own bonds?

Because, Thaler explained, most investors are "myopic" in that they focus on the short term. Combine that with our inherent aversion to loss, and you understand why people own investments that don't perform well in the long term because they are steadier in the short term. The short-term steadiness gives the illusion of safety but over the long haul runs a higher risk of not earning enough.

In his N-30D filing for the period ending March 1995, Miller wrote:

> The more short-term-oriented one is (the more "myopic"), the greater one's willingness to react to the risk of loss. . . .
>
> Since one's perception of the risk of stocks is a function of how often you look at your portfolio, the more aware you are of what's going on, the more likely you are to do the wrong thing. "Where ignorance is bliss, 'tis folly to be wise," said the bard, who understood myopic loss aversion centuries before the professors got hold of it.
>
> Suppose you buy a stock on Monday, and on Tuesday, while you are engrossed in the O.J. Simpson trial, it drops due to bad news. On Wednesday, though, it recovers to close higher than your purchase price. If you had been glued to CNBC on Tuesday when the news hit, and had observed the stock falling, you may have been prompted to act on the news, especially if the stock was reacting to it. If you missed the news until Wednesday, when the stock had recovered,

you are much less likely to sell it then, even though the fundamentals are the same as the day before.

That is myopic loss aversion at work. Put differently, you are not worried that IBM dropped overnight in Tokyo while you slept, if it closed up two points today in New York. You are worried if it drops today in New York though it's set to rise two points in Tokyo tonight while you sleep. . . .

For most investors, Thaler thinks, the appropriate advice is "Don't just do something, sit there."

Our investment approach in the Value Trust has been to use the myopic loss aversion exhibited by others to our shareholders' long-term benefit. We try to buy companies whose shares trade at large discounts to our assessment of their economic value. Bargain prices do not occur when the consensus is cheery, the news is good, and investors are optimistic. Our research efforts are usually directed at precisely the area of the market that the news media tells you has the least promising outlook ... and we are typically selling those stocks that you are reading have the greatest opportunity for near-term gain.

Money Management

Miller believes in what he calls factor diversification. He owns high P/E stocks alongside low P/E stocks, and considers that to be a strength because "we own them for the same reason: We think they are mispriced." Sometimes growth factors are favored, other times value factors are favored. By owning stocks in each factor group, he smooths his portfolio's fluctuations.

He doesn't think there's an inherent advantage in either concentrated or diversified portfolios. It depends on what you're considering. He wrote in his fourth-quarter 2006 shareholder letter, "If I am considering buying three $10 stocks, two of which I think are worth $15, and the third worth $50, then I will buy the one worth $50, since my expected rate of return would be diminished by splitting the money among the three. But if I think all are worth $15, then I should buy all three, since my risk is then lowered by spreading it around."

Because he researches his companies carefully and trusts his analysis, Miller's a believer in buying more when the price drops.

He doesn't usually buy all at once, and he's said that after the first buy he hopes the stock starts going down—a lot, and right away because he doesn't want it to drop two years later. If it drops immediately, he can begin lowering the average price he pays per share.

That leads to his famous quote, "Lowest average cost wins." He told *Barron's* in February 2003, "It's rare for us to pay up for anything, and it's common for us that if the stock goes lower after we buy it—and it always does—we will buy more of it."

Thoughts on the 2008 Recession

After Value Trust lost 55 percent in 2008, Miller changed his portfolio from concentrated bets in a few sectors, such as financials and technology, to a more diversified one with an emphasis on dividends and free cash flow.

He wrote in his January 2009 commentary, "We have been investing in banks and other financials for over a quarter of a century, and were involved in putting new capital into them during the last crisis around 1990. That worked out very well. We have also been part of the private capital that has put money into financials in this crisis, and that has been a disaster, for us and for every other investor who has done so. If we are typical, the appetite for private capital to go into banks now approaches zero, unless there are substantial changes in policy that are capital friendly."

He stood steadfast at the tiller:

I remain optimistic that the new administration, which is staffed with first rate financial talent, coupled with the Fed, will craft policies that will be effective in stabilizing the financial system and restoring the flow of credit.

Despite the raggedy start, I also think this will be a pretty good year for equity investors. Last year was the worst for U.S. (and most other) stocks since the 1930s. Pessimism and gloom abound. Short-term trading has replaced long-term thinking. The consensus is for economic growth to resume in the second half of the year, but of course no one knows. But growth will resume, and when it does equity prices will be much higher, in my opinion. Valuation based strategies had a strong December and early January and we performed very well, as one would expect when that is happening. The sell-off in financials and the market in the past two weeks has interrupted that trend, and the S&P 500 has now had its worst start to a new year ever. Fear has returned to the fore.

This too shall pass.

He expected performance to improve from the market's low valuations:

During the fourth quarter we added 15 new names to the fund, which is now exposed to every sector of the market for the first time in many years. Values abound and we believe we can broaden and diversify the portfolio without sacrificing future rates of return. . . . In my opinion, the long-term opportunities for the fund have never been better and the overall quality of the portfolio has never been higher. Financials are now under 10 percent of the market's capitalization for the first time since 1992, which was a great time to buy financials. This is also the best time to buy quality in my investing career; it has never been cheaper and we continue to look for, and to find, names with excellent financial strength, good and growing dividends, leading positions in their industry, and trading at five- or 10-year lows and at historically low valuations. We believe this should lead to quite satisfactory results over the next five to 10 years.

Looking Back from the Recovery

He was right. The subprime crash did pass and the abundant values in its wake did provide the best time to buy quality stocks, which are off to very satisfactory returns. When Miller and I emailed and spoke by phone in February 2012, the S&P 500 had more than doubled from the lows it reached shortly after he wrote the comments above.

In light of how far stocks crashed in 2008/09, I asked him whether he thought stops should play a critical role in portfolio management. He said they're "just one way to manage risk," sometimes effective, sometimes not. His team's analysis of its mistakes indicates that using time stops would have been better than using price stops. "If the investment case has not worked in two or three years, sell and move on." He still advocates buying more of a good idea that drops in price: "I do believe lowest average cost wins, on average and over time."

He finds one of the most useless aspects of common stock advice to be "the story given to explain stock price behavior, which is what is referred to as the narrative fallacy. We see some series of events or actions and we create a story to explain it. Stories always follow price." More often than not, though, the price *is* the story.

Too bad, then, that cacophony and short-term thinking dominate modern investing. "High-frequency trading makes up almost 70 percent of volume and has nothing to do with business fundamentals. Hedge funds are a significant part of the market and their client base is much shorter-term oriented than the usual institution or individual was 15 years ago. The 24/7 news cycle and stuff like CNBC shorten time horizons and amplify noise. So the environment now is much more difficult day-to-day or even year-to-year."

He didn't mention this, but an addendum is that the narrative most commonly presented is the opposite of what's helpful to investors. The media create fear as prices fall and greed as prices rise by telling stories of hardship in crashes and abundance in spikes. The pertinent stories for investors are the prices themselves, which should be bought after crashes and sold after spikes. You've seen this idea before. Warren Buffett teaches, "Be fearful when others are greedy, and be greedy when others are fearful."

I asked Miller if fundamental measures of value work in modern markets. Moreover, did he still consider a present value of future free cash flow to be the best measure of value? His answer was unequivocal: "The present value of future free cash flow is the *only* correct measure of value." He acknowledged that it's hard to estimate correctly and a tad impractical for the short term, which is why people "look at all kinds of other ways to try to predict the path of securities prices." Nonetheless, "Empirically, free cash flow yield is the single best predictor of excess return."

I said, "Pretend you and I sat down together at a stock

screener to find a short list of ideas to research further. What would the screen we built look like?" He replied that it "would sort for a combination of the following variables: high free cash flow yield, low P/E on projected one-year earnings, dividend yield greater than the market's, dividend growth rate greater than the market's, and an ROE greater than the market's." Later he added, "The best predictor of excess return in the market, across all factors and styles, is the combination of free cash flow yield and share repurchase. Companies that have the top decile of free cash flow yield and top decile of share repo at the same time have about a 1,200 basis point per year advantage on average. That's the highest of any quantitative factor in the market."

A basis point is 1/100 of a percent. It's a way of expressing small differences in performance that gets around cumbersome phrases like "0.02 percent" by saying "two basis points." Sometimes investors get so used to thinking in basis points that they use them even for larger percentages, as Miller did. The math is easy. How many basis points are in 1 percent? 100. So, the 1,200 basis point per year advantage that Miller described is equal to a 12 percent annual advantage. That's huge. Peter Lynch mentioned the importance of share repurchases, also called buybacks, earlier in this chapter, and you'll learn more about them in the next chapter as well.

A primary lesson that Miller and his team discovered when looking back on their experience in the subprime crash was that sector outperformance follows a sector reaching the lowest decile of its historical valuation range. From that discovery, they created a new rule: "Any time a sector is in the bottom decile of its historical valuation parameters, we'll be at least equal weight in that sector." Sectors that are low priced eventually become high priced. Knowing that and tagging any sector in its cheapest historical decile as "must own" prevents getting frightened off by whatever bad news created the bargain. History shows that no matter why the sector is on sale, once it reaches the cheapest decile of valuation, it's time to buy.

How, though, do Miller and his team define the historical valuation parameters? "We use all the major valuation factors like P/E, price-to-book, price-to-cash-flow, dividend yield, those kinds of things, then look at which of those have been the best predictor of a sector's future outperformance. So, for example, in financials it's price-to-tangible-book-value. In technology it's free cash flow yield." They created a grid of all market sectors displayed with their current valuation by major measurements, ranging from bottom deciles at the bottom to top deciles at the top for an instant visual message. "Whenever something drops down to the bottom decile on whichever measurement best predicts its longer-term outperformance, that's when we buy it."

He warned against a behavioral finance phenomenon identified by Richard Thaler as the "endowment effect," a tendency to look more favorably or forgivingly on a stock we own than on one we don't. As part of our loss aversion, we develop loyalty to what we decided to buy before and may therefore hold and hope too long. A firm analyzed the Miller team's portfolios from a behavioral finance standpoint and found evidence of the endowment effect. From that analysis, Miller learned that the "endowment effect has cost us money because if we'd just had a pure time stop—sell it after three years if it hasn't worked—that would have saved us a fair amount of grief."

What You Should Retain from Miller

Bill Miller finds bargains by comparing a stock's current price with its future prospects. He does not look only at historical data to see whether it's cheap based on its past. This sets him apart from traditional value investors. He is contrarian, often going against the crowd to buy what is hated because it is misunderstood or because others are unable to see through their fear of loss to a great opportunity. Other key points:

✔ Look forward, not back. Don't just compare a stock's current valuation with its past valuation. The past does not determine the future. Look ahead at its future prospects to see if it's cheap compared with those.

✔ He says, "The question is not growth or value, but where is the best value?" If traditional growth stocks are cheap, buy them. If traditional value stocks are cheap, buy them.

✔ Cheap doesn't necessarily mean bargain. It could mean worthless or, in stock jargon, value trap. In many cases, a stock's dropping price is just the market noticing its deteriorated prospects. It might be cheap compared with its past for a reason, and that's why you must look ahead. He tells his analysts, "100 percent of the value depends on the future."

✔ Use the present value of future free cash flow to determine whether a stock is a bargain.

✔ Be contrarian by looking at the long term in a short-term world.

✔ There are three types of competitive advantages:

- *Analytical, when you take the same information that others have, but process it differently and reach different conclusions.*

- *Informational, when you know something important that others don't.*

- *Behavioral, when you understand human behavior better than others and can use that understanding to exploit stock price movements.*

✔ Prospect theory shows that people hate losing more than they love winning. That makes them too risk averse so they "overweight recent trends relative to their long-term significance" and give greater weight to dramatic events "often out of all proportion to the probability of their occurrence." Use these tendencies to find bargains.

✔ Myopic loss aversion afflicts most investors, making them focus on the short term. However, a lot of short-term information is irrelevant in the long term. If you've bought solid companies, the best advice is often "Don't just do something, sit there."

✔ If you must do something, though, buy a good value as it gets even cheaper. Miller hopes that stocks he's started buying drop quickly and dramatically, so he has a chance to buy additional shares at lower prices. "Lowest average cost wins," he says.

✔ See through popular stories and understand what prices say. When they say a good company or a sector is undervalued, buy. When they say a good company or a sector is over-valued, sell. Tune out cacophonous media.

✔ Avoid the endowment effect of favoring what you own over what you don't. Analyze your portfolio dispassionately, and let go of ideas that aren't working.

Where the Masters Agree

Now that you've read a lot of advice from six great investors, let's take a moment to boil it down. You still have further reading ahead before I present this book's strategy, but pausing here to review what you should have picked up so far is time well spent.

Automate Your Strategy with Proven Criteria

No matter what investment strategy you create over the years, it should be clearly defined and measurable. This helps you instantly separate a company from its story, the latest buzz, and your inherent human frailty. None of us are immune to emotion, but we can use superior reasoning to counteract our emotions and make good decisions. Every great investor, from the most insistent value types to the most aggressive growth types, relies on a set of specific criteria to find superior companies. You should, too.

Look for Strong Income Statements and Balance Sheets

Every company is helped by high profit margins, lots of cash, and little or no debt. Each investor in this book wants to see these factors. They assure value investors that a beaten-down company has the wherewithal to recover, and they assure growth investors that a rising star will keep rising.

A high profit margin means the company keeps more of what it earns, plain and simple. If two companies each sell $10 million worth of products and one company spends $8 million to do it while the other spends only $4 million, you'd rather own the second company.

You would rather own a company that has a lot of cash on hand than a company that has a little. A big bank account means the company can expand easily, buy better equipment, pay off unexpected expenses, and buy back shares of its own stock.

Avoid debt. This applies to nearly every walk of life. Don't invest in companies with a lot of debt, don't go into debt yourself. Debt is a monster. It eats companies trying to prosper and it eats the futures of people like you and me. A company can go bankrupt only if it's in debt. *Debt* and *death* sound a lot alike, and that's no coincidence. You don't even need a finance book to arrive at this conclusion; all you need is a good literature class. Emerson wrote in *May-Day and Other Pieces*, "Wilt thou seal up the avenues of ill? Pay every debt, as if God wrote the bill." As an investor, you want those avenues of ill sealed up before you buy the stock.

Look for Insider Stock Ownership and Company Buybacks

Not everybody places a high value on this, but enough mention it to make it important. It makes sense that managers and employees will work harder to make their company successful if they own stock in it. Plus, nobody knows the fortunes and follies of a company better than the people who run it and work there. If a hot product is going to trounce every competitor, company insiders will know about it first. If a new service has produced the highest focus group scores in history, company insiders will know about it first.

Philip Fisher liked management teams that were honest with shareholders and were willing to sacrifice immediate profits for long-term gains. Like Fisher, Warren Buffett looks for a management team that communicates honestly and makes all decisions in the best interests of shareholders. There's a compelling reason to do so when managers themselves *are* shareholders. Peter Lynch writes, "There's only one reason that insiders buy: They think the stock price is undervalued and will eventually go up."

In addition to insider ownership, you want the company buying back shares of its own stock. Investing in itself indicates that the company believes in its future. The action also decreases the number of shares in circulation, which increases the earnings per share—as long as the company's earnings remain constant or grow. All in all, investors are left with more potent stocks after the buyback than they had before the buyback. Lynch explains,

"If a company buys back half its shares and its overall earnings stay the same, the earnings per share have just doubled. Few companies could get that kind of result by cutting costs or selling more widgets."

Bill Miller found that companies in the top decile of free cash flow yield and share repurchases at the same time have about a 12 percent annual advantage, which is huge.

Compare Stocks with a Proven Profile

In addition to the factors above, you should compare stocks you're considering with a profile of key measures that have uncovered winners in the past. Warren Buffett and Bill Miller look at the present value of future free cash flow, Peter Lynch emphasizes value measures such as P/E and price-to-book, William O'Neil focuses on earnings acceleration. We'll develop a set of specific criteria later in this book that you'll fill in after you . . .

Conduct Thorough Research

Every great investor believes in thorough research. Warren Buffett says to exercise the same scrutiny when buying shares in a company as you'd exercise when buying the company itself. When conducting research, don't forget your own circle of competence. You work in an industry, you consume products, and you talk to other consumers. Your life experience counts as research—use it! Your base knowledge is a great way to find leads. Follow those leads to more thorough research conducted through your library, the Internet, company investor relations departments, magazines, newspapers, and other investors.

Your style of research will vary based upon your personality and what you're looking for. Philip Fisher interviewed a company's customers, suppliers, former and current employees, and competitors to learn vital information. Peter Lynch likes to eat burritos, kick tires, watch consumers in stores, and feel hotel linen to confirm his interest in companies.

Whatever your research approach becomes, make sure that you conduct thorough research to find the information you need. Once you've assembled the information, you can determine whether to invest. Then you'll be prepared for the next section. . . .

Know Why to Buy

It's important to know the reasons that led you to buy a stock so you know the right time to sell. If you have no idea why you bought, the only information you can rely on to decide when to sell is the current price, which is subject to a million mysterious factors, and the current word on the street, which is about as reliable as kindergarten romance. Think of Warren Buffett, Peter Lynch, William O'Neil, and Bill Miller. If I asked any one of them why they held stock X, they would be able to answer me in a second.

If you own a stock because of the company's excellent earnings acceleration and high expectations for the future, know so. If it's because the company has been unfairly punished by the market and is selling for a ridiculously low P/E ratio, know so. If it's because you think the market misunderstands a company's future, know so—and know what you consider to be the real story. Then you can watch those earnings, watch that P/E, and watch that story for a change. As they change, you can reevaluate your decision to own the stock. If you're like Buffett, the factors may not involve price at all. If that's the case, know so and watch the company's management team, return on equity, and other non-price factors to make sure they don't erode.

I think the best way of forcing yourself to know why you buy is to recite a two-minute stock script, as Peter Lynch suggests on page 68. In two minutes, you should be able to run down the factors that made the stock attractive to you. That way you'll always know why you own your stocks and you'll avoid making rash decisions to either sell out or buy more.

Once you know the reasons to invest in a company, try to . . .

Buy at a Price Below the Company's Potential

At first this looks like advice for value investors only, but it's not. Every investor, whether value or growth, must buy stocks at a price lower than they sell them. Value investors try to buy low, sell high. Growth investors try to buy high, sell higher. Both look at a stock's current price and compare it to what they see as the company's potential to drive that price higher. The difference between the two types of investor lies in the information they use to determine a company's potential.

A value investor looks at a company's assets, how much it's sold, its profit margins, and other factors before determining whether the price is more or less than the company is worth. A growth investor looks at earnings per share, the acceleration or deceleration of those earnings, analyst expectations, and positive surprises. Warren Buffett and Bill Miller, investors with one foot in value and one foot in growth, look at future free cash flow.

William O'Neil relies on the components of his CAN SLIM system to select winning stocks. One of those components—the N—wants the stock to be pushing new price highs. However, he only buys if the other factors of CAN SLIM apply, too. The company must have accelerating earnings, a small supply of stock and high demand, a leading industry position, and moderate institutional sponsorship. What are these other factors looking at? The company's growth potential. O'Neil doesn't simply flip through the paper looking for stocks that are expensive. He looks for stocks that are expensive for a reason, and that reason is that they have the potential to grow and produce even more expensive prices.

Warren Buffett, the investor who blends growth and value better than anybody, bought GEICO after it declined from $60 to $2. He saw it being worth a lot more than $2 because of the company's unrewarded potential. He bought Coca-Cola in 1988 after it rose fivefold over the previous six years. Many thought it was overpriced, but he bought more than $1 billion worth because he saw that it held plenty of unrealized growth potential. He was right in both of these purchases, which appear to employ contradictory investment strategies. Dig a little deeper, though, and you see that they don't. Buffett is actually quite consistent. In both decisions, he projected the company's performance into the future, determined the company's potential, and bought at a price well below that potential. It's incidental that GEICO was on a path to recovery and Coca-Cola was on a roll. Both had potential beyond their current price.

Bill Miller also ignores growth and value labels. As he puts it, "The question is not growth or value, but where is the best value?" Sometimes stocks that look too expensive are just valuation illusions because they're bargains in light of their bright futures. He noted that both Microsoft and Wal-Mart were never cheap by traditional measures, but each produced tremendous gains. He sees value when the future is better than the stock price reflects.

Whether you tend toward value investing or growth investing, you must be able to estimate the potential of your investments. Of course, you'll never be able to do it perfectly, but by conducting thorough research and understanding a company's strengths, you should be able to form a decent forecast. Once you've assembled a portfolio of companies that you own . . .

Keep or Buy More of What's Working

Business owners constantly evaluate the different parts of their operation to see what's working and what's not. They put more money into the successful parts and slowly phase out the unsuccessful parts. Eventually, the business becomes a streamlined collection of winning pieces. Successful investors manage their portfolio in this same fashion. However—and this is key— different investors define *working* in different ways.

For Warren Buffett, a company is doing everything right if its fundamental strengths remain healthy. He watches things like the company's profit margins, its return on equity, and honest communication with shareholders. Buffett does not look at daily or weekly stock price fluctuations because they're too fickle. He wrote, "We don't need a daily quote on our 100 percent position in See's or H.H. Brown to validate our well being. Why, then, should we need a quote on our 7 percent interest in Coke?" If he bought a quality company and it still boasts all of its quality attributes, Buffett considers it a success and keeps it in his portfolio. He doesn't think of himself as an investor in his companies, he thinks of himself as an owner. He wrote, "An investor should ordinarily hold a small piece of an outstanding business with the same tenacity that an owner would exhibit if he owned all of that business."

For William O'Neil, the only measure of a successful stock is its performance. He watches the prices of his holdings, pyramids more money into the winners, and dumps the losers. O'Neil says the objective in the market is not to be right all the time but to make big money when you are right.

While you hope the stock of every strong company you own rises in price, it ain't always the case, not even for the pros. Every investor can recall a list of failures that taught them a lesson. I learned growing up in Colorado that "there are those who *have fallen* from a horse, those who *will fall* from a horse, and those who *don't ride* horses." The only people who never fall off a horse are those who don't ride. The only people who never own a falling stock are those who don't invest. The good news is that if you've chosen quality companies you can . . .

Take Advantage of Price Dips

Well now, doesn't this seem like an odd bit of advice following the previous section? I just finished showing that the experts keep or buy more of their winners, now it looks like I'm telling you to buy more of the losers, too. Bear with me a second and you'll see that these two pieces of seemingly incompatible wisdom can actually coexist, like darkness and light, or Democrats and Republicans.

Everything depends on your buying quality companies in the first place and knowing why you bought, as you read in "Know Why to Buy" on page 68. If you bought a company because of its outstanding new products, high profit margins, and accelerating growth rate and the company still boasts those attributes, there's no reason to sell. In fact, there's every reason to buy more—regardless of price. If the stock is marching steadily upward and the company is still a great company, the previous section advises you to take advantage of that by investing more money. What this section points out is that if the company is still great but its stock is dropping, that can be just as good a reason to buy more. You're getting a discount on additional shares of a great company. Remember, though, that the reasons you bought must still apply. Don't put more money into a falling stock that also has falling profit margins, falling sales, employees on strike, and a management team that sold all of its stock and quit the company for an extended vacation in Negril. Invest only in quality companies, whether buying your first shares in them or adding more shares to existing positions.

Benjamin Graham was a stickler on this point. He emphasized that nobody ever knows what the market will do but that you can profit by reacting intelligently to what it does do. Good companies drop in price every day, often for no apparent reason. A lawsuit perhaps, maybe a manufacturing glitch, or maybe just because the market's a weird place where you'd never want to hang out if there weren't so darned many ways to make money there. He said the market behaves like a voting machine in the short term but like a weighing machine in the long term.

Warren Buffett points out that time helps wonderful businesses but destroys mediocre ones. Even if the stock price is a bit down today—or this week, or this month, or this year—if the company is still the great company you bought, then this momentary price dip is an opportunity to invest more money at a bargain price. Robert Hagstrom Jr. wrote in *The Warren Buffett Way* that you've approached Buffett's level of investing if you look at the market and wonder only if something foolish happened to allow you to buy a good business at a great price. That could easily be additional shares of a good business you already own.

Bill Miller claims that he wants his stocks to drop in price so he can buy more shares to reduce his average cost. "Lowest average cost wins," he explains. If you are confident in your research, buy more when the price gets cheaper.

This section and the one before it underscore what should be clear by now: You must understand the strengths of your companies and the reasons you bought shares in the first place. Only then can you decide if rising prices mean you've got a winner and should invest more on the way up, or falling prices mean you've still got a winner and should invest more at a discount.

I know it's a fine line. Nobody said this was easy.

What You Should Retain from This Section

When excellent investors with different styles of investing agree on a few basic truths, it's worth paying attention. This section outlined powerful advice taken from the six master investors profiled. Specifically:

✔ Automate your strategy with proven criteria. Don't select stocks with your emotions, current hype, or stories from your friends. Use measurable information to compare stocks to a profile of key measures that have uncovered winners in the past.

- *Look for strong income statements and balance sheets.*
- *Look for insider stock ownership and company buybacks.*
- *Compare stocks with a proven profile.*

✔ Conduct thorough research. Warren Buffett sums it up best when he says to exercise the same scrutiny when buying shares in a company as you'd exercise when buying the company itself.

✔ Know why to buy. After conducting your thorough research on a company, outline exactly why you want to invest in it. Later you'll monitor the company to see if the factors that led you to buy deteriorate.

✔ Buy at a price below the company's potential. This applies to both value and growth investors because both look at a stock's current price and compare it with what they see as the company's potential to drive that price higher. The difference between the two types of investors lies in the information they use to determine a company's potential. Warren Buffett and Bill Miller look at future free cash flow. William O'Neil looks at earnings acceleration. Using your own thorough research, you should estimate a company's potential and buy at a price below it.

✔ Keep or buy more of what's working. Like a business owner looking at the different parts of your business, you should constantly evaluate the different stocks in your investment portfolio to see what's working and what's not. Put more money into the successful stocks and phase out the unsuccessful stocks.

✔ Take advantage of price dips. If all the reasons you bought a stock are still present but the price is dropping, that can be a good time to buy more. You're getting a discount on additional shares of a great company. As Bill Miller says, "Lowest average cost wins." Make absolutely sure, however, that it is still a great company. Don't buy more shares of a stock that's falling due to company failings.

3
How History Tells Us to Invest

In 1946, Benjamin Graham observed, "It is amazing to reflect how little systematic knowledge Wall Street has to draw upon as regards the historical behavior of securities with defined characteristics. . . . Where is the continuous, ever-growing body of knowledge and technique handed down by the analysts of the past to those of the present and future?" More than 60 years later, you can finally benefit from that perspective Graham desired.

Among the countless studies of stock market data completed since Graham's observation, one effort stands alone and is documented between the covers of a single book: *What Works on Wall Street* by James O'Shaughnessy, now in its fourth edition. His study explored 83 years of results from 1926 to 2009 using data from the Center for Research in Security Prices (CRSP), and 46 years of results from 1963 to 2009 contained in the Standard & Poor's Compustat database.

O'Shaughnessy gathered popular stock measures like the P/E ratio, price-to-book ratio, and relative price strength to see how they fared over the years when used to find both large and small companies. Then he combined the successful measures in master strategies. What he found—and what I'm delighted to share—is going to give you an advantage that has been available only recently. You, as a newcomer forming your own stock strategy, have more than eight decades of research to help you develop the correct habits.

Let's have a look inside *What Works on Wall Street*.

Testing Popular Measurements

Rather than take you laboriously through each measurement that O'Shaughnessy tested, I'm going to cut straight to the conclusions. Before I get started, though, you need to understand the ground rules of these studies. Bear with me if this gets complicated. The attention to detail should make you a believer in the results.

O'Shaughnessy separated the universe of stocks into two groups by company size. The first group he called "All Stocks." It consisted of all companies with an inflation-adjusted market capitalization of at least $200 million. Inflation-adjusted means that for any given year the companies were worth $200 million of 2009's dollars. After all, a $200 million company in 1935 was colossal. But by 2009's standards it was small, just $13 million. So the All Stocks group contained just that: all stocks of interest to this study.

He defined a second group of larger, better-known companies with market caps greater than the database average. This second group usually consisted of the top 17 percent of the database by market cap in any given year. These companies went into the "Large Stocks" group as well as the All Stocks group. The behavior of the Large Stocks group has been very similar to the S&P 500 index, which makes sense because the 500 is an index of large, well-known companies.

As you can see, the All Stocks group included both smaller companies and those companies found in the Large Stocks group. The Large Stocks group contained only the large stocks.

In each of the single-factor tests, O'Shaughnessy began with $10,000 hypothetically invested in the 10 percent of stocks from the All Stocks group and 10 percent of stocks from the Large Stocks group that best fit the criterion, then the polar opposite 10 percent that least fit the criterion for purpose of comparison. He called these groups the best decile and worst decile. Rather than following the long-term study convention of beginning portfolios on December 31, then tracking them through the following December 31 and calling it the one-year result, he rebalanced every month of each year in the study, composited the annual result of starting the portfolio in each of the 12 months of a year, then used the composite as the year's result. In his words, this technique addressed the reality that "investors invest continually throughout the year, not just on December 31."

For instance, when testing P/E ratios, O'Shaughnessy selected the 10 percent of stocks with the lowest P/E ratios from each group. He then rebalanced the hypothetical portfolios each month to invest in the new 10 percent of stocks with the lowest P/E ratios. The returns of each month's picks were followed for a year, then the one-year performances of all 12 months in the year were composited to come up with a good proxy for how an individual beginning the low-P/E technique sometime during that year would have fared.

O'Shaughnessy's study used data from January 1, 1927, to December 31, 2009. During that time period, the All Stocks group averaged 10.5 percent per year and the Large Stocks group averaged 9.7 percent, which is almost exactly the S&P 500's average of 9.8 percent. O'Shaughnessy sometimes tested factors over smaller time frames within the larger period studied.

The Best Value Measures

In the first three editions of his book, O'Shaughnessy studied a smaller set of data contained in the Compustat database alone, and tested various value measures by tracking their performance from December to December only. When he introduced the larger dataset and more sophisticated monthly composite tracking methodology, the winning value measure changed.

"Uh oh," said critics. "If more data and a different way of looking at it produce different conclusions, what's the point? Who's to say the conclusions won't change in the next edition and every one thereafter?" While understandable, the objection misses a useful consistency in O'Shaughnessy's results. The specific value measure claiming top-dog status may change with different datasets, different time frames, and different testing methods, but the spirit of the conclusion doesn't change: It's important to buy cheap stocks. In this section, we'll look at the previous and current champions. Later, we'll see how different measures in combination work better than a single measure by itself, which relieves pressure to find the one shining winner. The best combination of factors is another lesson from O'Shaughnessy's work that's useful when managing our own portfolios.

Price/Sales

This was the former champion among value measures, with the 50 lowest P/S stocks from the All Stocks group returning

15.95 percent a year, better than the group's return of 13 percent. The 50 lowest P/S stocks from the Large Stocks group returned 14.30 percent, better than the group's return of 11.71 percent. Conversely, the 50 highest P/S stocks from each group greatly underperformed the group.

The new, expanded study confirmed the trends. From January 1, 1964, to December 31, 2009, the 10 percent of the All Stocks group boasting the lowest P/S ratios returned 14.5 percent a year, better than the group's return of 11.2 percent. Also, as before, the highest P/S stocks performed terribly.

O'Shaughnessy concluded, "While no longer the king of the hill, stocks with low price-to-sales ratios beat the market consistently over time." It's interesting to note that O'Shaughnessy found P/S more reliable than P/E, the most popular stock measurement around.

CONCLUSION: Look for stocks with low P/S ratios.

EBITDA to Enterprise Value

So, then, what *is* the current king of the hill? An odd-looking measure called EBITDA to enterprise value, or EBITDA/EV. Don't know what either of those terms mean? Don't worry, you're not alone. They're not exactly mainstays of daily conversation.

EBITDA stands for earnings *before* interest, taxes, depreciation, and amortization. It's the number you get when you add money lost to interest, taxes, depreciation, and amortization back to net income. Those four expense categories can be misleading when trying to compare companies, because finance and accounting methods vary widely from place to place. Thus, EBITDA strips out those vagaries to look at raw profitability. To sound like a pro when discussing it, say *ee bitdah* with emphasis on the *ee*. Don't say the letters.

Enterprise value is not the price of Captain Kirk's ship, but rather a more complete picture of a company's worth than you get by looking at market capitalization alone. It's calculated as market cap minus cash but plus debt, minority interest, and preferred shares. The reason it's more accurate than market cap alone is that somebody buying the whole company would need to pay its enterprise value, not its market cap. They would bank its cash but become responsible for its debt, so those need to be factored into the company's value.

When we combine the two to get the EBITDA/EV ratio, we're looking at how much profit is produced by the place's value. The more, the better, so a high EBITDA/EV is what we're after. It's a more nuanced look at value than we get with price/sales, price/ earnings, or price-to-anything, according to O'Shaughnessy's work. By the way, with price/whatever measurements, smaller is better because we're paying less for what we're getting. Even though EBITDA/EV is a value measure, it switches positions of the "price" and the benefit so that a bigger number shows us a better value.

From January 1, 1964, to December 31, 2009, the 10 percent of the All Stocks group boasting the highest EBITDA/EV returned 16.6 percent a year, better than the group's return of 11.2 percent and the lowest P/S decile's return of 14.5 percent. As with P/S, the worst decile of stocks by EBITDA/EV performed dismally, returning just 5.3 percent.

Unfortunately, EBITDA and EV are missing from many stock databases, and the EBITDA/EV ratio is even harder to find. However, you can approximate the results by using other more common measurements. Free cash flow is a decent substitute for EBITDA, and market cap will do in a pinch when you can't find enterprise value. If all else fails, you could run a free-cash-flow/market-cap screen to get a group of stocks to further investigate. As you'll find out later in this section, combining various measures is the best approach anyway.

CONCLUSION: Look for stocks with high EBITDA/EV ratios.

The Best Growth Measure—
Relative Price Strength

Next, O'Shaughnessy examined measures of growth. "Generally, growth investors like *high* while value investors like *low*," he notes. "Growth investors want high earnings and sales growth with prospects for more of the same. . . . Growth investors often award high prices to stocks with rapidly increasing earnings."

O'Shaughnessy's characterization of value and growth investors is consistent with the styles of our master investors profiled in the previous chapter.

I could run you through the studies O'Shaughnessy conducted on a variety of growth measures including earnings-per-share change, profit margin, and return on equity. But guess what? Only relative price strength proved to be a useful measure, so let's focus on just that one.

Remember from page 35 that relative price strength looks at a stock's price history. Did it rise or fall last year? Momentum growth investors think you should buy stocks that have risen, many value investors think you should buy stocks that have fallen.

From January 1, 1927, to December 31, 2009, the 10 percent of the All Stocks group boasting the highest six-month price appreciation returned 14.1 percent a year, better than the group's return of 10.5 percent. The decile of stocks with the worst six-month price appreciation could start a club called Losers Anonymous. They returned just 4.2 percent.

How about that? In the short term, Newton's first law of motion seems to apply to large stocks as well as physical objects: Prices in motion tend to stay in motion. The winners keep winning and the losers keep losing.

O'Shaughnessy concluded that "relative strength is among the only pure growth factors that actually beats the market consistently, and by a wide margin." He believes the reason is that it "conveys different information about the prospects of a stock and is a much better indicator than factors such as earnings growth rates. Many look at the disappointing results of buying stocks with the highest earnings gains and wonder why they differ from the best price performers. First, price momentum is the market putting its money where its mouth is. Second, the common belief that stocks with strong relative strength also have the highest P/E ratios or earnings growth is incorrect. When you look at the top performers over time, you find that they are *rarely* the highest valued in terms of P/E or P/S."

The only times when price momentum did not work were bubble market tops and bear market bottoms. When everybody agrees that stocks will keep going up forever, the highest fliers are poised for the biggest crash. When everybody agrees that stocks will never recover, the stocks that have crashed hardest bounce back highest immediately after the tide turns. O'Shaughnessy explained the latter: "This happens because investors collectively realize that all the companies that they had priced for extinction may in fact not go out of business, so they rush in and quickly bid up their prices." For example, he found that between February 2009 and December 2009, when the market staged a steep recovery from the subprime mortgage crash, the worst 6-month price performers from the All Stocks group shot up 132.2 percent, turning $10,000 invested in February into $21,647 just 11 months later. The best decile of 6-month performers fared much worse, gaining only 32 percent in the same time period and turning the $10,000 into just $12,868.

CONCLUSION: Except for moments of extreme optimism and initial recoveries from extreme pessimism, buy stocks with the best six-month relative price strength.

Combining the Measurements

People rarely make decisions with a single factor. A woman in search of an evening gown probably has a certain color in mind. Perhaps all black dresses are prettier to her than all red dresses, but within the black dress universe there are still plenty of choices. She narrows down the field by specifying a certain cut, a certain fabric, a certain overall panache. Soon she's presented with a handful of choices from which to make her final selection.

So it is with stocks. Single measurements are a start, but that's all. Combining measurements yields far better results by either reducing risk, increasing performance, or both. O'Shaughnessy experimented with several different combinations to come up with an ideal value strategy and an ideal growth strategy, then combined *those* into a single super strategy. I'm going to skip the research process and focus on the single super strategy, which O'Shaughnessy calls Trending Value.

The Value Recipe

O'Shaughnessy's winning recipe included these value measures:

• Price-to-book

• Price-to-cash-flow

• Price-to-earnings

• Price-to-sales

• EBITDA/EV

• Shareholder yield

He calls this group of measures Value Factor Two. Value Factor One didn't work as well, so I won't bother telling you about it. Stocks evaluated by Value Factor Two receive a score based on the six measures, as explained by O'Shaughnessy: "If a stock has a P/E ratio that is in the lowest 1 percent for the universe, it receives a rank of 100; if a stock has a P/E ratio in the highest 1 percent for the universe, it receives a rank of 1. We follow a similar convention for each of the factors. . . . For shareholder yield and EBITDA/EV, those stocks in the 1 percent of the universe with the *highest* values are ranked 100, whereas those within the lowest 1 percent are ranked 1. Once all the factors are ranked, we add up all their rankings and assign the stocks to deciles based upon their overall cumulative ranking."

Thus, the best decile of stocks by these measures boasted the lowest price-to ratios, the highest EBITDA/EV ratios, and the highest shareholder yields. Stocks in the worst decile shamed themselves at the other extreme.

Got it, you're thinking, *but what's shareholder yield?* Glad you asked. It combines the value of dividends with the benefits of a company buying back shares of its own stock. As you learned from Peter Lynch in Chapter 2, company share buybacks leave fewer shares in circulation, so each share has a higher earnings per share than before the buyback. Also in Chapter 2, Bill Miller mentioned the power of buybacks. Now you're encountering them for the third time. Reason enough to pay attention? I'd say so. Both dividends and buybacks benefit investors, so it's useful to combine them into one measure. Here's O'Shaughnessy's explanation:

> . . . to create shareholder yield, you add the current dividend yield of the stock to any net buyback activity the company has engaged in over the prior year. If, for example, a company trading at $40 a share is paying an annual dividend of $1, the company would have a dividend yield of 2.5 percent. If that same company engaged in no stock buybacks over the year, its shareholder yield would equal 2.5 percent, the same as the dividend yield. If, however, the company had 1,000,000 shares outstanding at the beginning of the year and 900,000 at the end of the year, the company's buyback yield would be 10 percent. Adding this to the dividend yield of 2.5 percent, you would get a total shareholder yield of 12.5 percent. This formula allows us to capture all of a company's "payments" to shareholders, and it is indifferent as to whether those payments come in the form of cash dividends or buyback activity. This is important because, like all other things in life, trends come in and out of favor on Wall Street. There are times when buybacks are all the rage, and times when cash dividends are in favor. Shareholder yield captures them both.

While shareholder yield is not a measurement commonly found in publications or on websites, its two components of dividend yield and share buybacks are. Following the idea of it is easy to do. One way is to look for high dividend yields among the biggest, best companies on the market, and then see which of those are engaged in stock buyback plans.

About this idea, O'Shaughnessy wrote, "Investors who want to use dividend yields as a sole determinant of value should stick to large, better-known companies, since those companies typically have stronger balance sheets and longer operating histories. . . . When you include other criteria such as strong cash flows, large sales, and large numbers of shares outstanding, large stocks with high dividend yields offer excellent risk-adjusted returns. . . . We've found that investors interested in high dividend yields are best served by limiting their search to market-leading stocks, and then concentrating on those with the highest dividend yields."

You may be wondering how to locate the biggest, best companies on the market yourself. After all, you don't have access to the Compustat database from your living room. You'll be thrilled to know that a tiny group of 30 market-leading large companies is listed everywhere you look. The returns of this group are averaged every day and posted for the world to see. Can you guess what I'm referring to? The stocks of the Dow Jones Industrial Average. On page 129 you're going to learn how to use the Dow with high-yield strategies.

Let's see how O'Shaughnessy's Value Factor Two performed. Remember, it's the group of six value measures shown at the beginning of this section. From January 1, 1964, to December 31, 2009, the 10 percent of the All Stocks group boasting the best overall score by the six measures returned 17.3 percent a year, better than the group's return of 11.2 percent. The decile of stocks shaming themselves with the highest price-to ratios and the worst EBITDA/EV fell apart almost completely, returning less than 3 percent.

Trending Value

We know now how to find the best-performing stocks by value measures alone. What if we added a growth component to the stocks found with Value Factor Two? Would that identify the highest potential of the lowest-valued stocks? Yes.

Recall that the best growth factor is six-month relative price strength. When O'Shaughnessy ran it against the best 10 percent of stocks by Value Factor Two, he discovered a super strategy. I'll let him introduce it:

> One of the consistent themes of my research is the efficacy of uniting value and growth factors. Doing so allows you to smooth out the jags of a pure momentum strategy by tempering it with the best of value. Over long periods of time, the data proves conclusively that value trumps growth. Yet, there is also evidence that value strategies can get seriously out of sync during runaway bull markets. . . . When the market is in love with the concept of a company, as it was in the late 1990s with dot-com stocks, companies that have excellent financials and are modestly priced tend to be

ignored. For example, the best decile of stocks from All Stocks in Value Composite Two (those with the best valuations) went up a mere 4.12 percent in 1999, a year that saw the best decile from All Stocks by six-month price appreciation soar by more than 100 percent. Thus, what we will attempt with our next strategy is to find the best value stocks that are also trending up sharply in price, what we call Trending Value.

Value Composite Two is just the set of stocks found by Value Factor Two. The best Trending Value strategy bought the 25 stocks with the highest six-month price appreciation from the 10 percent of stocks found cheapest by Value Factor Two. You won't believe how well the 25 stocks chosen this way performed.

From January 1, 1964, to December 31, 2009, the 25-stock Trending Value portfolio returned 21.2 percent a year, far better than the All Stocks return of 11.2 percent. It turned $10,000 into $69,098,587 with less risk and a lower maximum decline than the All Stocks group, which turned $10,000 into only $1,329,513. Trending Value beat the All Stocks group in 85 percent of single years, 99 percent of rolling three-year periods, and 100 percent of rolling five-year, seven-year, and ten-year periods. Plus, it never lost money over a five-year span.

While Trending Value offers superb long-term results, O'Shaughnessy offers some words of warning about the difficulty—but also importance—of sticking with a strategy over many years:

> [Out-of-sync years] might try your patience. Most notably that would have been in 1998 and 1999, the two biggest speculative years since 1967. During these two sizzling years, speculative stocks soared—the biggest six-month price appreciation gainers from All Stocks soared more than 100 percent, whereas the 25-stock version of Trending Value earned just 14.12 and 7.41 percent, respectively, in 1998 and 1999. Thus, while Trending Value is a great long-term strategy, my point is that by the end of 1999 you likely would have

been deeply frustrated with its modest returns, especially as you watched other growth and momentum stocks soar.

. . . the single greatest threat to our success as investors is our own human nature. In hindsight, it may be easy to convince yourself that you would have stuck with this strategy and remained a systematic, dispassionate investor, but having lived through the period and working with many clients, I can tell you that the odds of this happening are small indeed. We are unfortunately our own worst enemies when it comes to letting a strategy work over the entire market cycle, and I urge every reader to contemplate this when the next "new, new" thing gets investors' imaginations ignited. It is at just those times that it can be the most difficult to stick with even the best of strategies.

. . . while I have no idea what the names of the winning and losing stocks of the future will be, I have a very good idea of what factors will define them. No doubt we will see new fads that will push individual stocks and industries to unsustainable highs, and commentators and investors will invent very exciting and seemingly plausible stories for why it is different "this time" for these new stocks and industries. Yet I believe—*like every time in the past*—that these story-stocks will go on to devastate investors as they crash back to earth.

Another issue with running a portfolio of stocks found with Trending Value is that most will be unfamiliar to you. Headline-making, famous companies rarely make the cut, and the "nobody from nowhere" companies might not be as much fun or feel as right to you as owning what everybody else is talking about. "Perhaps," O'Shaughnessy writes, "this is why the portfolio does as well as it does—for the most part, huge, well-known companies are not the engines of phenomenal year-in and year-out growth." It's one thing to read that and grasp it in your mind, quite another to feel it in your heart when emotions are high. Know that in advance.

Here's a breakdown of benchmarks and Trending Value over the 44 years from August 31, 1965, to December 31, 2009, ranked by return:

Strategy	Compound Annual Return	$10,000 Became	Standard Deviation
S&P 500	9.33%	$522,661	15.31%
Large Stocks	10.06%	$701,190	16.75%
All Stocks	11.01%	$1,025,389	19.26%
Trending Value 25	21.08%	$48,246,947	17.66%

Standard deviation measures the amount an investment has deviated from its normal, or standard, return. A low number indicates steady returns while a high number indicates widely varying returns. Thus, a high standard deviation means high risk. Looking at the table above, notice that Trending Value returned 47 times as much as the All Stocks group with less risk. O'Shaughnessy's work paid off.

To somebody looking for a way to win in the stock market, this table should have brought the crescendo from Beethoven's "Ode to Joy" flooding to your ears. If you need to pause your reading to dab the corners of your eyes, I understand. These moments in life are rare.

What You Should Retain from History's Lessons

Benjamin Graham wished for a historical perspective on the stock market. Now we've got it, thanks to the work of James O'Shaughnessy and data from the CRSP and Standard & Poor's. Near the end of *What Works on Wall Street*, O'Shaughnessy wrote that "the data prove the stock market takes purposeful strides. Far from chaotic, random movement, the market consistently rewards specific strategies while punishing others." Here are the prevailing lessons of those purposeful strides:

✔ The best all-purpose value measure is EBITDA/EV, which can be approximated with free-cash-flow/market-cap.

✔ EBITDA is earnings *before* interest, taxes, depreciation, and amortization. Those four expense categories can be misleading when trying to compare companies because finance and accounting methods vary widely from place to place. EBITDA strips out those vagaries to look at raw profitability.

✔ EV stands for enterprise value, which is market capitalization minus cash but plus debt, minority interest, and preferred shares. It's more accurate than market cap alone because somebody buying the whole company would need to pay its enterprise value, not its market cap.

✔ Dividend yield is a great value measure against large, market-leading companies.

✔ The best growth measure is relative strength. Specifically:

   • *Six-month relative strength is best.*

   • *Do not buy relative strength winners in moments of extreme optimism.*

   • *Relative strength losers perform well only during initial recoveries from extreme pessimism at bear market bottoms.*

✔ Shareholder yield combines the value of dividends with the benefits of company share buybacks. Large, market-leading companies with high shareholder yields outperform their low-yield peers.

✔ The simplest and one of the best value strategies is to buy large, market-leading companies with high dividend yields. You'll learn a way to automate this strategy in the next chapter.

✔ The winning value recipe finds the cheapest stocks by these measures:

   • *Price-to-book*

   • *Price-to-cash-flow*

   • *Price-to-earnings*

   • *Price-to-sales*

   • *EBITDA/EV*

   • *Shareholder yield*

✔ Using six-month relative price strength to find upward movers among the cheapest stocks flagged by the winning value recipe produces the best risk-adjusted return. This super strategy combining value and growth is called Trending Value.

✔ It's essential to stick with proven strategies through complete market cycles, even though they'll underperform in some years.

4
Permanent Portfolios

Our goal is to beat the market over time. This chapter looks at various approaches to doing so and will form the core of your portfolio.

Value averaging provides a framework to lock in constant growth from the market, and we'll use it against an index of small companies to gain 3 percent per quarter. That's 20 percent more than the S&P 500's long-term average.

Once you have that going, it's time to move on to other permanent techniques to boost performance even more. The Dow dividend strategies are methods of beating the Dow by investing in its most undervalued companies, so we'll start there. Then we'll examine how leveraging the entire Dow to double its daily performance outperforms the Dow dividend strategies in most markets. Next we'll apply that same approach to the S&P Mid-Cap 400 index of medium-sized companies for even better results. Finally, we'll look at the downside of leverage and use charts to limit losses and increase returns.

Value Averaging for Steady Growth

The market fluctuates. Can we accept that and devise a way to put the fluctuations to work in our favor, instead of fearing them?

Yes.

The best way I've found is called *value averaging*, or VA. It was introduced in a 1988 article by Michael Edleson, who later expanded the concept in his book *Value Averaging: The Safe and Easy Strategy for Higher Investment Returns*.

The most popular way to invest periodically is called *dollar-cost averaging*, or DCA. It's simply investing the same dollar amount on a regular basis, such as $50 per week or $100 per month or $500 per quarter. It forces your money to buy more shares when they're cheap and fewer shares when they're expensive. Your $100 spent in January when the price is $20 buys five shares. Your $100 spent in March when the price is $10 buys ten shares. Over time, buying more cheap shares than expensive shares lowers your average cost to less than the average price of the investment during the time period.

Simplicity makes DCA appealing, because it can be automated. Tell your broker to transfer $100 per month until otherwise instructed, and you're done.

However, value averaging is better. It's a little more complicated but well within your grasp and worth the effort.

VA poses this question: If buying more shares when they're cheap is a good idea, then isn't it an even better idea to send extra money when the price is cheap and less when it's expensive? Of course, and that's what VA does, even to the point of selling shares when the price rises beyond the performance level you want.

In the DCA example above, you spent $100 per month no matter the investment's price. You bought five shares at $20 in January and ten shares at $10 in March. It would be smarter, however, to spend less than $100 to buy only two shares in January and more than $100 to buy 15 shares in March, wouldn't it? Then you'd have even fewer of the expensive shares and even more of the cheap ones.

The way you achieve that with VA is by specifying a rule for how much you want your investment to grow in a time period. Monthly is common, but I prefer quarterly because it requires less work and gives the market time to move around.

My rule is for my permanent portfolio to grow at 3 percent per quarter. That becomes an annual growth rate of 12.6 percent, which is 20 percent higher than the S&P 500's long-term rate of 10.5 percent. That level of outperformance—thanks to the magic of compounding—turns a substantial profit over time.

Unlike DCA, which just sends more money no matter what's happening, VA sometimes sells shares when the investment's performance exceeds the growth rule. If the first quarter sees 5 percent growth, you would sell the required number of shares to get your account down to the value needed to be 3 percent higher than at the end of the previous quarter. If, on the other hand, the quarter goes badly and your account does not grow 3 percent, then you would buy the required number of shares to bring your account up to the value needed to be 3 percent higher than at the end of the previous quarter.

In choosing what investment to use with VA, we look for one that brings enough potency to meet and sometimes exceed the 3 percent quarterly growth target. A bank account, for example, wouldn't work. It's essentially flat, so the entire 3 percent quarterly growth would come from new money. That's not investing, it's saving.

So, the plan needs firepower. The ideal investment to use with VA is one that's reasonably volatile and as cheap as possible. One idea is the Vanguard Total Stock Market exchange-traded fund (ETF), symbol VTI. It has the lowest expense ratio of any ETF, just 0.07 percent. However, it tracks the 1,300 stocks on the MSCI US Broad Market index and therefore provides returns similar to those of the Dow and S&P 500.

A better bet, and the one we'll use, is the iShares S&P Small-Cap 600 ETF, symbol IJR, which charges a higher 0.20 percent but makes up for it with more kick. Also, its expense ratio may be higher than VTI's but is still well below the median ETF expense ratio of 0.50 percent. Another benefit of IJR is that it's tradable without commission at several popular brokerage firms such as Fidelity and TD Ameritrade. If you have an account at Vanguard, its Small Cap ETF, symbol VB, is a good alternative to IJR for this plan, as it tracks IJR's returns almost identically, charges a tiny 0.12 percent expense ratio, and is commission-free when traded at Vanguard. To keep our plan universally applicable, however, we'll stick with IJR.

As you saw back on page 13, small- and medium-sized companies outperform large companies over time. You can see that in the historical record of these two ETFs. From mid-April 2002 to the end of September 2002, VTI fell 28 percent and IJR fell 30 percent—about the same. From there to early July 2007, VTI rose 103 percent while IJR rose 144 percent, then they fell the same 48 percent from the end of that July to the end of February 2009. From the end of January 2009 to the end of January 2012, they gained 74 percent and 93 percent, respectively. Such outperformance by small companies is typical, and is the reason we're using IJR. We'll tap medium-company strength in a different strategy later.

Let's run IJR through a real-world value-averaging example from December 31, 2007, to December 30, 2011, a time frame that includes the crash of '08 and its recovery. Say you decided to start your plan with an initial investment of $10,000. Here are IJR's closing prices at the end of each quarter, and the action you needed to take to sustain a 3 percent quarterly growth rate:

Quarter Ending	IJR Price	Shares Held	Current Value	Shares Needed for 3% Growth	Action to Take	Cash Flow	New Cash Balance	New IJR Balance
Dec 2007	$65.02	0	$0.00	NA	Buy 154 shrs	-$10,013	$0	$10,013
Mar 2008	$59.93	154	$9,229	172	Buy 18 shrs	-$1,079	$0	$10,308
Jun 2008	$60.17	172	$10,349	176	Buy 4 shrs	-$241	$0	$10,590
Sep 2008	$59.51	176	$10,474	183	Buy 7 shrs	-$417	$0	$10,890
Dec 2008	$43.97	183	$8,047	255	Buy 72 shrs	-$3,166	$0	$11,212
Mar 2009	$36.39	255	$9,279	317	Buy 62 shrs	-$2,256	$0	$11,536
Jun 2009	$44.43	317	$14,084	267	Sell 50 shrs	+$2,222	$2,222	$11,863
Sep 2009	$52.34	267	$13,975	233	Sell 34 shrs	+$1,780	$4,002	$12,195
Dec 2009	$54.72	233	$12,750	230	Sell 3 shrs	+$164	$4,166	$12,586
Mar 2010	$59.45	230	$13,674	218	Sell 12 shrs	+$713	$4,879	$12,960
Jun 2010	$54.14	218	$11,803	247	Buy 29 shrs	-$1,570	$3,309	$13,373
Sep 2010	$59.09	247	$14,595	233	Sell 14 shrs	+$827	$4,136	$13,768
Dec 2010	$68.47	233	$15,954	207	Sell 26 shrs	+$1,780	$5,916	$14,173
Mar 2011	$73.56	207	$15,227	198	Sell 9 shrs	+$662	$6,578	$14,565
Jun 2011	$73.32	198	$14,517	205	Buy 7 shrs	-$513	$6,065	$15,031
Sep 2011	$58.54	205	$12,001	264	Buy 59 shrs	-$3,454	$2,611	$15,455
Dec 2011	$68.30	264	$18,031	233	Sell 31 shrs	+$2,117	$4,728	$15,914

See how the plan forces you to add money as the price drops, and to take profits as the price rises? The more the price falls, the more money you spend to buy a lot of the cheap shares; the more the price rises, the more shares you sell to take profit off the table.

Look at the seventh row, June 2009. In the previous three months, your $11,536 in IJR grew to a current value of $14,084. That's more than the $11,882 you needed to achieve 3 percent growth in the quarter. Dividing $11,882 by the then-current IJR price of $44.43 showed that you needed just 267 shares to be at a value of $11,882. Because you owned 317 shares, you could sell 50 and still be on track at 3 percent.

Even in this awful time period, the plan became self-sustaining that June, after just five quarters. From June 2009 onward, it maintained a positive cash balance that could fund later purchases without external cash. By the end of December 2011, the overall plan balance reached $20,642, a gain of 20.2 percent on the $17,172 put into it between December 2007 and March 2009—not bad for this period that saw many people bail out at the bottom. Plus, IJR kicked off an additional $514 in dividends in this example. That brings the grand total ending balance to $21,156, a much better 23.2 percent gain from $17,172.

By the way, the new IJR value figures don't show precisely 3 percent growth because we're rounding shares to whole numbers. Rounding gets us close enough and is probably what you'll do in real life anyway. Fractional share amounts are a hassle.

It's possible in abysmal quarters like the one ending December 2008 that you would lack the cash needed to keep the plan going precisely. You could have run the numbers, though, seen that it was a time to add as much as you could afford, and kept the plan going in spirit. That shouldn't happen often, however. Bear markets like the one in 2008 are rare enough that you'll have time between them to save cash from your job or business, and could use that capital to jump on extremely low prices when the plan says to do so, as it did in March 2009 when IJR traded at a dirt cheap $36.39.

In Appendix 3, I present the table at left starting at the end of 2005 and continuing to the end of 2011. After the initial investment, the plan stayed mostly self-funded for two years. Then its buy signals into the subprime crash required extra cash to keep on track. You probably would have been able to fund it. People interested enough in finances to buy this book set aside capital from their income over time. You're one of those people, and that's why I think you would have had the cash.

IJR with value averaging to guarantee 3 percent quarterly growth is a great core portfolio strategy. It automates the process of buying low and selling high. That gives your emotions a rest as the market fluctuates and headlines sensationalize.

Once you have your core portfolio in place, it's time to try potentially more profitable strategies, which we'll explore next.

A Short, Sweet Look at the Dow

The Dow Jones Industrial Average, or DJIA, was created by Charles H. Dow in 1884. He chose 11 very active stocks, nine of which were railroads. At the end of each trading day, he simply added up their closing prices and divided by 11 to get that day's measure of the market. In 1896, *The Wall Street Journal* published the first real industrial average, which measured a whopping 12 companies. One of them, General Electric, remains on the Dow today. In 1916, the Dow increased to 20 stocks and in 1928 it grew to 30 stocks.

The Dow is a benchmark for the entire stock market. It's an imperfect one, but popular because of its simplicity. Other indexes like the S&P 500, NASDAQ Composite, and Wilshire 5000 capture larger cross sections of the market and provide better benchmarks for comparing the performance of mutual funds, hedge funds, and other stock pools. But the Dow persists. It's listed in every paper, reported by talking heads on the news every evening, and whizzes past lightscreens in brokerage offices every few minutes. When the Dow broke 3,000 for the first time, then 4, then 5, then 6, then 12, the whole world knew about it. Few could tell you where the S&P 500 stood on those days.

And, impressively, the Dow keeps pace with the S&P 500. They've both returned an average annual 10.5 percent over the past 75 years or so. More recently the Dow has performed better. Over the 10 years ended December 31, 2007, the S&P 500 returned 51 percent, but the Dow returned 68 percent. Want to see the difference a year can make? Over the 10 years ended December 31, 2008, the S&P 500 lost 27 percent, but the Dow lost 4 percent. The 2008 recession was a doozy, depressing historical returns for years.

Over the 10 years ended December 30, 2011, the S&P 500 returned only 10 percent, but the Dow returned 22 percent. The Dow's out-performance during both good and bad times provides rousing testimony to the dominance of the 30 Dow companies. Each is powerful enough in its industry to stand for its competitors not listed on the Dow.

Think of the Dow as a mini senate representing the various parts of our economy. The senators vote daily on how the market is doing. There are senators from the computer industry (Cisco Systems, Hewlett-Packard, IBM, Intel, Microsoft), the food industry (Coca-Cola, Kraft, McDonald's), the healthcare industry (Johnson & Johnson, Merck, Pfizer), the retail industry (Home Depot, Wal-Mart), the entertainment industry (Disney), the aerospace industry (Boeing), the financial industry (American Express, Bank of America, JPMorgan Chase, Travelers), and so on.

Here are the 30 current Dow companies and their ticker symbols:

Alcoa AA	DuPont DD	McDonald's MCD
American Express AXP	Exxon Mobil XOM	Merck MRK
AT&T T	General Electric GE	Microsoft MSFT
Bank of America BAC	Hewlett-Packard HPQ	Pfizer PFE
Boeing BA	Home Depot HD	Procter & Gamble PG
Caterpillar CAT	IBM IBM	3M MMM
Chevron CVX	Intel INTC	Travelers TRV
Cisco Systems CSCO	Johnson & Johnson JNJ	United Technologies UTX
Coca-Cola KO	JPMorgan Chase JPM	Verizon Communications VZ
Disney DIS	Kraft Foods KFT	Wal-Mart WMT

Heard of any of them? If not, put down this book, pick up your wooden staff, and head back to the mountaintop. You've risen to a plane of existence beyond the needs of commerce and profit.

The defining characteristic of all 30 Dow companies is their gargantuan size. To take one example, Wal-Mart had sales of $450 billion in 2011, a full 3 percent of America's gross national product. It employs more than two million people worldwide. Each Dow company does billions of dollars in annual sales, most are diversified into a bunch of different businesses, and they're international contenders. Even though the list reads like a who's who in American business, you probably spend even more money with these companies than you think.

Let's say you created invitations to your daughter's birthday party using Microsoft Windows and Microsoft Word on your Hewlett-Packard computer running Intel inside. After you knew how many kids were coming, you went to Wal-Mart to buy supplies on your Bank of America credit card. On the day of the party you received a phone call from a mother on your Verizon Wireless phone, but it cut out so you called back on your AT&T landline. Then, one little boy spilled his glass of Powerade and a little girl spilled her glass of Hi-C. Powerade and Hi-C are owned by Coca-Cola. You served up Happy Meals from McDonald's. The kids finished their Happy Meals and went outside to play while you spruced up the kitchen with Mr. Clean. At halftime of the back-yard football game, you passed around a pack of Oreo cookies, patched up some skinned knees with Band-Aids, and rubbed Bengay on the quarterback's shoulder. All the excitement left you with a slight headache, so you popped a couple of Tylenols. Oreos are made by the Nabisco division of Kraft Foods. Johnson & Johnson makes Band-Aids at its consumer products division, and Bengay and Tylenol at its McNeil operating company. Next, your daughter opened her presents and powered each of the electronic ones with Duracell batteries. The final event of the party was to watch the newest DVD from Disney. After the kids went home, you wrapped the leftover food in Reynolds Wrap aluminum foil. That's owned by Alcoa. Your daughter brushed her teeth with Crest, and went to bed. You laundered her grass-stained shorts with Tide, fed the dog some Iams and the cat some Eukanuba, and finally relaxed with a cup of Maxwell House coffee. After that, you washed your face with Olay if you're a woman or Old Spice soap if you're a man, and brushed your teeth with an Oral-B brush. Maxwell House is a division of Kraft Foods. Procter & Gamble owns Mr. Clean, Duracell, Crest, Tide, Iams, Eukanuba, Olay, Old Spice, and Oral-B.

I'd bet my bottom dollar that your grandchildren will do business with Dow companies. In fact, I'm sure of it because editors of *The Wall Street Journal* periodically update the Dow by eliminating laggards and welcoming current market leaders. For example, on April 18, 2004, American International Group,

Pfizer, and Verizon replaced AT&T, Eastman Kodak, and International Paper. On December 1, 2005, AT&T returned when it merged with former Dow component SBC Communications and the combined company began trading with AT&T's symbol, T. On February 19, 2008, Chevron and Bank of America replaced Altria Group and Honeywell. On September 22, 2008, former Altria subsidiary Kraft Foods replaced American International Group. At most points in history, the Dow represents the best of the big guns.

There you have it. Dow companies are enormous, pervade all parts of our lives, tread internationally, and they don't easily disappear. If you're looking for battleships in a market full of kayaks, look no further than the Dow.

Of course, even battleships can be sunk, as 2008 reminded us. Former Dow component General Motors saw its stock fall 91 percent from October 2007 to the end of 2008. Former Dow component American International Group's stock sank 98 percent in the same time. From just September 8, 2008, to September 22, 2008—the day it was removed from the Dow—AIG's stock lost 78 percent.

The Dow Dividend Strategies

Dow companies are strong. Not invincible, but strong. (See: "School of Hard Knocks, Year 2008.") Because of their strength, buying them when they are cheap is usually a way to safely get a good price. With weaker companies, buying cheap can be dangerous because there's a good chance that the company will fail. With Dow companies, the chance of failure is small. Not zero, but small.

Using Dividend Yield to Find Bargains

So, how should you determine if a Dow stock is cheap? By looking at its dividend yield. As you read in Chapter 3, James O'Shaughnessy's study of 83 years on Wall Street found that an effective strategy was to buy large, well-established companies with high dividend yields.

When applied to the Dow, that approach is known as the Dow dividend strategy. Although the idea has been around for decades, the basic strategy is best presented and validated in the 1991 book *Beating the Dow*, by Michael O'Higgins with John Downes. Here we go with another O'lesson from one of those guys. First O'Neil, then O'Shaughnessy, and now O'Higgins. That's O'kay, though. They all know how to make money.

All Dow companies pay a steady dividend, which makes the dividend yield a reliable indicator of how good a bargain their stock prices are at any given time. Remember from page 27 that you determine a stock's dividend yield by dividing its annual dividend by its price. So a $100 stock paying $5 a year in dividends has a yield of 5 percent (5 divided by 100 gives you .05, or 5 percent). Even though it's a piece of cake to calculate dividend yield, you'll be pleased to know that you won't need to do it. It's printed for you in the paper each day and is widely available online.

Because there are only two numbers involved in the dividend yield, if one number remains constant, then the other number drives any changes. With Dow companies, the dividend payout remains fairly constant. These big companies don't like to shock people by reducing the dividend and they don't like to throw their books out of whack by giving too much money away. So they sit comfortably within a narrow range. That leaves us with only one other number to influence dividend yield: stock price. It changes daily and its relationship to the dividend is immediately reflected in the dividend yield.

Now, watch the magic as our 30 Dow darlings fluctuate in price. Say IBM is trading at $86 a share and is paying a dividend of $.35 per quarter, or $1.40 per year. You could look up its dividend yield in the paper or online, or calculate it yourself: $1.40 divided by $86 equals .016, or 1.6 percent. In the next few months, IBM declines to $42 a share but maintains the same $1.40 dividend: $1.40 divided by $42 equals 3.3 percent. Aha, it's a higher dividend yield because the stock price dropped. A lower stock price for the same company is a bargain and could indicate that a turnaround is on the way. Do you think IBM is going out of business because its stock dropped over 50 percent? Probably not. Dow companies don't usually stay down and out forever. IBM is going to find a way to climb back up to its former glory prices and you might as well accompany it on the journey by purchasing a few shares. When it reaches high prices again and its dividend yield goes down to reflect that, you know it's time to move your money to one of IBM's 30 Dow brethren with a low price and a high yield to accompany it on the path to recovery.

How to Invest in High-Yield Dow Stocks

Now you're thoroughly convinced of the reliability of Dow companies and you understand why high dividend yields are a good indicator of bargain stock prices. It's time to look at how the Dow dividend strategies seek to harness that information for profit.

The plan is to spend 15 minutes once a year finding the 10 highest-yield Dow stocks, then invest in each of the 10 or a select number of the 10. Every year thereafter, you repeat the process and adjust your portfolio by selling the stocks that no longer make the select group and buying the ones that replaced them. Your eyes haven't failed you—this is, indeed, an investment strategy requiring 15 minutes of research *once per year*. O'Higgins wrote that each Dow strategy "involves reviewing and updating your portfolio once a year and fastidiously and deliberately ignoring it in between." For convenience, historical returns tracking the Dow dividend strategy begin on January 1, but you can begin your plan on any day of the year.

First, I'll show how to list the 10 highest-yielding Dow stocks. Then I'll review five popular strategies.

On the day you begin your Dow dividend strategy investment program, visit Finance.Yahoo.com, click the Dow index, then click Components. You'll see all 30 current Dow stocks and can click each of their symbols for more info. Click through the list and write down each stock's dividend yield and price. Using your keen faculties of observation and a process of elimination, circle the 10 highest-yield Dow stocks on your list. If there's a tie among the dividend yields, choose the stock with the lower price. Rank the 10 circled stocks 1 to 10 from lowest to highest stock price and write the rank beside each one. The cheapest stock will have a 1 beside it, the second cheapest a 2, and so on.

Too much clicking and writing? A quicker way to get the information is by visiting www.dogsofthedow.com, which shows each company's dividend yield, price, and so on. It even ranks them, so you don't have to.

List on a sheet of paper the company names, symbols, dividend yields, and prices of all 10 stocks in the order you just ranked them. On December 30, 2011, my sheet looked like this:

	Company Name	Symbol	Dividend Yield	Price
1	General Electric	GE	3.80%	17.91
2	Pfizer	PFE	3.70%	21.64
3	Intel	INTC	3.46%	24.25
4	AT&T	T	5.82%	30.24
5	Kraft Foods	KFT	3.10%	37.36
6	Merck	MRK	4.46%	37.70
7	Verizon	VZ	4.99%	40.12
8	DuPont	DD	3.58%	45.78
9	Johnson & Johnson	JNJ	3.48%	65.58
10	Procter & Gamble	PG	3.15%	66.71

All Dow dividend strategies are based on investing in the 10 Dow stocks chosen in this manner.

Let's discuss stock 2 for a second. Michael O'Higgins calls the second-lowest-priced stock the *Penultimate Profit Prospect*, or *PPP*. In case your SAT study sessions have worn off, penultimate means next to last. It's the stock that has historically returned more than all the other Dow stocks. The lowest-priced stock is often facing genuine trouble, which is the reason for its low price. The second-lowest-priced stock, on the other hand, is not usually in trouble. It's simply the most bargain priced of the high yielders that are faring well, and therefore has the best prospects for stock performance. As you'll see, however, when it does badly, it does very badly.

Here's how you would allocate $10,000 among the 10 stocks according to four popular Dow dividend strategies:

- **Dow 10** simply buys an equal amount of each stock. You would invest $1,000 in each of the 10 stocks.

- **Dow High 5** buys the five highest yielding of the 10 stocks. You would invest $2,000 in each of AT&T, Verizon, Merck, General Electric, and Pfizer.

- **Dow Low 5** buys the five lowest priced of the 10 stocks. O'Higgins advocates this strategy because the lower prices should lead to higher percentage gains. You would invest $2,000 in each of stocks 1 to 5.

- **Dow 1** puts all of your money on stock 2, the penultimate profit prospect. You would invest $10,000 in stock 2, which is Pfizer in this case.

Performance

The table below, from investment advisor Mark Pankin at Pankin.com, summarizes how the four Dow dividend strategies performed in the 40 years ended December 30, 2011. It details price change only and does not take into account income from dividend payouts:

Strategy	Average Annual	Best Year	Worst Year
Dow 10	7.9%	48.1%	–41.6%
Dow High 5	7.3%	61.2%	–48.8%
Dow Low 5	9.6%	60.8%	–51.5%
Dow 1	4.6%	183.4%	–87.1%
Dow Jones Ind. Avg.	6.8%	38.3%	–33.8%

Three of the four strategies were effective at beating the Dow over time. The one that wasn't, the Dow 1, killed itself by owning General Motors in 2008 and Bank of America in 2009. GM fell 87 percent in 2008; Bank of America fell 82 percent from the end of 2008 to its Feburary 2009 low, and even after recovering, it ended the year up only 7 percent compared with the Dow's 19 percent. In 2010, the Dow 1 was Kraft and in 2011 it was Intel. They returned a respective 16 percent and 15 percent in their years, compared with the Dow's 11 percent and 6 percent, respectively. The Dow 1 is useful for finding a place to spec-ulate with part of your money but is not a good portfolio strategy. The best approach is the original, the O'Higgins Low 5.

The strategies show dividend yield to be a good way to find undervalued Dow companies.

Doubling the Dow

As good as the Dow dividend strategies have been, there's a way to beat them all. First, some background.

When I began researching Dow strategies, it occurred to me that an easy way to outperform the Dow would be through leverage, a technique that magnifies an investment's perfor-mance. There seemed to be no reason to go through the process of winnowing out the high dividend yielders when I could just own the whole Dow and magnify its performance to a bigger return than any of the dividend strategies had achieved.

However, at the time of this book's first publication, there was no practical way for the individual investor to own the whole Dow. You could have bought all 30 Dow stocks and constantly rebalanced them, but that would have been too much work. You could have matched the Dow with an index mutual fund, but your return would have been less than the return posted by the dividend strategies. So the dividend strategies were the best way for individuals to beat the Dow and, therefore, the only strate-gies I showed in the book's first edition.

The introduction of two investment products since then has made leveraging the Dow not only possible, but easy. The prod-ucts are:

- ✔ The Ultra Dow 30 ETF from ProShares. The security, symbol DDM, is available through any broker. It trades exactly as a stock, and uses leverage to achieve roughly twice the performance of the Dow.

- ✔ The Ultra Dow 30 mutual fund from ProFunds. The fund, symbol UDPIX, is available through most brokers. It uses leverage to achieve roughly twice the performance of the Dow.

Both of these products make it easy to double the Dow. Doing so produces results better than the dividend strategies in most market environments.

In this section, I show how leverage works and then explain three ways to double the Dow.

Pros and Cons of Leverage

Most people are familiar with leverage because they use it when buying a house. Let's say you bought a house for $200,000 with a down payment of $40,000. Five years and two lawn mowers later, you sell the house for $250,000. The value of the house increased 25 percent. Not bad. But the value of your $40,000 investment in the house increased 125 percent to a total of $90,000.

How did that happen? Through the use of a mortgage. You borrowed $160,000 from a lender and put just $40,000 of your own money into the house. You controlled a $200,000 investment with just $40,000.

It works the same way with stocks, except that you borrow money from your broker instead of from a mortgage lender. The borrowed money is not called a loan, it's called *margin*. You would say, "I bought 250 shares of General Electric on margin," by which you would mean that you borrowed the money from your broker to buy the 250 shares.

You could buy $5,000 worth of GE, borrow another $5,000, and then control a $10,000 investment in General Motors. Without the leverage, a 20 percent rise in your $5,000 investment in GE would give you $1,000 profit. With the leverage, however, a 20 percent rise would give you $2,000 profit, which is a 40 percent return on your investment.

What's the catch? That leverage magnifies losses as well as gains. If GE loses 20 percent, your $10,000 position is now worth just $8,000. You lost $2,000 of your $5,000 investment, which is -40 percent. In addition to that loss, you need to pay interest to your broker when you borrow money. For example, Fidelity's margin rate for amounts under $10,000 is 8.6 percent.

I almost always discourage leverage. Everybody chooses the wrong stocks at the wrong time at least once in their investment career. Magnifying the losses in those cases can be devastating.

Why, then, would I advocate leveraging the Dow? Because it's not one stock, it's 30 of the best stocks available. That does not mean that leveraging the Dow won't produce big losses at times—it will—but over the long haul, the Dow will rise. Magnifying that rise will be profitable.

Three Ways to Leverage the Dow

You can leverage the Dow by following the example above. Apply for a margin account at your broker and then buy shares of the Diamonds Trust, symbol DIA, just as you would buy any stock. It's an ETF that tracks the Dow. You might want to just buy it with cash to get used to watching your money fluctuate along with the Dow. Later, when you've had a chance to feel the Dow's performance in your bones as you watch the gains and losses, you might decide that doubling the behavior is right for you. In your margin account, you would simply double the number of shares you own by purchasing more with money borrowed from your broker.

However, I recommend that you take advantage of either the ProShares Ultra Dow 30 ETF or the ProFunds Ultra Dow 30 mutual fund. Instead of borrowing the money from your broker, you just invest your cash. Leave the details of leveraging up to the fund to double the performance of the Dow.

Of the two, I suggest the ETF as the better approach if you'll be selling shares more than a couple of times per year in an attempt to time the market, as we'll discuss below. I suggest the mutual fund as the better approach if you plan to make frequent contributions and stay invested most of the time. Many people continue investing every month or every quarter. Doing so in a mutual fund results in no extra commissions. It's free to add money. With an ETF, you pay a commission each time you buy more shares, just as you do with a stock.

Ultra Dow 30 doubles the Dow by using leveraged investment techniques such as futures, options, and swaps. Explaining those techniques is beyond the scope of this book and irrelevant to the discussion anyway. All you really need to know is that the fund returns roughly twice what the Dow returns each day, whether positive or negative.

The fund is not precise, but it strives to be and it comes close in the short term. The longer the time frame, the more its performance degrades because magnified losses add up. To offset that, we'll look at ways to guard against extreme loss.

Here's how the Dow, the Dow 1, and Double the Dow performed from December 31, 2002, to December 30, 2011, and includes the growth of an initial $10,000 investment:

	The Dow (DIA)	The Dow 1 (different each year)	Double the Dow (UDPIX)
Dec. 30, 2011	$14,480 (+5% in 2011)	$2,102 (+15% in 2011)	$14,451 (+9% in 2011)
Dec. 31, 2010	$13,741 (+11% in 2010)	$1,823 (+16% in 2010)	$13,251 (+22% in 2010)
Dec. 31, 2009	$12,368 (+19% in 2009)	$1,573 (+7% in 2009)	$10,835 (+37% in 2009)
Dec. 31, 2008	$10,401 (-34% in 2008)	$1,470 (-87% in 2008)	$7,905 (-63% in 2008)
Dec. 31, 2007	$15,752 (+6% in 2007)	$11,432 (-17% in 2007)	$21,097 (+7% in 2006)
Dec. 29, 2006	$14,805 (+17% in 2006)	$13,779 (+11% in 2006)	$19,642 (+29% in 2006)
Dec. 30, 2005	$12,710 (-0.5% in 2005)	$12,412 (-13% in 2005)	$15,265 (-4% in 2005)
Dec. 31, 2004	$12,776 (+3% in 2004)	$14,312 (-1% in 2004)	$15,906 (+5% in 2004)
Dec. 31, 2003	$12,427 (+24% in 2003)	$14,479 (+45% in 2003)	$15,094 (+51% in 2003)
Dec. 31, 2002	$10,000	$10,000	$10,000

You can see a current version of the chart above at www.jasonkelly.com/resources.

The first thing you'll notice is the ferocity of the 2008 recession. As you read above, the Dow 1 stock that year was General Motors, which declined 87 percent as it teetered on the edge of bankruptcy. GM single-handedly invalidated the Dow 1 strategy, because in one year it wiped out decades worth of gains. I keep tracking it for purposes of comparison but don't recommend it for the bulk of your portfolio, and never have. After 2008, it's easy to see why.

Ultra Dow didn't do much better that year. Its 63 percent loss erased more than five years' worth of gains and proved the need for downside protection in the strategy. In this time frame, the best bet was the plain old Dow via DIA. It ended the nine-year span higher than Ultra Dow, and with a lot lower pulse rate. However, we're seeking to beat the Dow, not just match it. Notice how, if not for 2008, Ultra Dow was by far the best choice. Wouldn't it be nice to find a way to avoid years like 2008 while benefiting from the extra oomph provided by leverage in ordinary years? You bet. More on that below.

Ultra Dow 30 is cheaper than seeking your own leverage through a margin account. At the beginning of 2008, Fidelity's interest on amounts under $10,000 was 8.6 percent. The annual expense of Ultra Dow 30 is just 1.7 percent.

Ultra Dow 30 is also safer than seeking your own leverage through a margin account. Why? Because investing in the mutual fund does not require borrowing money. With margin investing, you can lose more than 100 percent of your investment by losing not just your own money but also losing the money you borrowed. That cheerful situation leads to your needing to pay back the borrowed money that you lost, with interest. In Ultra Dow 30, the most you could lose is 100 percent of your money, no more.

That will never happen with the Dow. The companies are not all going to go bankrupt at the same time, and if they ever do you'll have a lot more to worry about than the value of your portfolio. Something will have gone seriously wrong in the world.

Maximum Midcap

You've seen the power of the solid companies of the Dow, the usefulness of the Dow dividend strategies to find the stocks from the Dow with the most potential for short-term appreciation, and a way to beat both the Dow and the dividend strategies by leveraging the entire Dow to twice its performance.

Now, let's apply the same leveraging approach you read about in "Doubling the Dow" above to a different index. The goal is to do better than the Dow, but there's no rule saying we need to restrict ourselves to only Dow stocks to do so. Why not beat the Dow using an entirely separate group of stocks?

That group should lose less than the Dow during falling markets, make more than the Dow in rising markets, or both. I found an index that does both. It's the S&P MidCap 400. It tracks 400 stocks with a medium-sized market capitalization. They're not large caps, such as those on the Dow and S&P 500, nor are they small caps, such as those on the Russell 2000 and S&P Small Cap 600. They're just right, sandwiched in the middle, the sweet spot of the stock market. You saw this for yourself on pages 40 and 41.

In researching even better ways to beat the Dow, I compared long-term and short-term charts of various indexes in search of a Dow beater. They all had their moments of outperformance coupled with moments of underperformance, but the MidCap 400 rose consistently near the top of the list. For example, it was not devastated by the bursting of the Internet bubble and it performed briskly during the ensuing recovery.

Look at its total returns compared with the total returns of the Dow as of December 30, 2011:

Index	3-Year	5-Year	10-Year
S&P MidCap 400 Index	63%	9%	73%
Dow Jones Ind. Avg.	39%	-2%	22%

The MidCap 400 is not immune to bad times, of course, and no recent year says bad times better than 2008, when all stocks suffered. That year, the MidCap 400 lost 37 percent and the Dow lost 34 percent. These are their total returns as of December 31, 2008:

Index	3-Year	5-Year	10-Year
S&P MidCap 400 Index	-27%	-7%	37%
Dow Jones Ind. Avg.	-18%	-16%	-4%

As you can see, the midcap index has handily outperformed its larger cap brother over time, despite lagging recently. It's not hard to see why midcaps do well. Large caps are established in their industries. They're large because they've already grown a lot. They could still do well, but not nearly as well as they did in their early years.

Small caps have a lot of potential, but a lot of danger. For every one that goes on to become Starbucks or Microsoft or Pfizer, there are hundreds that become nothing. Investors lose their money. Employees lose their jobs. Dreams go up in smoke. That's the nature of small cap investing, and entrepreneurship in general.

With midcaps, we get companies that have cleared their first hurdles without exhausting their growth potential. They've proven that they have a good thing going, but they haven't grown old and stodgy. They provide a lot of potential for a relatively small amount of risk.

Now, let's apply leveraging to them as we did earlier to the Dow.

To leverage the Dow, I suggested using either ProFunds Ultra Dow 30 (UDPIX) or ProShares Ultra Dow 30 (DDM). To leverage the MidCap 400 index, I suggest using either ProFunds Ultra MidCap (UMPIX) or ProShares Ultra MidCap 400 (MVV).

As with the Dow, the benefit of the mutual fund is that it allows you to invest more each month without paying a commission. The benefit of the ETF is that it allows you to buy and sell immediately as you do with stocks.

According to my tracking in *The Kelly Letter*, the table on the next page shows how Maximum Midcap via UMPIX compared to Double the Dow via UDPIX from December 31, 2002, to December 31, 2011.

Look very carefully and see if you can find the year you'd most like to remove from the list. Time's up. Did you choose 2008? Good. Then you're qualified to move on to the next section.

Year	Maximum MidCap	Double the Dow
2011	-13%	9%
2010	50%	22%
2009	65%	37%
2008	-68%	-63%
2007	6%	7%
2006	10%	29%
2005	19%	-4%
2004	29%	5%
2003	60%	51%

The Downside

If there's one thing that's clear in the above background, it's that the elephant in the china shop of these strategies is an extreme bear market. The enemy of all leverage is the downside. In fact, that's what caused the recession of 2008. Banks got themselves into big trouble with leverage in the housing market, and it changed the world.

One conclusion could be to skip leveraging and just own the Dow or S&P 500 through a plain vanilla index fund. Many advisors suggest that. By definition, you'll be guaranteed market performance over time and your research will be done. You will not beat the market, but nor will you lose to it.

Our goal, however, is to beat the market, so let's keep exploring ways to get around the downside weakness of these strategies.

Recently, the number of leveraged investment products has exploded. They now cover not just the Dow and S&P MidCap 400 but many other indexes targeting domestic stocks of every company size, foreign stocks, sectors such as finance and energy, commodities such as oil and gold, and currencies. They don't just double performance anymore, either. They now offer triple leverage for three times the performance of the target index and even inverse double and triple leverage for steroid-pumped performance in the opposite direction of the target index. There are hundreds of new ways to profit no matter which way the market is moving. I've provided a collection of them in Appendix 2.

Most of these leveraged products are designed to achieve their goal day to day. They track the *daily* movements of their target indexes, which is why their accuracy degrades as the time frame lengthens, especially when volatility is high but the net performance is flat. It's possible to get the long- or medium-term forecast right, choose the right leveraged product, and still just match or even lose to the index.

Let's say you own MVV, which doubles the daily return of the S&P MidCap 400 index. In one random sample week, Monday to Friday, the midcap index posts these returns: -5 percent, -3 percent, +4 percent, +3 percent, +2 percent. The index is up 0.7 percent for the week. Because you're doubling the index, you should be up 1.4 percent, right? Right, but you're not because you're doubling each daily performance, not the weekly performance. Run those daily tallies at twice the numbers and you get a weekly net performance of precisely 0.7 percent—the same as the plain index but with twice the volatility and heart rate. If the leveraged advantage slipped in just one week, imagine how far offtrack it can get over months and years.

This doesn't mean the leverage is useless, though. The market rises two-thirds of the time, and adding money to a line that's rising more steeply than the market itself works. On the next page, look at the recent growth of $10,000 in Maximum Midcap, Double the Dow, and the Dow itself through the Diamonds Trust, symbol DIA.

In the five years ended December 31, 2007, leverage took Maximum Midcap 81 percent higher than the Dow, and Double the Dow 34 percent higher. The devastation of 2008, magnified by leverage, took Maximum Midcap to an overall 12 percent lower than the Dow, and Double the Dow 24 percent lower. See the degradation over time? Over these six years, the Dow gained 4 percent, so we would expect Double the Dow to have gained about 8 percent. Due to slippage from the adverse effect of a magnified downside, it instead *lost* 21 percent.

Now, before you pack your bags and leave leverage for good, consider that table up to the end of 2007. Wouldn't it have been nice to have owned Maximum Midcap for most or all of that five-year period? What about 148 percent growth from 2008 to 2010? Wouldn't that have been nice to own? Sure it would, so let's see if we can know when to get out and avoid years like 2008.

Date	Maximum Midcap	Double the Dow	Dow (via DIA)
12/30/2011	$19,754	$14,450	$14,481
12/31/2010	$22,768	$13,250	$13,741
12/31/2009	$15,173	$10,835	$12,368
12/31/2008	$9,168	$7,905	$10,401
12/31/2007	$28,495	$21,097	$15,752
12/29/2006	$26,961	$19,642	$14,805
12/30/2005	$24,418	$15,265	$12,710
12/31/2004	$20,604	$15,906	$12,776
12/31/2003	$16,035	$15,094	$12,427
12/31/2002	$10,000	$10,000	$10,000

Limiting the Downside with Charts

We can boost the long-term performance of these permanent portfolios by trying to avoid the downside. You've now arrived at the most controversial of all market topics: timing. "Nobody can do it," says one group. "Baloney," says another.

I'll present three chart indicators that have worked fairly well together and let you decide for yourself whether timing is worth the effort. In my view, those who swear off timing and those who swear by timing both make good points. Timing is, if not impossible, very difficult. We can all agree on that. However, we can also probably agree that anything offering a chance to avoid years like 2008 is worth exploring.

The three indicators we'll consider are not perfect, but they're better than nothing. They are SMA, MACD, and RSI. We'll look at each one individually, with help from charts provided by Online Trading Concepts, then pull them together in an example that includes the crash of 2008 on charts provided by StockCharts.com.

Simple Moving Average

A *simple moving average*, or SMA, price line smooths out an investment's path to show its trend more clearly. If closing prices over the last five trading days were $32, $36, $34, $35, and $31, then the SMA would be $33.60, arrived at by adding the five numbers to get 168 and then dividing that by five. If we do that the next day, and the next, and the next, we'll create a five-day SMA line that we can watch for trends. We can set the interval wherever we want. Typical settings for SMA are 20 days, 50 days, and 200 days.

A price line's relationship to its SMA shows you its trend. If the price is staying above the SMA at a rising angle, that's a rising trend, or *uptrend*. If the price is staying below the SMA at a falling angle, that's a falling trend, or *downtrend*.

The easiest way to get buy and sell hints from this measure is to watch for when the investment's price line crosses above or below its SMA. When the investment is moving up, the SMA acts as a support line, and the price dipping below the line and moving back up signals a buy. That's shown on the following chart of a 20-day SMA of the Dow Jones Industrial Average ETF, symbol DIA:

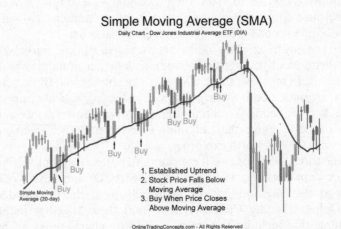

Simple Moving Average (SMA)
Daily Chart - Dow Jones Industrial Average ETF (DIA)

Simple Moving Average (20-day)

1. Established Uptrend
2. Stock Price Falls Below Moving Average
3. Buy When Price Closes Above Moving Average

Notice how much smoother the SMA is than the price. See how well it shows the upward trend, and then the abrupt change to a downtrend? That's helpful.

When the investment is moving down, the SMA acts as a resistance line, and the price popping above the line and moving back down signals a sell. That's shown in this chart:

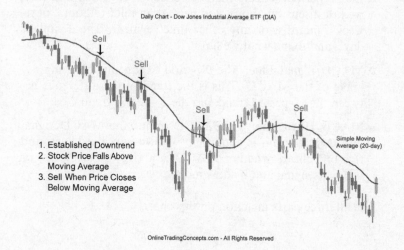

Daily Chart - Dow Jones Industrial Average ETF (DIA)

Sell

Sell

Sell

Sell

Simple Moving Average (20-day)

1. Established Downtrend
2. Stock Price Falls Above Moving Average
3. Sell When Price Closes Below Moving Average

OnlineTradingConcepts.com - All Rights Reserved

Many traders use several moving averages together, such as a 20-day, a 50-day, and a 200-day and watch for them to cross over each other for hints on future price direction.

We'll keep it easy, however, by watching just the price and the 50-day SMA for crossover signals in the 2008 example on page 148.

MACD

This measurement shows trends in an investment by looking at the difference between fast and slow *exponential moving averages*, or EMAs, of its closing prices. An exponential moving average is similar to the simple moving average we looked at above, but it places more weight on recent prices than on past ones, making it react more quickly to trend changes. *Fast* and *slow* refer to the time periods used, with fast being a short one and slow being a long one. As these averages come together and move apart, they send hints about future direction. That's why the name of the measurement is *moving average convergence divergence*, or MACD.

The MACD message is comprised of three parts:

- ✔ **MACD:** The 12-period exponential moving average minus the 26-period. This is the difference between fast and slow we just discussed above, and *period* can refer to hours, days, weeks, months, or any other time segment. The default is days, and that's what we'll use.

- ✔ **MACD Signal Line:** The 9-period exponential moving average of the MACD. This is the trend of the difference between the 12-period trend and the 26-period trend.

- ✔ **MACD Histogram:** The MACD minus the MACD signal line. A histogram is commonly known as a bar chart, and this one shows whether MACD is above, the same as, or below its signal and by how much.

See all three parts in action on this chart:

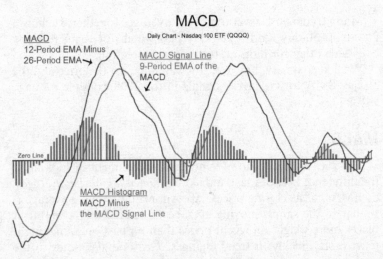

MACD

Daily Chart - Nasdaq 100 ETF (QQQQ)

MACD
12-Period EMA Minus
26-Period EMA

MACD Signal Line
9-Period EMA of the
MACD

Zero Line

MACD Histogram
MACD Minus
the MACD Signal Line

That's just the bottom part of the chart. Next, let's expand the scope to include the full chart with the investment's price line.

The main way to use MACD is by watching for the moving averages to cross over each other. A buy signal happens when the fast 12-period EMA crosses over the slow 26-period EMA, which causes MACD to cross over the zero line. A sell signal happens when the fast 12-period EMA crosses below the slow 26-period EMA, which causes MACD to cross below the zero line.

Another way to use this curious collection of lines is to watch for the MACD to cross the MACD signal line, which flips the histogram to the opposite side of the zero line. Flipping above it is a buy signal; flipping below it is a sell signal.

Seeing it is easier than reading about it, so witness all parts at work on the chart below.

I find the bars of the histogram to be the friendliest way to follow MACD. Look how simple they are. Their depth or height tells us how stretched the investment is getting either down or up, their moves back toward zero show that something is changing, and their crossing over or under the zero line shows us a new trend has begun.

Notice that any way you choose to follow MACD will have

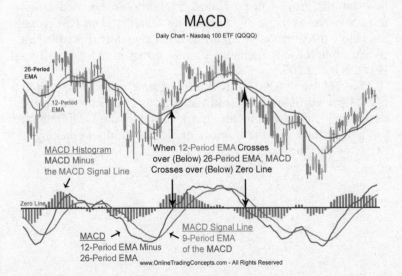

MACD

Daily Chart - Nasdaq 100 ETF (QQQQ)

26-Period EMA

12-Period EMA

MACD Histogram
MACD Minus
the MACD Signal Line

When 12-Period EMA Crosses
over (Below) 26-Period EMA, MACD
Crosses over (Below) Zero Line

Zero Line

MACD
12-Period EMA Minus
26-Period EMA

MACD Signal Line
9-Period EMA
of the MACD

www.OnlineTradingConcepts.com - All Rights Reserved

you missing the very tops and bottoms of the price line but catching the bulk of the next trend. That's the goal. If you're happy only when catching absolute bottoms and absolute tops, you'll rarely be happy. Give yourself a break by seeking most of a move, not all of it.

RSI

Relative strength index compares an investment's current price with its past performance to gauge current strength. Be careful about a fine distinction at work here. RSI compares an investment's current situation with its own history. A different measurement that sounds the same, *relative price strength*, compares a stock's price action with the price action of all other stocks. We looked at that in Chapter 3 and will see it again in the *Investor's Business Daily* section of Chapter 6.

The idea with RSI is that we can know from an investment's history when it tends to reverse direction, either up from a low or down from a high. RSI is easy to understand. It fluctuates between 0 and 100, with readings over 70 indicating overbought and due for a fall, and readings under 30 indicating oversold and due for a bounce. You're supposed to wait for the reversal to happen before either selling or buying because you never know how far the move will go before reversing. So, an RSI crossing above the oversold 30 line is a buy signal, and an RSI crossing below the overbought 70 line is a sell signal. RSI is called an oscillator because it oscillates up and down in a wave pattern between 0 and 100.

Like SMA and MACD, RSI needs a time frame. The default is a 14-period time frame, and the periods can again be hours, days, weeks, or anything else, but are usually days. Shortening the period increases the number of signals, and lengthening it decreases the number.

The following chart shows RSI signals for eBay:

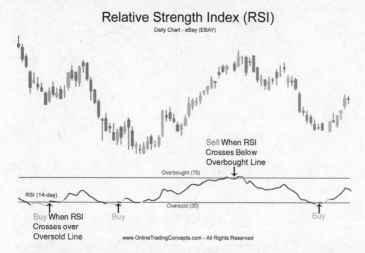

Relative Strength Index (RSI)
Daily Chart - eBay (EBAY)

Sell When RSI
Crosses Below
Overbought Line

Overbought (70)

RSI (14-day)

Oversold (30)

Buy When RSI
Crosses over
Oversold Line

Buy

Buy

www.OnlineTradingConcepts.com - All Rights Reserved

Look at the very left of the chart. See that when RSI first crossed under the oversold line, eBay had further to fall? That's why you wait for RSI to move back over before buying, because it hints that the worst is over and improvement is at hand. Sometimes it gets even more extreme. I've seen RSIs get as low as 15 before turning back up and as high as 90 before turning back down.

Using Them Together

Now, let's see how SMA, MACD, and RSI together would have helped you avoid the 2008 downturn in our Maximum Midcap strategy. Getting the same signal from two of the three measurements is usually enough to warrant taking action. Getting the same signal from all three is quite convincing.

The chart on the next page shows UMPIX from December 29, 2006, to December 31, 2008, and includes SMA, MACD, and RSI with the default periods we discussed above.

At the end of February 2007, both MACD and RSI said to sell, even though the price and SMA showed an uptrend. MACD crossed below its signal line and RSI crossed below 70. The price crossed below the SMA, then bounced around it for a couple of weeks, showing that a trend change had not occurred. Within a month, both MACD and RSI suggested getting back in. Notice

UMPIX (ProFunds Ultra MidCap) USMF   © StockCharts.com
31-Dec 2008   Op 16.40 **Hi** 16.40 **Lo** 16.40 **Cl** 16.40   **Chg** +0.71 (+4.53%) ▲

that they gave conflicting signals during the 25 percent run higher from early March to early June, but SMA showed the uptrend to be intact. That's why using three measurements is a good idea.

Early June 2007 was the best time to sell before the crash of 2008. UMPIX reached a high of $62.40 on June 4. RSI hit 70 that day and began backing off—a sell signal. Three days later, MACD slipped below its signal line and the histogram flipped below the zero line—a second sell signal. The price fell to the SMA, too—a caution flag.

RSI began giving buy signals at the end of July but wasn't confirmed by an MACD buy signal until the third week of August.

On October 9, RSI hit 69 and backed off—close enough to be considered a sell signal if confirmed by MACD. A week later,

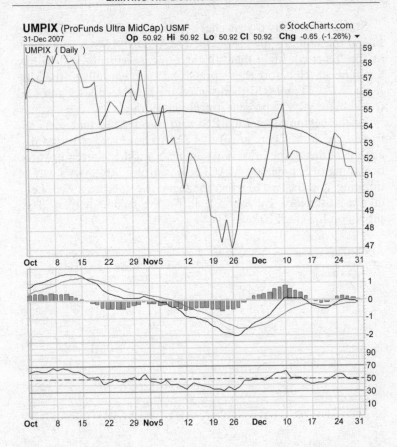

MACD slipped below the signal line and the histogram flipped under the zero line—the sell signal was confirmed. In early November, the price slipped convincingly below the SMA to signal a downtrend. All of this is more clear on the chart zoomed to the fourth quarter of 2007, shown above.

After issuing dual buy signals at the end of November 2007, MACD and RSI did not agree on a time to sell before the early 2008 tumble. MACD said to sell at the end of December, but RSI did not. However, the price reversing off the overhead SMA in December was another sell signal. That was two out of three, and would have gotten you out of UMPIX for most of the December-to-January sell-off shown on the two-year chart on the facing page.

Staying on the two-year chart, both MACD and RSI said to buy at the January 2008 lows; then MACD and SMA said to sell at the February high; then all three measurements said to buy again in March before the impressive 25 percent rally to the May highs. MACD and RSI then sensed the nosebleed level and said to sell before the 16 percent drop to late June.

At the beginning of July, RSI said to buy, and that was confirmed by MACD in mid-July. SMA, however, strongly disagreed, showing the price nowhere near another uptrend. At the beginning of September, MACD came around to SMA's way of thinking, and the two together made a powerful case to sell. Let's take a closer look by zooming in on the second half of 2008, shown on the chart below.

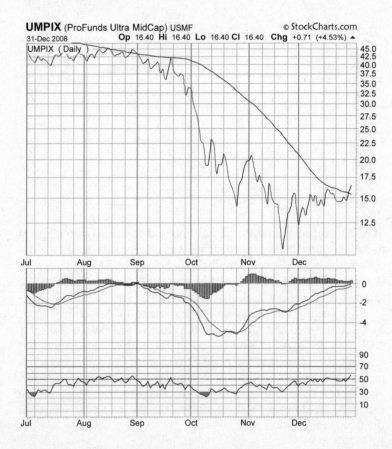

Notice that just when MACD tagged its signal line at the end of August and the histogram played along the zero line, the price of UMPIX popped above its SMA and then reversed back down. Meanwhile, we could understand why RSI wasn't showing overbought. UMPIX was already in a downtrend shown by the downward-sloping SMA line, and it was about to get much worse. It didn't go from a lofty high to a lower high; it went from a low to a much lower low. RSI can't catch that because its signals come from overbought and oversold conditions, and UMPIX never became overbought to issue an RSI sell signal in summer 2008.

The other two did, though, and two out of three is good enough for us. The credit market panic swept in and took UMPIX down 77 percent from its August high to its November low. At the October and November lows, both MACD and RSI said to buy, but SMA disagreed.

As you can see, SMA, MACD, and RSI together caught a lot of good turning points in this two-year span and spared investors the brunt of 2008's wrath. Their buy suggestions in October and November were hard to follow amid some of the worst financial headlines ever printed, but paid off fairly quickly.

Stay Put Most of the Time

When we time the market correctly, it's wonderful. It's the holy grail of the stock world: getting out just before a big crash and getting back in just before a big recovery. It's hard to do even one time, though, much less consistently year after year. I promise you that the guy on TV being praised for calling the most recent move correctly got the last one or two wrong and will one day be wrong again. Why do I know? Because I'm one of those guys.

Chances are quite good—I dare say, certain—that you will experience the same spotty record when trying to time the market on your own. If not, if you get it right consistently year after year, email me. I'll have a few questions.

The good news is that most of the time it's best to just stay put in MVV or UMPIX because the market rises more than it falls. Big bear markets are the exception, not the rule. Staying put on a rising line benefits from compounding as gains build upon prior gains, and you watch profits mount.

While staying put, keep an eye on SMA, MACD, and RSI for indications of big trouble ahead. Because it's hard to determine when trouble is big and when it's small, you'll sometimes get it wrong. Know that in advance and give yourself a break. With the above tools in hand you'll do a pretty good job. That's more than we can say for the billion-dollar banking geniuses who ran their firms to insolvency in 2008.

What to Expect

If you decide to leverage either the Dow or the S&P MidCap 400, expect a wild ride. The price you pay for enjoying higher highs is suffering lower lows. Shooting higher and falling lower than a target index isn't for everybody.

If you can change your way of thinking to see lower lows as opportunities amid crisis, you'll love these doubling strategies. If instead you see lower lows as abject failure while the world ends, you'll hate these doubling strategies. Know that the downside will happen, and expect it. Do not be shocked by it.

Value averaging teaches us that buying more when the price is down eventually pays off—as long as recovery is assured. That last part is key. If the investment is on its way to zero, no method of buying it makes sense. You can keep lowering your average cost all the way into the dirt, but you'll still end up with nothing. You will have bought oblivion on sale. I hope that's obvious. People who owned certain large, supposedly too-big-to-fail financial firms rediscovered that in 2008 when those firms went bankrupt.

The beauty of basing a permanent portfolio on an index is that recovery is assured. The investment relies not on one company but on 400 in the case of Maximum Midcap. They're not all going to disappear.

Think of the doubling strategies as crazy discount stores that sell the same product that other stores sell, but at absurdly low prices now and then. The "same product" is eventual recovery. For example, when Maximum Midcap and Double the Dow dropped 40 percent from June 2002 to October 2002, the Dow dropped only 20 percent.

Usually, a person looking at that would point to the Dow as the better investment. For the long-term investor, however, the doubling strategies were better. Why? Because they eventually recovered, too, but investors had a chance to get them at twice the discount during the sale period.

It didn't take long to pay off. When Maximum Midcap gained 127 percent from March 2003 to March 2004, the Dow gained only 37 percent.

From early May 2006 to mid-July 2006, Maximum Midcap fell 25 percent while the Dow fell only 6 percent. You see that and think, "I should have put all my money in baseball cards." But by now you know what came next, right? Over the next 12 months, Maximum Midcap gained 58 percent while the Dow gained only 28 percent.

In the 2008 crash and recovery, the numbers became even more extreme. From their June 2008 highs to their March 2009 lows, Maximum Midcap fell 84 percent while the Dow fell just 49 percent. Over the ensuing 25 months to their April 2011 highs, Maximum Midcap gained 493 percent while the Dow gained only 100 percent. A perfectly timed investment of $10,000 at the March 2009 lows to the April 2011 highs became $59,300 in Maximum Midcap but only $20,000 in the Dow.

What I am pointing out here is that extreme volatility coupled with assured recovery is a potent combination. It's why I continue believing in these strategies through good times and bad, but especially during bad. When most of what you hear is complaining about the stock market, get out your checkbook. Eventual recovery is on sale.

Putting it all together, then, your core portfolio will have two parts:

✔ Value averaging the S&P SmallCap 600 via IJR to achieve steady 3 percent quarterly growth.

✔ Leveraging the S&P MidCap 400 index via MVV or UMPIX. You'll stay put most of the time to compound strong performance, but keep an eye on the chart to see if SMA, MACD, and RSI warn of big trouble ahead. When they do, you'll get out and wait for buy signals to take advantage of recovery on sale.

On top of this core portfolio, you'll choose individual stocks with the potential to perform even better. That's what we'll explore next.

To see the current performance of these and other strategies, visit my website at www.jasonkelly.com/resources.

5
Get Ready to Invest

This chapter contains the planning you need to do before investing. I discuss opening a brokerage account, putting money into it, and placing trades.

Choose a Discount Broker

As you read on page 17, I like discount brokers a lot. After reading this book and conducting your own research on companies, you don't need the expensive opinion of a full-service broker. Save some money, consolidate your investments, and continue forming your own opinions.

The brokerage business changes quickly, so this section is deliberately light on specifics. Most brokers charge commissions between $5 and $30 with various incentive plans that come and go. Most brokers offer major stock research from firms like Standard & Poor's for free. Visit each broker's website for current details.

If you choose a broker that has an office near your home, such as Fidelity or Scottrade, you can always walk in and talk to a live human being. Some people actually prefer that.

E*Trade

E*Trade is a financial bazaar with everything from banking and bill management to shopping and taxes. Oh yeah, and they can trade stocks and mutual funds, too.

Contact Information: www.etrade.com

Fidelity

Fidelity is a good choice if you're looking for a place to assemble a mutual fund portfolio together with your stocks. The company's FundsNetwork program gathers leading names into one place without loads or transaction fees. An advantage that FundsNetwork has over other supermarkets is that it includes Fidelity's own funds, which is significant because Fidelity is the biggest fund company in America. It maintains offices throughout the country.

Contact Information: www.fidelity.com

Firstrade

Firstrade offers a flat-fee system. It has won honors in surveys for its low prices, simple interface, and attentive customer service. It's free to transfer your account, there's no minimum deposit, and there are no inactivity fees. It's a friendly place.

Contact Information: www.firstrade.com

Schwab

Schwab's OneSource mutual fund supermarket runs neck and neck with Fidelity's. Although Schwab can't offer Fidelity funds, it tends to gather higher-quality names from other fund families including its own Schwab funds. It maintains offices throughout the country.

Contact Information: www.schwab.com

Scottrade

Scottrade is consistently well ranked in surveys for its low prices, the convenience of its branch offices across the country, and its tolerance of low account balances and inactivity. Its website page load speed is among the fastest in the business.

Contact Information: www.scottrade.com

TD Ameritrade

TD Ameritrade receives high praise for its slick trading inter-face, extensive mutual fund network, innovative research tools, and competitive prices. Its trading platforms show what the portfolio and stocks you're watching are worth this very second.

Contact Information: www.tdameritrade.com

TradeKing

TradeKing ranks high in surveys for its low price, $4.95 per stock trade. That's the whole story. In its own words, "We don't have a pricing structure, we have a price."

Contact Information: www.tradeking.com

Super Discounters

BuyandHold, ShareBuilder, and Zecco are super discounters. They offer cheap single trades, free trades under certain conditions, and monthly subscription trading packages. Make sure you understand the limitations of their various plans. If the price is cheap and you can still manage your investments the way you want, it could be worth a try.

Contact Information: www.buyandhold.com, www.sharebuilder .com, and www.zecco.com

Place Orders

Once you've chosen a discount broker and you've got money in your account, you're ready to invest. This section explains the bid, ask, and spread, and discusses different types of orders available to you.

Bid, Ask, and Spread

The *bid* is the highest quoted price that buyers are willing to pay for a security at any specific moment. In that same specific moment, the *ask* is the lowest quoted price that sellers are willing to accept for the security. The bid is the price you get when you sell the stock, the ask is the price you pay to buy the stock. The *spread* is the difference between the two numbers and is kept by a dealer who's called a "market maker" on the OTC and a "specialist" on one of the exchanges. The dealer maintains fair and orderly trading by keeping an inventory of stock to satisfy demand when buyers and sellers can't be matched up. He's a middleman just like the owner of the bookstore where you bought this fine title. All middlemen purchase inventory at a price lower than they sell it. The spread is biggest for stocks that are thinly traded because it takes fewer dealers to satisfy demand. Fewer dealers means less competition and, thus, bigger spreads. Now you have career advice for your children: become dealers in thinly traded stocks.

Let's take a closer look at these three numbers. If Mister Magazine asks $15.50 and bids $15, the spread is 50 cents. Placing a market order buys your shares at $15.50. The instant after you buy your shares, they're worth only $15 because that's the price other sellers are asking. In one of my investment seminars, a gentleman questioned whether he could ask for the extra 50 cents to recoup his purchase price. Ahem, well, no. First of all, nobody's actually asking anybody for anything. It's a figure of speech. The market knows the bid and ask prices based only on supply and demand. Second, even if you could ask for a higher price, nobody would pay it. If everybody but you is selling at $15.50, why would I pay $16 to buy from you?

As you see, the spread can translate into a serious investment cost if you sell right away. In our Mister Magazine example, 50 cents represents a full 3.2 percent of the $15.50 bid price. A flat brokerage commission of $18 on a 100-share trade is only a 1.2 percent cost. The spread is more than $2\frac{1}{2}$ times the expense of the commission! Before you get too riled up and embark on a dealer hunt, remember that you don't actually suffer the burden of the spread unless you sell right away. Hopefully, your stock will appreciate far beyond the spread and it will become irrelevant. Always be aware of the spreads, though, because your stock must move beyond the combined spread and commission costs just to break even.

Orders

Giving an order to your broker is a thrilling moment. It means you've done your research, thought about your situation, and are ready to take action. There are two types of orders: market and limit.

Market

A *market order* is the simplest type. It instructs your broker to buy a security at the current ask price. That's it. Your buy price is whatever the thing is trading for when the order reaches the floor. With today's fast communications, that price is going to be fairly close to where it was when you placed the order, if not the exact same price. For instance, say Mister Magazine is trading at $15.50 per share and you place a market order for 100 shares. If you don't buy your shares for precisely $15.50, you'll probably pick them up somewhere between $15.40 and $15.60.

Limit

A *limit order* instructs your broker to buy or sell a security at a price you specify or better. That means if you say to sell a stock at $10, your broker will sell either at $10 or at a higher price. If you say to buy a stock at $20, your broker will buy either at $20 or at a lower price.

Limit orders and stop orders (next section) have a time period associated with them. When you place a limit order, it is either a *day order* or a *good-till-cancelled* (*GTC*) order. A day order expires at the end of the current trading day regardless of whether or not its conditions were met. A GTC order remains open until its conditions are met, which might never happen.

I love limit orders and use them almost exclusively. There's no better way to remain calm about the markets than to evaluate a company, decide on a fair price to pay for its stock, specify that price to your broker in a GTC limit order, and forget about it. If the stock hits your buy price, the broker buys and sends you a confirmation statement. If not, you never hear about it. It works the same on the sell. If a stock you own is bouncing around what you consider to be a good sell price, just log into your brokerage account and specify your sell price and number of shares to sell. Then forget about it. A few days later, perhaps, the stock will spike up for a brief moment, hit your sell price, and go about on its way up or down. You'll receive a statement confirming your sale.

You shouldn't literally forget about your limit orders, of course. The last thing you want is for a stock to hit its buy limit when you don't have any money sitting in your core account. You'll get to know your broker real well if that happens. When I say to forget about your limit orders, I mean to relax and let the market do its silly thing. Nine times out of 10, my limit orders come through and I never sweat a drop waiting for the precise right time to buy and sell. I specify it in the limit order. If it happens, great. If not, I let it go.

Of course, this is pure hooey to some people. They would say it's lunacy to place limit orders and forget about them. They are assuming that they can watch a stock and pick the right time to buy and sell. If you bought Mister Magazine at $15.50 and it rose to $30, would you sell? You could reevaluate and, if you thought it might go higher, place a limit order to sell half your shares at $31. Some would say that's foolish because the stock might rise to $35. Might, could, would have, almost did, it happened once to a friend of mine, nearly came through—anybody can surmise this way forever. I would be happy to have tacked on an extra $1 to my sell price and to have kept half my shares. Then you could place another limit order for the remainder at $36. Ah, the critics say, but what if it rises to $40? Then you made a mistake.

In truth, you shouldn't be playing the markets like that. You should always examine the worth of the companies you own and determine whether they're still worth owning. Who cares what the market says they're worth? Think like Warren Buffett and treat your stocks like your own companies. They *are* your own companies, a certain percentage of them at least. When you do decide to buy and sell, consider using limit orders. They take away some of the pressure and usually allow you to save a few bucks on the buy and make a few extra on the sell.

Stop

A stop order becomes a market order when a price you specify is reached. Like limit orders, stop orders are either good for the day or good-till-cancelled. If you own a stock and instruct your broker to sell it at a price lower than it currently trades for, that's called a *stop loss* because you're stopping your potential loss and protecting the profit you've already gained. You can use a stop order in the other direction, too. Technically it would be called a stop gain, but nobody calls it that because it sounds silly. What you're really doing is ratcheting up the point that you want to sell.

When the price you specify in a stop order is reached, the stop order becomes a market order. That means your broker will then trade the stock at its current price. If the price is moving quickly, that might be higher or lower than your stop. This is an important distinction between limit orders and stop orders. A limit order trades the stock at the price you specify or better; a stop order trades the stock at its current price after it touches the price you specify. Thus, with a stop order, your trade might occur at a price better or worse than the stop price.

To get around this inherent problem with stop orders, you can use a *stop limit order*. As its name implies, it combines the features of a stop order and a limit order. First, you specify the price at which you want the stop order to kick in. Then you specify the price at which you want the limit order to trade. If the price you specify in the limit order isn't reached, your order never executes. That guarantees that you won't trade at a price worse than you specify in the limit order.

Let's run through an example. Say you're eyeing Mister Magazine at $15.50 per share. You want to buy 100 shares if it starts moving upward considerably. You could place a stop order at $17. That means that if Mister Magazine suddenly spikes up to $19, your stop order will become a market order to buy 100 shares. If the price is moving quickly, the order might not go through until Mister Magazine asks $18. Perhaps that's fine with you because you just want to pick up your shares when the stock breaks out. It's more important that you actually buy the 100 shares than it is to buy them at a specific price.

On the other hand, it might annoy you to pay more for Mister Magazine than you think it's worth. You still want to buy 100 shares if it starts moving up. You could place a stop limit order with the stop at $17 and the limit at $17.50. If the stock hits $17, your stop order becomes a limit order to buy 100 shares at $17.50 or better. If your broker can only get $18, the order won't execute.

Once you buy your 100 shares, let's think positive and say they rise to $30. You don't want to lose the profits you've already gained, so you place a stop loss at $28. If Mister Magazine hits the skids and plummets to $18, your order will kick in at $28 and sell at the next opportunity, which might be lower than $28. That really bugs you, so on further consideration you decide to cancel the stop order and replace it with a stop limit order with a stop at $28 and a limit at $28 as well. Now if Mister Magazine plummets to $18, you might go with it. Why? Because your limit order to sell at $28 or better won't kick in if the price hits $28 and immediately falls lower without ever coming back up. Know what you want to do and place the right kind of order.

Trailing Stop

This is another type of stop order, but I put it in a separate section because it deserves distinction. The trailing stop is a tool I've come to love over the years, as it offers one of the least stressful ways to maximize profits.

If the price of a stock you own is rising but you think it's getting a little topped out, what should you do? If you sell now and it keeps rising, you'll be upset. If you don't sell now and it reverses direction and drops, you'll be upset. Oh dear.

You want to own the stock as long as its uptrend continues, and that's the specialty of trailing stops. They "trail" behind the price as it rises upward but lock into place when the price begins to fall. You specify in your order the price, or percentage distance, at which the stop order to sell kicks in. As with all stop orders, this one can be a market, to sell immediately, or a limit, to sell at a specified price.

When you set the price, you do so with either a dollar amount or a percentage distance. I prefer the latter. The bigger the dollar amount or the wider the percentage, the less likely the order is to trigger but the more loss you're willing to accept before you sell. A typical order might be a 10 percent trailing stop.

Here's how that would work. You buy 2,000 shares of Mister Magazine at $15.50 for a total of $31,000. It rises over six months to $26 per share. Fantastic! However, you know that a 68 percent gain in six months is vulnerable to a pullback. Earnings are coming up, though, and you think they'll be good and might give one last pop to the price before it settles. You decide on a 10 percent *trailing stop-loss market order* and place it at your broker.

Mister Magazine does indeed beat earnings estimates—blows them away, as the headline reads—and the stock rockets up to $31. You were smart to stay in but also smart to know that no rising trend stays steep forever. When you first placed the 10 percent trailing stop, its trigger price was $23.40, which was just 10 percent below the $26 trading price. Now, after the post-earnings pop to $31, the trailing stop's new trigger price is $27.90. You think, though, that the stock is more vulnerable than ever because of the quick shot higher on earnings, so you "tighten up" the stop to 5 percent. After that, the new trigger price is $29.45.

The stock rises to $32 the next day, which moves your trigger up to $30.40, then falls back to $29, then to $26, and then to $20 before flattening out. Where did you sell? At $30.40, right where the 5 percent trailing stop locked in place.

See why I love trailing stops?

By the way, you can use a trailing stop at any time, not just when you're sitting on a profit. Sometimes a stock drops immediately after you buy it, and you want to limit the loss but are willing to give it a little more play before cutting it off. You might be down 10 percent and set a trailing stop at 5 percent to limit your loss to 15 percent. That's a trader's mind-set, though, and in most cases you'll be better served by an investor's mind-set. If you did thorough research and believe in the company, it should be better to buy more shares at the cheaper price, not to dump the first ones.

Not always, though, and in cases where you want to stop the loss but leave room for recovery, a trailing stop will be your friend.

6

Research to Riches

It's time for you to learn how and where to conduct research, the most critical part of investing. Every master investor swears by it. Your returns will be directly proportional to the quality of the companies you buy. That quality depends on your research.

Have no fear! There is more information available to you than you can use. Peter Lynch wrote in *One Up on Wall Street*, "I can't imagine anything that's useful to know that the amateur investor can't find out. All the pertinent facts are just waiting to be picked up." After reading this chapter, you'll laugh at people who say they can't invest because they don't know where to get information. I submit that it is now more difficult to avoid investment information than to get what you need. It's everywhere: from your Christmas list to your library to the magazine rack at your local grocery store, investment research is there for you to snatch up, file away, and turn into profit.

This chapter shows where to get the information. The next chapter shows what to do with it.

Personal Experience

Follow your money to find great companies. It works for Peter Lynch and it can work for you, too. If you need to jog your memory, take a look at your last few credit card statements or your checkbook register. Where do you repeatedly spend money? Life's necessities can turn up great companies. Take food, for example. You might not want to invest in your local grocery chain, but what about that restaurant chain you keep visiting? All your friends like it, the paper gave it a four-star rating, it's always packed, and the food is wonderful and reasonably priced. It's worth checking into. That's how an investor friend of mine found Starbucks Coffee when it sold split-adjusted at 75 cents in August 1992. In November 2006, it reached $40. His $10,000 investment became $533,000.

He might have been happy to read the previous section on trailing stops. Like most stocks, Starbucks was devastated by the crash of 2008. It closed that year at $9.46, down 76 percent from its high in November 2006. A wide trailing stop to give long-term winner Starbucks room to fluctuate, perhaps 20 percent, would have sold at $32. Even if he had set the 20 percent trailing stop one year earlier, in November 2005, it still would have sold at $31.90 in August 2006, after Starbucks spiked up to $39.88 in May 2006, locking in the trailing stop at $31.90. He would have felt bad as Starbucks recovered back up to $40 in the next three months but pretty good during the two-year slide that followed and took Starbucks to a low of $7.06 in November 2008. What was the move to make then? Buy, of course, and there was plenty of time to do it. The stock languished under $10 until March 2009 when it embarked on a steady recovery to $50 in early 2012, putting my friend's fortune at the fascinating balance of $666,666.67. "The devil's brew," he called it.

How about clothing? Like me, you might enjoy watching people in public places such as a shopping mall. What are they wearing? One year, I noticed kids wearing Tommy Hilfiger clothes more and more frequently. It didn't take a genius to know the clothing was from Hilfiger because the name was emblazoned across the front of every T-shirt and sweatshirt. I went into the department stores and looked for racks of Hilfiger clothing. Much to my intrigue, I found entire sections of the stores devoted to Hilfiger. In a local Macy's, "Hilfiger" hung in huge gold letters against the wood paneling and throngs of kids stood under the sign holding shirts up to each other for first looks. That's darned interesting to an investor, wouldn't you say? I checked out the company's numbers and recommended Hilfiger to friends in spring 1993. A buddy picked up shares at $10.50 in July. At the end of 1996, he sold them for $48.

I have a more recent clothing story for you. We'll call it rags-to-riches-to-rags. My mother and sister visited me in Japan in May 2006. My mother wore a pair of Crocs sandals that she raved about the entire visit as we walked around Tokyo and flower parks near my home in the countryside. She told me that Crocs were invented in Colorado, where we're from, and that everybody back home had a pair. When my friends in Japan saw the sandals, they asked about them, tried them on, and wondered if I would buy some for them on my next trip back to the States. An actionable tip? You bet. Shares of Crocs were less than a split-adjusted $12 that May. In October 2007, they broke $75 for a gain of more than 525 percent in less than two years. I have a feeling Peter Lynch would love this story . . . up to this point. Along came 2008. If the crash did what it did to Starbucks, imagine what it did to the much smaller Crocs. At its November 2008 low, Crocs traded for just 79 cents. *Cents* mind you. In 11 months, the stock fell 99 percent. Note to self: trailing stops.

Do you think it died there, bankrupt in a sea of cheap imitation footwear? That's what its detractors said it would do, but the company kept growing and the stock crawled out of the mud. It hit a high in August 2011 of $32.47, a 4,010 percent gain from that 79-cent low in November 2008. If you'd have put $10,000 into it at 79 cents (nobody did, but let's live a little), you'd have had $411,000 just 33 months later.

Food, clothing, and other necessities are good places to start looking for companies. Once you've exhausted them, think about where you spend your discretionary dollars, that is, for things you don't absolutely need. Perhaps you love home movies and notice that some companies just won't go away. One might be the place you rent videos, maybe Netflix. You could have bought it split-adjusted for less than $5 in fall 2002 and sold it for $300 in July 2011. Another might be the movie company Disney. If you decided back in summer 2002 to get more out of Disney than a mouse cartoon and a few roller coasters, you could have purchased its stock for $14 and sold it in February 2012 for $40. That's a 5,900 percent gain in less than 9 years with Netflix and a 186 percent gain in less than 10 years with Disney, both of which you would have found by just vegging out on home movies. Who says couch potatoes can't get ahead?

If your company is making an officewide computer upgrade, somebody is going to research which computers to buy. Ask that person why he or she chose Acer, Apple, Dell, HP, or Sony. Maybe your friends use the same brand. If your family needs a personal computer, conduct research yourself and pay attention to the things that are important to you. What matters to you and your family probably matters to millions of others. If one company meets your every need, check it out. You might find a kaleidoscope of big-name players and decide to research all of them. One will probably surface as a clear leader. If not, consider investing in more than one.

Getting investment ideas from your personal experience is an easy way to start your Stocks to Watch worksheet, which we'll cover in the next chapter. Keep buying what you buy, but observe what you buy and who else is buying it with you. Your tendencies will often prove to be the tendencies of a lot of people. If you love a product, so will others. Of course, you need to keep your wits about you and always conduct further research before investing. Don't buy stock in every company you ever patronize. Even companies you love can lose money, like we just saw with Crocs, and not every successful product will produce a soaring stock. As Peter Lynch points out, a product that is a tiny part of a company's business can't move the stock very much. So no matter how much your kids love the lunar ball you bought for them, if it's only one of 800 toys made by Whacky Whimsicals, you don't have much reason to invest. Maybe the company's Mars mittens are causing hives to break out on little hands everywhere and little lawyers are filing little papers. Always look beyond your first impressions.

The Investment Grapevine

Just past your personal experience lies the investment grapevine. After I noticed everybody packed into the Hilfiger clothing section, I conducted further research and decided Hilfiger was a stock worth buying. Notice that I didn't actually buy it myself, but I did tell a friend. He bought it and made a killing.

Where did he learn about Hilfiger? From my personal experience. He harvested the investment grapevine to find a great company.

Be careful of stories that are too good. It's human nature to talk about our triumphs and usually to build them up bigger than they really are. Remember those fishing stories your grandpa used to tell every Christmas while your grandma rolled her eyes? They were probably a lot closer to the truth than his investment stories. Always remember that any company you hear about is only a lead, that is, something to look into further. You probably wouldn't hire a babysitter at the advice of a friend who heard about her from his manager who talked to his brother who saw an ad tacked to a telephone pole. Don't invest on that kind of reference, either. Best friends, colleagues, and especially relatives are notorious for their hot tips that freeze over the moment after you buy. Be warned and conduct your own due diligence.

Instead of tuning in to somebody else's success, listen for people lamenting an investment gone bad. If somebody conducted thorough research on a company, decided it was a great investment, and happened to buy at the wrong time, you can take advantage of the situation to buy that great company at a discount. Unfortunately, most people prefer telling others about their winners. Too bad for the listener because knowing somebody's runaway, high-flying stock isn't nearly as useful as knowing which of their holdings are down. My friends and I have made a point of disclosing everything in our portfolios to each other. That way, when one of us gets in at the wrong time, others can use that information to buy a good stock at a bargain price. And, of course, the person who got in at the wrong time can always buy additional shares to profit on the way back up.

It pays to listen to tales of woe. The next time somebody comes up to you and starts bragging about their latest triumph, ask about their most disappointing stock. Ask if they're planning to buy additional shares at the lower price. Let other people make mistakes with their money while you show up in time for the recovery. If you keep investing long enough, I guarantee you'll have an opportunity to return the favor.

Premium Research

Investment information is highly specialized, requires a great deal of work by smart people, and the best of it makes money for you. That's why it's expensive. Prices change all the time, so I use the following four categories to describe the price range of products in this section:

- Low—less than $100 per year

- Average—$100 to $250 per year

- High—$251 to $500 per year

- Very High—more than $500 per year

Magazines

The first money you spend on investment research should go toward a magazine subscription. They're cheap and they're packed with helpful how-to articles and some pretty darned good investment advice. Nobody considers it cool to get a good stock lead from a $5 magazine purchased along with a carton of yogurt, but I've found some good investments that way. One of my favorite techniques is to monitor the model portfolios shown for different money managers or a list of stocks chosen by the magazine editors for one reason or another. The magazines monitor the performance of their picks, making it easy to wait for some of them to decline in price.

These are my two favorite investment magazines, and a good newsmagazine:

SmartMoney

This is the online *"Wall Street Journal* Magazine," and it's excellent. Reading through the magazine gives you an impression of quality. There's no tabloid feel to it like you'll find in many investment magazines. *SmartMoney* runs articles on every aspect of investing, but does a particularly good job with mutual funds and stocks. The editors hold themselves accountable for their stock picks and are always striving to improve their methods. By following their progress, your own skills will improve along with theirs.

Contact Information: 800-444-4204, www.smartmoney.com. Price: low

Kiplinger's

This magazine has a broader scope than *SmartMoney*. Instead of talking just about investing, *Kiplinger's* moves into other issues of personal business such as credit card spending, loans, college tuition, and vacation planning. The magazine's real claim to fame, however, is its mutual fund surveys. With clear graphics and easily digested tables, they lead the industry year after year. Its columns are nothing to sneeze at, either.

Contact Information: 800-544-0155, www.kiplinger.com. Price: low

The Week

A big part of investing is keeping your finger on trends. For that, you need an efficient way to stay informed. My favorite news magazine is *The Week*. It condenses the best-written stories from the U.S. and international media into a tidy magazine that you can read in a single sitting. Rather than churn out long, in-depth coverage, it prints only the highlights from several angles.

Contact Information: 877-245-8151, www.theweekmagazine.com. Price: low

Newspapers

Just about every newspaper includes stock tables, but there are times when you need more than a quote or volume information. During those times, it's a good idea to check out one of the four papers in this section.

The Wall Street Journal

This is certainly the big kahuna among investment newspapers. Everybody who's anybody glances at *The WSJ* from time to time. It's a good idea for you to do the same.

The front page contains top news summaries in a section called "What's News." A quick skim of the summaries will alert you to items of interest. You can follow a page number to read the complete article.

The heart of the paper is section C, "Money & Investing." That's where you can see how the Dow is performing, what interest rates are doing, whether the dollar is falling or rising against foreign currencies, where commodities are headed, and a slew of other information. Read the top investment stories, get quotes on every stock you own, and track the performance of your mutual funds.

Contact Information: 800-568-7625, www.wsj.com. Price: high for print edition, average for online edition

Investor's Business Daily

Investor's Business Daily is the result of William O'Neil's frustration at the lack of what he considered the most important information about stocks. Because he couldn't find it anywhere, he decided to publish it himself and thus was born *Investor's Business Daily*. You can read all about O'Neil's investment approach on page 71.

IBD covers news in an executive news summary on the left side of the front page. It contains key national and international news in single paragraphs. The right side of the front page covers important news stories in depth. Inside the front page is a feature called "To the Point," and it gets there quickly. You'll find dozens of news items that you can cover in a glance. The streamlined front page combined with to-the-point summaries gives you "twice as many news items in a page and a half as you'll find in 60 pages of other publications," in *IBD*'s own words. The paper prints a ton of features too numerous to outline here. I have never purchased an issue of *IBD* that was worthless. There's always something good.

IBD's stock tables are O'Neil's main reason for starting a new paper. They contain five SmartSelect measurements you won't find anywhere else: earnings per share rank for the past five years, relative price strength rank for the past 12 months, industry group relative strength, an overall evaluation of sales and profit margin and return on equity, and accumulation/distribution for the past three months. The five measurements are combined into a composite rating that gives the most weight to earnings per share and relative price strength. The paper also shows a daily percentage change in volume. Here's a snapshot of the measurements from *IBD*'s Chipotle Mexican Grill listing on February 10, 2012:

SmartSelect Composite Rating	E P S	Rel Pri Str	Ind Rel Str	Sales Profit ROE	Acc Dis	Stock & Symbol	Vol Percent Chg
97	97	91	B	A	B+	Chipotle CMG	-5

Let's have a closer look at the measures from *IBD*.

SmartSelect Composite Rating

This is a stock's overall score from 1 to 99, with 99 being the best. The composite tallies *IBD*'s five SmartSelect measurements, with extra weight given to earnings per share and relative strength. Chiplotle scored a 97.

Earnings per Share Rating

This measurement compares the earnings growth of all companies and then ranks them from 1 to 99, with 99 being the strongest. Thus, by looking at this one simple number, you know how Chipotle's earnings growth stacks up against IBM's, Hewlett Packard's, Pfizer's, and Home Depot's.

The paper takes each company's earnings per share for the two most recent quarters and computes their percentage change from the same two quarters a year ago. That result is combined and averaged with each company's three- to five-year earnings growth record and the final figures for every company are compared with each other. Thus, a company with an EPS rank of 95 has earnings figures in the top 5 percent of all companies in the tables.

Chipotle had a 97, placing its earnings growth in the top 3 percent.

Relative Price Strength Rating

This measurement looks at a stock's price performance in the latest 12 months. That's it. It doesn't look at stories, earnings, or price ratios. It simply reports the hard numbers and answers the question, how did this stock perform compared to all others?

IBD updates the numbers daily, compares all stocks to each other, and ranks them from 1 to 99, with 99 being the best. That means a company with a relative price strength of 90 outperformed 90 percent of all other stocks in the past year.

Chipotle had a 91. It outperformed 91 percent of all stocks.

Industry Group Relative Price Strength Rating

This measurement compares a stock's industry price performance in the latest six months with the performance of all other industries. The industry then receives a letter grade from A+ to E, with A+ being the best.

You know by glancing at this grade whether a stock is operating in a dominant or struggling industry. *IBD* says that roughly half of a stock's performance is traced to the strength of its industry, the theory being that a rising tide lifts all boats and vice versa. Who's doing better, computer hardware manufacturers, food processors, home improvement retailers, or tobacco companies? This measurement will tell you.

To see all the industries ranked over the past six months, find the Industry Group Rankings table in the newspaper. The top 10 performers from yesterday are printed in bold and the bottom 10 are underlined.

Chipotle's industry, Restaurants, had a letter grade of B.

Sales + Profit + ROE Rating

This measurement combines a stock's recent sales growth, profit margins, and return on equity to provide a quick snapshot of company health. The stock gets a grade from A to E, with A being the best.

Chipotle had an A, placing it among the healthiest companies on the market.

Accumulation/Distribution Rating

This measurement looks at whether a stock is being heavily bought or sold by comparing its daily price and volume over the past 13 weeks. The stock receives a grade from A to E, with A being the best. An A grade means the stock is under heavy accumulation, or being bought frequently. An E grade means the stock is under heavy distribution, or being sold frequently.

IBD is trying to convey the direction that the price is likely to head as a result of trading trends. In other words, is the trend one of accumulation where the price should rise as a result of high demand, or is the trend one of distribution where the price should fall as a result of low demand?

Chipotle was graded B+. That's good accumulation.

Volume Percent Change

IBD calculates the average daily trading volume of each company's stock during the last 50 trading days. Then it compares each day's trading volume to the 50-day average and prints the difference as a percentage.

Chipotle's daily volume was 5 percent lower than usual.

Contact Information: 800-831-2525, www.investors.com. Price: high

Financial Times

If you're craving a global perspective, consider the *Financial Times* of London. The so-called pink pages, named after the distinctive color of the paper, bring you news, editorial, and global market prices with commentary.

One of my favorite features is the single-topic special reports. Each one covers a country, an investment trend, a new business strategy, an industry breakthrough, or something similarly focused. If you happen to get the paper when it's focused on something of interest to you, the briefing will be very useful. Other times, you might just discover something you hadn't considered before.

Another nice feature for those too busy to read every day is the Saturday *Weekend FT* that summarizes the week's key events.

Contact Information: 800-628-8088, www.ft.com. Price: high

Barron's

If *The Wall Street Journal* lost your business, *Barron's* might catch your fancy. Either way, you're dealing with Dow Jones & Company. It owns both papers.

The center of each paper contains "Market Week," the meat and potatoes data. It shows vital signs of the economy, the week's biggest winners and losers from each exchange, and superbly designed stock and fund tables. Unlike the typical paper's crunched, overlapping columns, *Barron's* prints tables that have white space between different pieces of information. Though the tables don't contain data as valuable as that in *IBD*, they do display the most recent earnings and compare them with earnings from a year ago. The mutual fund tables show performance for the last week, year-to-date, and three years. Finally, "Market Laboratory" will give you plenty to think about for the next week as you ponder how every relevant index performed, how much volume the markets moved, every economic indicator, and so on.

Contact Information: 800-568-7625, www.barrons.com. Price: average

Newsletters

A newsletter should be a trusty friend who accompanies you through good times and bad. It's important that you like the relationship that a newsletter editor builds with you. He or she should be honest, admit mistakes, and work hard to help you get ahead. Nobody is perfect in the stock business, but somebody who can provide you with a steady stream of good ideas in an understandable manner will prove worth the subscription price.

This section shows six good stock newsletters. For a list of others, visit www.jasonkelly.com/resources.

Dick Davis Investment Digest

The *Dick Davis Investment Digest* pioneered the newsletter digest approach on the theory that no single investment advisor has all the best ideas. The *Digest* is chock-full of information. Companies covered in each issue are listed alphabetically on the back page, making it easy for you to monitor the latest on stocks you own or are watching. The stories assemble expert information from other newsletters into this one convenient source. For casting a wide net, it's hard to beat the *Dick Davis Digest*.

Contact Information: 800-654-1514, www.dickdavis.com. 24 issues per year, 12 pages. Price: average

Grant's Interest Rate Observer

If you're looking to read what the pros read and to use the information better than they do, consider *Grant's*, self-described as "the financial information medium that least resembles CNBC." It publishes some of the most insightful market commentary I've found. In a wry tone, the editors deliver a careful look at balance sheets, CEO comments, analyst recommendations, and the disposition of the market. In their own words, "Not knowing exactly what the future may bring, we try to identify change where it most frequently occurs: at the margin."

Contact Information: 212-809-7994, www.grantspub.com. 24 issues per year, 12 pages. Price: very high

The Kelly Letter

Want to read my take on financial markets every Sunday morning? In *The Kelly Letter*, I manage a three-tier portfolio that value averages a small-cap index in Tier 1 (page 119), leverages a midcap index in Tier 2 (page 136), and trades individual stocks in Tier 3. It applies all the advice contained in this book to financial events happening right now. I interpret the week skeptically in search of things mispriced, and build relationships with readers by emphasizing discussion over data. One subscriber wrote, "This newsletter remains the most understandable review of the market I've ever read." Many claim, "There's no better way to start a Sunday." If you like this book, you'll love the letter.

Contact Information: www.jasonkelly.com. More than 48 issues per year, online delivery. Price: average

Morningstar StockInvestor

Morningstar is an industry heavyweight, first making its name in mutual funds and then moving on to stocks. Its *StockInvestor* newsletter contains aggressive and conservative portfolios, analyst commentary, and a list of stocks to sell. The publication focuses on strategies used by successful investors and tries to put those strategies into a usable form. The smart table design and astute writing make this one of the most enjoyable reads on the marketplace, and profitable, too.

Contact Information: 866-910-1145, www.morningstar.com. 12 issues per year, 24 pages. Price: average

The Outlook Online

Published by Standard & Poor's, *The Outlook* is one of the most widely read investment newsletters. S&P analysts provide clear market commentary, stock updates, stock screens based on S&P's STARS rankings and Fair Value rankings, and investment recommendations. You can find *The Outlook* in a three-ring binder at most public libraries. Just ask for it at the reference desk. Most individual investors subscribe to the more affordable online edition. To read more about STARS and Fair Value, see "S&P STARS/Fair Value" on page 231.

Contact Information: 800-523-4534, www.spoutlook.com. 45 issues per year, online delivery. Price: average

Outstanding Investor Digest

Of *Outstanding Investor Digest*, Warren Buffett wrote, "I'd advise you to subscribe. I read each issue religiously. Anyone interested in investing who doesn't subscribe is making a big mistake." That's about as much endorsement as any publication should ever need. *Outstanding Investor Digest* is a collection of the best ideas from the brightest investment minds around. It prints exclusive interviews, excerpts from letters to shareholders, conference call transcripts, and other "inside" scoops. The front table of contents shows the names of investors featured in that issue and an alphabetized list of companies covered inside. Next to the table of contents are the beginning paragraphs from several key articles. *Outstanding Investor Digest* is an eclectic publication that varies in length and is delivered on a sporadic schedule. It's an investment gold mine.

Contact Information: 212-925-3885, www.oid.com. 10 issues, 32 pages. Price: average

Value Line

Value Line publishes the premier stock research tool, *The Value Line Investment Survey*. It covers around 1,700 companies. Almost everything you could want to know about each company is condensed to a single page. When you get to this book's strategy and begin filling out the Stocks to Watch worksheet in the back, you'll use Value Line exhaustively.

Begun by Arnold Bernhard during the Great Depression, *Value Line* boasts more than 100,000 subscribers today. If you count the number of people who look at reports from libraries or photocopies from brokers, *Value Line*'s users number in the millions. The company's analysts have learned a thing or two about stock research over the past seven decades. Let's take a closer look at *The Value Line Investment Survey*. First, we'll look at

IBM's profile back in 1997, then we'll look at its profile in 2012. Seeing how a company evolves over time is helpful.

The Parts of a *Value Line* Page

Let's say that back in January 1997 you got a hot tip from your neighbor that IBM had fully recovered from its dark days in 1993 and was poised for great things. You decided to check it out by looking up IBM in *Value Line*. What you would have found is on pages 182 and 183.

Doesn't that look like light reading? Actually, it is once you familiarize yourself with the most important parts—which I've conveniently numbered and highlighted for you. Now I'll take you on a tour of IBM's *Value Line* page.

1. The Rankings

Value Line ranks every stock from 1 to 5 for timeliness and safety, with 1 being the best. Timeliness is a gauge of the stock's projected performance over the next 12 months as compared with all other stocks followed by *Value Line*. The measure examines a company's earnings momentum and the stock's relative strength. The rankings are distributed along a bell curve. Stocks ranked 1 or 5 each account for about 5 percent of all stocks, those ranked 2 or 4 each account for about 17 percent of all stocks, and the remainder get the average 3 rank.

The safety measure looks at a stock's volatility and financial stability, then assigns a rank of 1 to 5 just like the timeliness rank. Stocks ranked 1 for safety are the least volatile and most stable, those ranked 5 are the most volatile and least stable.

Are the rankings foolproof? No. If they were, stock research would consist of simply choosing stocks from those ranked 1. *Worth* ran a story on *Value Line*'s ranking system in February 1997. *Value Line*'s former research chairman, Samuel Eisenstadt, remarked on the usefulness of the ranks: "Just get rid of the fours and fives from your portfolio and you'll do well. The system almost does better at signaling the poor stocks than at picking out the winners." He also said, "If you randomly select from the group 1's—don't concentrate in one industry group—I think you stand a decent chance. To cut down on turnover, we generally recommend holding No. 1's even if they go to No. 2.

Once they go down to 3's, we suggest finding another group 1. Why settle for an average stock?"

You can see on the sheet that IBM was ranked 2 for timeliness and 3 for safety. Evidently, *Value Line* agreed with your neighbor about IBM's bright future.

2. Price Projections and Insider Decisions

Here you read *Value Line*'s projections for the stock price over the next three to five years, and the annual percentage return that it translates to. You'll record the projected price high and low on your worksheet.

Below the projections is a box for insider decisions. It lists the buy and sell activity of company insiders for each of the past nine months. You'll write the buys on your worksheet.

IBM was projected to gain as much as 80 percent in the next three to five years. The worst-case expectation was a 20 percent gain. In the last nine months, three insiders chose to buy stock.

3. P/E Ratio and Dividend Yield

Because P/E and dividend yield are so commonly used, *Value Line* prints the current measurements boldly at the top of the page. You see on your sheet that IBM was currently trading with a P/E of 14 and a dividend yield of 0.8 percent. To give you a barometer reading of IBM's typical P/E, *Value Line* prints the median P/E from the past 10 years. IBM's was 15, thus the stock was just slightly cheaper than usual.

4. Price History Chart

The chart plots stock price over the past decade or so. The overall trend line is comprised of little vertical lines for each month. The top of each vertical line indicates the month's price high, the bottom indicates the month's price low. The price highs and lows for each year are printed at the top of the graph.

In addition to the price history, there are two other lines on the graph. The solid black line is cash flow, a very important measure of a company's financial strength. It shows how much money was actually coming into the company over the years. The dotted line is relative price strength. That line shows you how the stock was performing compared with all other stocks. It usually follows roughly the same pattern as the stock price itself. That is, when the stock is falling it is performing poorly compared with other stocks. Makes sense, right?

Looking at IBM's chart, you saw that your friend was right about another thing: The stock had definitely roared back from its dismal 1993.

5. Historical Financial Measurements

Here's the data dump. *Value Line* prints a company's financial measurements for the past 16 years or so. There's something for everybody such as earnings per share, dividends per share, average annual dividend yield, and net profit margin. I've put arrows next to the measurements that show up on your Stocks to Watch worksheet.

This section is excellent for spotting trends. For instance, if the company's net profit margin is slipping from year to year, that's a bad sign. If working capital is decreasing and debt is increasing, that's another bad sign. If earnings are growing steadily from year to year, that's a great sign.

As for IBM, it looked pretty good. Its 1996 earnings per share were just 2 cents below 1995, which was the best year on the chart. Both years were a far cry from 1993's loss and 1994's measly 4.92. The net profit margin was 8.1 percent in 1996, a gain from the year before and one of the best over the previous five years. It's always nice to see an improving profit margin. Also, 1996 debt was $8.5 billion, down from $9 billion in 1995 and the latest in a steady debt decrease from 1993's $15.245 billion. Hmm, perhaps your neighbor was onto something.

6. Capital Structure

This is where you see how much debt the company carries and how much stock is outstanding. Debt is critical in evaluating a company, as you should know by now. Every one of the master investors in Chapter 2 says to avoid companies with excessive debt. You'll write the company's total debt on your worksheet.

IBM's long-term debt was $9.669 billion.

7. Current Position

A company's current position shows its short-term health. It looks at assets that can be quickly turned into cash and liabilities that are due within a year. You'll use information from this section to compute the current ratio on your worksheet.

IBM had current cash of $7.002 billion, current assets of $39.379 billion, and current liabilities of $31.071 billion. Those numbers translated into a current ratio of 1.27 (current assets divided by current liabilities). That was adequate, I suppose, but nothing to sound trumpets about. I like to see current ratios of at least 2. What was most disturbing to me about IBM's 1996 numbers is that they were worse than 1994 and 1995. In both prior years, cash and current assets were higher, and current liabilities were lower. Overall debt was coming down, however, so maybe some of those current assets were going to good stuff. Still, this was a tarnish on IBM's otherwise sterling report.

8. Annual Rates

In this handy box, *Value Line* computes rates of change for important measures like revenues, cash flow, and earnings. Included are the rates of change over the past ten years, past five years, and projected rates for the next five years. You'll write projected revenue and earnings on your worksheet.

IBM had definitely turned itself around, judging from the annual rates. Its earnings had fallen over the past 10 and five years. However, they were projected to increase by 23.5 percent over the next three to five years. That's excellent.

9. Quarterly Financials

For the past five years, *Value Line* prints quarterly figures for sales, earnings, and dividends. You can look over these tables to see if a company's business is seasonal or steady all year long. IBM's numbers were consistent from quarter to quarter. I guess people buy technology and related services all year long.

10. Business

This humble little box in the center of the page summarizes the basics about a company. You read about its main business, sideline businesses, how much of the company is owned by its directors, and where to contact the company.

From reading this information, you would have learned that IBM was the world's largest supplier of big-time computer equipment. It also made 18 percent of its money from software

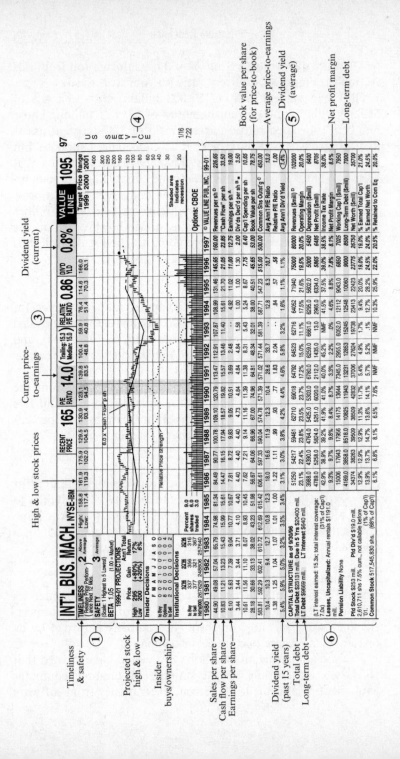

Timeliness & safety ① · Projected stock high & low · Insider buys/ownership ② · Sales per share · Cash flow per share · Earnings per share · Dividend yield (past 15 years) · Total debt · Long-term debt ⑥

High & low stock prices · Current price-to-earnings ③ · Dividend yield (current)

Book value per share (for price-to-book) · Average price-to-earnings ④ · Dividend yield (average) ⑤ · Net profit margin · Long-term debt

INT'L BUS. MACH. NYSE-IBM   RECENT PRICE **165**   P/E RATIO **14.0** (Trailing: 15.3 / Median: 15.0)   RELATIVE P/E RATIO **0.86**   DIV'D YLD **0.8%**   VALUE LINE **1095**

TIMELINESS 2 Above Average (Relative Price Performance Next 12 Mos.)
SAFETY 3 Average (Scale: 1 Highest to 5 Lowest)
BETA 1.05 (1.00 = Market)

1999-01 PROJECTIONS
	Price	Gain	Ann'l Total Return
High	295	(+80%)	17%
Low	200	(+20%)	6%

Insider Decisions
	F M A M J J A S O
to Buy	0 0 2 1 0 0 0 0 0
Options	8 2 0 0 0 0 0 0 4
to Sell	8 2 0 0 0 0 0 0 2

Institutional Decisions
	1Q96	2Q96	3Q96
to Buy	337	356	316
to Sell	377	321	367
Hld'g(000)	267629	248806	257640

CAPITAL STRUCTURE as of 9/30/96
Total Debt $23131 mill. Due in 5 Yrs $20400 mill.
LT Debt $9609 mill. LT Interest $640 mill.
(LT interest earned: 15.3x; total interest coverage: 7.0x) (31% of Cap'l)
Leases, Uncapitalized: Annual rentals $1191.0 mill.
Pension Liability None

Pfd Stock $253 mill. Pfd Div'd $19.0 mill.
2,610,711 shs 7.5% cum., not callable before '01.
Common Stock 517,545,830 shs. (68% of Cap'l)

© VALUE LINE PUB., INC. 99-01

Options: CBOE

	1980	1981	1982	1983	1984	1985	1986	1987	1988	1989	1990	1991	1992	1993	1994	1995	1996	1997	© VALUE LINE PUB., INC.	99-01
Revenues per sh D	44.90	49.08	57.04	65.79	74.98	81.34	84.49	90.77	100.78	109.10	120.79	113.47	112.91	107.87	108.99	131.46	145.65	160.00		226.65
"Cash Flow" per sh D	10.83	11.21	13.23	15.43	15.99	16.11	14.47	15.70	17.94	19.82	19.57	18.65	13.46	11.40	15.61	21.70	21.00	23.85		33.50
Earnings per sh A	6.10	5.63	7.39	9.04	10.77	10.67	7.81	8.72	9.83	9.05	10.51	3.69	2.48	4.92	11.02	11.00	12.75			19.00
Div'ds Decl'd per sh B ■	3.44	3.44	3.44	3.71	4.10	4.40	4.40	4.40	4.40	4.73	4.84	4.84	4.84	1.58	1.00	1.00	1.30	2.00		3.50
Cap'l Spending per sh	10.61	11.56	11.10	8.07	8.93	10.45	7.62	7.21	9.14	11.16	11.39	11.38	8.31	5.43	5.24	8.67	7.75	8.40		10.65
Book Value per sh B	28.18	30.66	33.13	38.02	43.23	51.98	56.67	64.06	66.96	67.00	74.96	64.81	48.34	32.01	38.00	40.51	45.65	53.00		78.75
Common Shs Outst'g C	583.81	592.29	602.41	610.72	612.69	615.42	606.61	597.33	590.04	574.78	571.39	571.02	571.44	581.39	587.71	547.23	515.00	500.00		450.00
Avg Ann'l P/E Ratio	10.4	10.3	9.4	12.7	10.8	12.3	18.0	16.6	11.9	12.3	10.4	28.6	33.7	—	12.8	8.3	10.7			13.0
Relative P/E Ratio	1.38	1.25	1.04	1.07	1.01	1.00	1.22	1.11	.99	.93	.77	1.83	2.04	—	.84	.57	.66			1.00
Avg Ann'l Div'd Yield	5.4%	5.9%	5.0%	3.2%	3.5%	3.4%	3.1%	3.0%	3.8%	4.2%	4.4%	4.6%	5.8%	3.2%	1.6%	1.1%	1.1%			1.4%
Revenues ($mill)	25192	29070	34364	40180	45937	50056	51250	54217	59461	62710	69018	64792	64523	62716	64052	71940	75000	80000		102000
Operating Margin	23.1%	23.8%						22.4%	23.8%	23.5%	23.7%	17.2%	15.0%	11.1%	17.5%	21.6%	19.5%	20.0%		20.0%
Depreciation ($mill)	3988.0	4389.0						4390.0	4764.0	5425.0	5303.0	6780.0	6259.0	6661.0	6295.0	5602.0	5000	5450		6400
Net Profit ($mill)	4789.0	5700.0						5258.0	5824.0	5251.0	6020.0	2112.0	1435.0	13.0	2965.0	6334.0	5865	6485		8705
Income Tax Rate	42.9%	45.0%						38.9%	39.2%	41.9%	41.0%	40.0%	45.2%	0%	41.5%	37.5%	39.0%	38.5%		38.0%
Net Profit Margin	9.3%	9.5%						9.7%	9.8%	8.4%	8.7%	3.3%	2.2%	—	4.6%	8.8%	7.8%	8.1%		8.5%
Working Cap'l ($mill)	15006	14175						17643	17956	14175	13844	7345.0	2955.0	6052.0	12112	9043.0	6850	7025		7950
Long-Term Debt ($mill)	4169.0	2610.0						3858.0	8518.0	10825	11943	13231	12853	15245	12548	10060	9000	6500		7900
Net Worth ($mill)	34374	38263						38263	39509	38509	42832	37006	27624	19738	23413	22423	23775	26750		35700
% Earned Total Cap'l	12.9%	13.0%						12.9%	12.9%	11.3%	11.7%	5.7%	4.9%	.1%	9.4%	20.0%	19.0%	19.0%		21.0%
% Earned Net Worth	13.9%	14.1%						13.7%	14.7%	13.6%	14.1%	5.7%	5.2%	.1%	12.7%	28.2%	24.5%	24.0%		24.5%
% Retained to Com Eq	6.1%	6.4%						6.8%	8.1%	6.5%	7.6%	NMF	NMF	NMF	10.3%	25.9%	22.0%	20.5%		20.0%

97   US SERVICE   1/16   7/22
Target Price Range 1999 2000 2001

Shaded area indicates recession

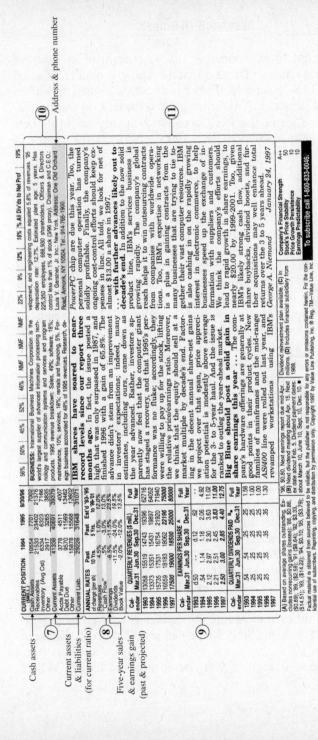

% All Div'ds to Net Prof															
56%	50%	45%	52%	46%	NMF	NMF	NMF	NMF	22%	9%	12%	16%			19%

CURRENT POSITION	1994	1995	9/30/96
Cash Assets	10554	7701	7902
Receivables	21533	23402	21376
Inventory (Avg Cost)	6334	6323	7168
Other	257	3265	3835
Current Assets	41338	40691	36379
Accts Payable	3778	4511	4007
Debt Due	9570	11569	13462
Other	15878	11568	13602
Current Liab.	29226	31648	31071

ANNUAL RATES of change (per sh)	Past 10 Yrs.	Past 5 Yrs.	Est'd '93-'95 to '99-'01
Revenues	4.5%	3.0%	12.0%
"Cash Flow"	-.5%	-5.0%	22.5%
Earnings	-6.5%	-11.5%	23.5%
Dividends	-11.5%	-24.0%	19.5%
Book Value	-2.0%	-12.0%	13.5%

Calendar	QUARTERLY REVENUES ($ mill)				Full Year
	Mar.31	Jun.30	Sep.30	Dec.31	
1993	13058	15519	14743	19396	62716
1994	13373	15351	15431	19897	64052
1995	15735	17531	16754	21920	71900
1996	16559	18183	18062	22196	75000
1997	17500	19000	18500	25000	80000

Calendar	EARNINGS PER SHARE A				Full Year
	Mar.31	Jun.30	Sep.30	Dec.31	
1993	d.50	...	d.12	62	...
1994	.54	.14	.18	2.06	4.92
1995	2.12	2.97	2.30	3.63	11.02
1996	2.21	2.51	2.45	3.83	11.00
1997	2.50	3.00	2.85	4.40	12.75

Calendar	QUARTERLY DIVIDENDS PAID B				Full Year
	Mar.31	Jun.30	Sep.30	Dec.31	
1993	.54	.54	.25	.25	1.58
1994	.25	.25	.25	.25	1.00
1995	.25	.25	.25	.25	1.00
1996	.25	.25	.35	.35	1.30
1997					

BUSINESS: International Business Machines Corporation is the world's largest supplier of advanced information processing technology and communication systems and services and imaging products. 1995 revenue breakdown: Sales, 49%; software, 18%; maintenance, 10%; services, 18%; rentals and financing, 5%. Foreign business accounted for 48% of 1995 revenues. Research, development, and engineering costs equaled 5.8% of revenues. '95 depreciation rate: 12.7%. Estimated plant age: 5 years. Has 225,360 employees, 668,930 shareholders. Officers & Directors control less than 1% of stock (396 proxy). Chairman and C.E.O.: Louis V. Gerstner, Jr. Inc.: New York. Address: One Old Orchard Road, Armonk, NY 10504. Tel.: 914-765-1900.

IBM shares have soared to near-record levels since our report three months ago. In fact, the issue posted a high that was only surpassed in 1987, and finished 1996 with a gain of 65.8%. The advance didn't stem from an improvement in investors' expectations; indeed, many estimates, including ours, came down as the year advanced. Rather, investors apparently now feel that the computer giant has staged a recovery, and that 1995's performance was no fluke; accordingly, they were willing to pay up for the stock, lifting the relative price/earnings ratio. Moreover, we think that the equity should sell at a market multiple by decade's end. Factoring in the decent annual share-net gains we project over that span, price appreciation potential is modestly above average for the 3- to 5-year haul. And the issue is ranked to outleg the year-ahead market.

Big Blue should post a solid gain in share earnings this year ... The company's hardware offerings are generally at good points in their product cycles. New families of mainframes and the mid-range AS/400 line were rolled out last year, and revamped workstations using IBM's PowerPC chip are due this year. Too, the personal computer operation has turned solidly profitable. Finally, the company's ongoing cost-control efforts should keep expenses in line. All told, we look for net of almost $13.00 a share in 1997.

... with further advances likely out to decade's end. In addition to the now solid product line, IBM's services business is growing rapidly. The company's global reach helps it to win outsourcing contracts from companies with worldwide operations. Too, IBM's expertise in networking is a plus in gaining contracts from the many businesses that are trying to tie together their vast computer resources. IBM is also cashing in on the rapidly growing interest in electronic commerce, to help businesses speed up the exchange of information with suppliers and customers. We think the company's efforts should lead to rapid growth in share earnings, to nearly $20.00 by 1999-2001. Too, given IBM's likely strong cash flow, additional share buybacks, dividend boosts, and further acquisitions may well enhance total returns over the 3 to 5 years ahead.
George A. Niemond   January 24, 1997

(A) Based on average shares outstanding. Excludes noncurring gains (losses): '88, $0.86; ($0.69); '89, ($2.58); '91 ($8.64); '92, $3.33; ($14.51); '93, ($14.22); '94, $0.10; '95, ($3.79); about March 10, June 10, Sept. 10; Dec. 10.

(B) $0.80. Next earnings report due mid-Apr. Next dividend meeting about Apr. 15. Next ex date about Feb. 5. Dividend payment dates:

'96, $0.80. Dividend reinvestment plan available (C) In millions. (D) Includes financial subsidiary from 1988.

Company's Financial Strength	A+
Stock's Price Stability	50
Price Growth Persistence	10
Earnings Predictability	10

To subscribe call 1-800-833-0046.

and 10 percent from services. A full 48 percent of its business came from overseas. That's great to know if you're worried about the U.S. economy. Finally, directors owned less than 1 percent of the stock. That's not good to hear. You want directors to own a lot of the stock because then they act in its best interest. If your investment ship sinks, you want the people in charge of the company to get wet, too.

11. Analysis

One of *Value Line*'s securities analysts follows every stock. In this section, the analyst gives his or her opinion on the company's current status and future prospects.

IBM's *Value Line* analyst, George Niemond, said the company was doing better than he expected. He said IBM would post solid earnings in 1997 and should continue doing so through the end of the decade. One thing he didn't mention directly but you could infer from the last paragraph was that IBM was well positioned to exploit the growing popularity of the Internet. Mr. Niemond pointed out that IBM already had a powerful global business network in place, he acknowledged the company's expertise in networking, and he highlighted IBM's interest in electronic commerce. All three of those strengths were going to help IBM own some of the Internet. If you thought the Internet had a future, perhaps IBM would have made a good investment for you.

At the very least, your time spent with *Value Line* would have given you some real meat to chew with your neighbor. Your opinions would be based on hard evidence, not just tips whispered over your fence while the lawn mower idles.

Let's say that after reading the *Value Line* information, you decided to buy 100 shares of IBM on February 3, 1997, at $155. On May 28, 1997, the stock split 2-for-1 and you had 200 shares. On May 27, 1999, the stock split 2-for-1 again and you had 400 shares. By February 17, 2012, with IBM at $193 per share, your initial $15,500 was worth $77,200. That's a 15-year gain of 398 percent without even including the dividends you received. During that same time, the S&P 500 gained just 73 percent, so you're pretty happy.

You wonder, though, if you should hold on longer. Where

should you look to see how IBM's doing now? *Value Line*, of course.

The January 2012 *Value Line* Profile

What you find is that your old pal George Niemond was replaced by Theresa Brophy. Her January 6, 2012, installment is on the next page.

The format should look familiar. In our ever-changing world, isn't it nice to know that some things remain the same?

As it was back in 1997, IBM was still ranked 2 for timeliness, but its safety rank improved to 1. Move your eyes down and notice a small change in the profile, the addition of the technical rank below the safety rank. It looks at the stock's relative price performance over the past 52 weeks and then ranks the stock based on how well it should perform against the market in the near term. Stocks ranked 1 or 2 should outperform the market in the next quarter or two, stocks ranked 3 should follow the market, and stocks ranked 4 or 5 should underperform the market.

The technical rank probably seems a lot like the timeliness rank to you. The way they're different is that timeliness considers the company's earnings when projecting near-term performance; the technical rank does not. It considers only stock price performance. Which should take precedent? Timeliness. Straight from *Value Line*'s glossary comes this handy tip: "Under no circumstances should the technical rank replace the timeliness rank as the primary tool in making an investment decision. Over the years, the timeliness rank has had a superior record." Of course, seeing both ranked 1 or 2 would be best of all.

IBM's technical rank was 3. That's neutral, but its timeliness was positive. All told, the ranking box gave IBM a green light.

The stock was projected to gain as much as 55 percent in the next two to four years. The worst-case projection was a 25 percent gain.

IBM's P/E ratio was 13.6, just about where it was in 1997. Notice the trend. From 1997, it increased to almost 29 in 1999, stayed in the 20s until 2003, then began declining. In the 2008 recession IBM became a great bargain. In 2012 it was a decent bargain.

INT'L BUS. MACH. NYSE-IBM

RECENT PRICE	184.95	P/E RATIO	13.6 (Trailing: 14.6 / Median: 16.0)	RELATIVE P/E RATIO	0.94	DIV'D YLD	1.7%	VALUE LINE

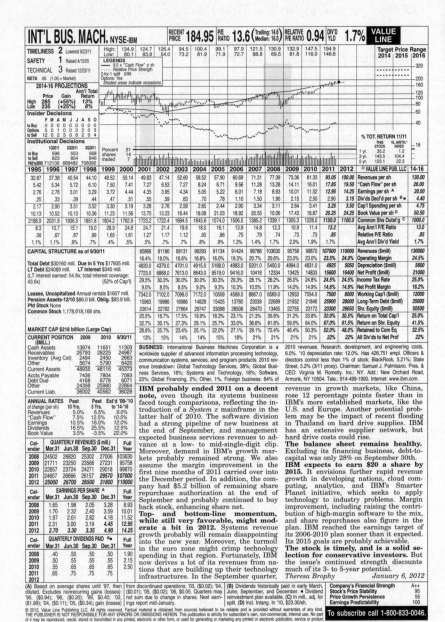

TIMELINESS	2	Lowered 9/23/11
SAFETY	1	Raised 4/15/05
TECHNICAL	3	Raised 12/23/11
BETA	.85	(1.00 = Market)

2014-16 PROJECTIONS

	Price	Gain	Ann'l Total Return
High	285	(+55%)	13%
Low	235	(+25%)	8%

Insider Decisions

	F	M	A	M	J	J	A	S	O
to Buy	0	0	0	0	0	0	0	0	0
Options	5	0	1	0	0	3	2	0	3
to Sell	12	0	2	5	0	6	2	0	4

Institutional Decisions

	1Q2011	2Q2011	3Q2011
to Buy	596	553	568
to Sell	823	854	846
Hld's(000)	712139	688482	708392

High/Low range by year:
	1995	1996	1997	1998	1999	2000	2001	2002	2003	2004	2005	2006	2007	2008	2009	2010	2011
High				134.9	124.7	126.4	94.5	100.4	99.1	97.9	121.5	130.9	132.9	147.5	194.9		
Low				80.1	83.8	54.0	73.2	81.9	71.9	72.7	88.8	69.5	81.8	116.0	146.6		

Target Price Range 2014 2015 2016

LEGENDS
- 9.5 x "Cash Flow" p sh
- ---- Relative Price Strength
- 2-for-1 split 5/99
- Options: Yes
- Shaded areas indicate recessions

% TOT. RETURN 11/11
	THIS STOCK	VL ARITH.* INDEX
1 yr.	35.2	1.2
3 yr.	143.5	104.4
5 yr.	123.1	22.3

	1995	1996	1997	1998	1999	2000	2001	2002	2003	2004	2005	2006	2007	2008	2009	2010	2011	2012	© VALUE LINE PUB. LLC	14-16
Revenues per sh	32.87	37.38	40.54	44.10	48.52	50.14	49.83	47.14	52.60	58.52	57.90	60.69	71.31	77.39	73.36	81.33	93.05	100.00		130.00
"Cash Flow" per sh	5.42	5.34	5.72	6.10	7.50	7.41	7.27	6.53	7.27	8.24	8.71	9.56	11.28	13.28	14.11	16.01	17.85	19.50		26.00
Earnings per sh A	2.76	2.76	3.01	3.29	3.72	4.44	4.35	3.95	4.34	5.05	5.22	6.01	7.18	8.93	10.01	11.52	12.95	14.25		20.00
Div'ds Decl'd per sh B ■	.25	.33	.39	.44	.47	.51	.55	.59	.63	.70	.78	1.10	1.50	1.90	2.15	2.50	2.90	3.15		4.40
Cap'l Spending per sh	2.17	2.90	3.51	3.52	3.30	3.19	3.28	2.76	2.59	2.65	2.44	2.90	3.34	3.11	2.64	3.41	3.25	3.50		4.75
Book Value per sh D	10.13	10.52	10.10	10.36	11.23	11.56	13.70	13.23	16.44	18.08	21.03	18.92	20.55	10.06	17.43	18.87	20.25	24.25		50.50
Common Shs Outst'g C	2188.9	2031.9	1936.5	1851.8	1804.2	1762.9	1723.2	1722.4	1694.5	1645.6	1574.0	1506.5	1385.2	1339.1	1305.3	1228.0	1150.0	1100.0		1000.0
Avg Ann'l P/E Ratio	8.3	10.7	15.1	19.0	28.9	24.8	24.7	21.4	19.6	18.0	16.1	13.9	14.8	12.3	10.9	11.4	13.2			13.0
Relative P/E Ratio	.56	.67	.87	.99	1.65	1.61	1.27	1.17	1.12	.95	.86	.75	.79	.74	.73	.73	.85			.85
Avg Ann'l Div'd Yield	1.1%	1.1%	.9%	.7%	.4%	.5%	.5%	.7%	.7%	.8%	.9%	1.3%	1.4%	1.7%	2.0%	1.9%	1.7%			1.7%

CAPITAL STRUCTURE as of 9/30/11

Revenues ($mill)	85866	81186	89131	96293	91134	91424	98786	103630	95758	99870	107000	110000		130000

Total Debt $30160 mill. **Due in 5 Yrs** $17935 mill.
LT Debt $24089 mill. **LT Interest** $340 mill.
(LT interest earned: 54.8x; total interest coverage: 43.6x) (52% of Cap'l)

Operating Margin	16.4%	18.0%	16.6%	16.8%	16.0%	19.3%	20.7%	20.6%	23.0%	23.0%	23.5%	24.0%		24.5%
Depreciation ($mill)	4820.0	4379.0	4701.0	4915.0	5188.0	4983.0	5201.0	5450.0	4994.0	4831.0	4925	5050		5800
Net Profit ($mill)	7723.0	6868.0	7613.0	8643.0	8519.0	9416.0	10418	12334	13425	14833	15600	16400		21000

Leases, Uncapitalized Annual rentals $1607 mill.
Pension Assets-12/10 $86.0 bill. **Oblig.** $93.9 bill.
Pfd Stock None
Common Stock 1,178,618,168 shs.

Income Tax Rate	29.5%	30.3%	30.0%	30.3%	30.0%	30.3%	29.3%	28.1%	26.2%	26.0%	24.8%	24.5%		25.0%
Net Profit Margin	9.0%	8.5%	8.5%	9.0%	9.3%	10.3%	10.5%	11.9%	14.0%	14.9%	14.6%	14.9%		16.2%
Working Cap'l ($mill)	7342.0	7102.0	7098.0	7172.0	10509	4569.0	8867.0	6569.0	12933	7554.0	7500	8000		12000
Long-Term Debt ($mill)	15963	19986	16986	14828	15425	13780	23039	22689	21932	21846	25900	28000		35000
Shr. Equity ($mill)	23614	22782	27864	29747	33098	28506	28470	13465	22755	23172	23300	26650		50500

MARKET CAP $218 billion (Large Cap)

Return on Total Cap'l	20.5%	16.7%	17.5%	19.9%	18.3%	23.1%	21.3%	35.6%	31.2%	33.8%	32.0%	30.5%		25.0%
Return on Shr. Equity	32.7%	30.1%	27.3%	29.1%	25.7%	33.0%	36.6%	91.9%	59.0%	64.0%	67.0%	61.5%		41.5%
Retained to Com Eq	28.6%	25.7%	23.4%	25.1%	22.0%	27.1%	29.1%	72.4%	46.4%	50.3%	52.0%	48.0%		32.5%
All Div'ds to Net Prof	15%	15%	14%	14%	15%	18%	21%	21%	21%	21%	22%	22%		22%

CURRENT POSITION

(SMILL.)	2009	2010	9/30/11
Cash Assets	13974	11651	11303
Receivables	26793	28225	24987
Inventory (Avg Cost)	2494	2450	2663
Other	5674	5790	6420
Current Assets	48935	48116	45373
Accts Payable	7436	7804	7093
Debt Due	4168	6778	6071
Other	24398	25980	22864
Current Liab.	36002	40562	36028

BUSINESS: International Business Machines Corporation is a worldwide supplier of advanced information processing technology, communication systems, services, and program products. 2010 revenue breakdown: Global Technology Services, 38%; Global Business Services, 18%; Systems and Technology, 18%; Software, 23%; Global Financing, 2%; Other, 1%. Foreign business: 64% of 2010 revenues. Research, development, and engineering costs, 6.0%. '10 depreciation rate: 12.0%. Has 426,751 empl. Officers & directors control less than 1% of stock; BlackRock, 5.21%; State Street, 5.2% (3/11 proxy). Chairman: Samuel J. Palmisano. Pres. & CEO: Virginia M. Rometty. Inc.: NY. Add.: New Orchard Road, Armonk, NY 10504. Tele.: 914-499-1900. Internet: www.ibm.com.

ANNUAL RATES

of change (per sh)	Past 10 Yrs.	Past 5 Yrs.	Est'd '08-'10 to '14-'16
Revenues	5.0%	6.5%	9.0%
"Cash Flow"	7.5%	12.5%	10.5%
Earnings	10.5%	16.0%	12.0%
Dividends	16.5%	25.5%	12.5%
Book Value	3.5%	-3.5%	22.0%

QUARTERLY REVENUES ($ mill.)

Cal-endar	Mar.31	Jun.30	Sep.30	Dec.31	Full Year
2008	24502	26820	25302	27006	103630
2009	21711	23250	23566	27231	95758
2010	22857	23724	24271	29018	99870
2011	24607	26666	26157	29570	107000
2012	25000	26700	26500	31800	110000

EARNINGS PER SHARE A

Cal-endar	Mar.31	Jun.30	Sep.30	Dec.31	Full Year
2008	1.65	1.98	2.05	3.28	8.93
2009	1.70	2.32	2.40	3.59	10.01
2010	1.97	2.61	2.82	4.18	11.52
2011	2.31	3.00	3.19	4.45	12.95
2012	2.70	3.30	3.35	4.90	14.25

QUARTERLY DIVIDENDS PAID B ■

Cal-endar	Mar.31	Jun.30	Sep.30	Dec.31	Full Year
2008	.40	.50	.50	.50	1.90
2009	.50	.55	.55	.55	2.15
2010	.55	.65	.65	.65	2.50
2011	.65	.75	.75	.75	
2012					

IBM probably ended 2011 on a decent note, even though its systems business faced tough comparisons, reflecting the introduction of a *System z* mainframe in the latter half of 2010. The software division had a strong pipeline of new business at the end of September, and management expected business services revenues to advance at a low- to mid-single-digit clip. Moreover, demand in IBM's growth markets probably remained strong. We also assume the margin improvement in the first nine months of 2011 carried over into the December period. In addition, the company had $5.2 billion of remaining share repurchase authorization at the end of September and probably continued to buy back stock, enhancing share net.

Top- and bottom-line momentum, while still very favorable, might moderate a bit in 2012. Systems revenue growth probably will remain disappointing into the new year. Moreover, the turmoil in the euro zone might crimp technology spending in that region. Fortunately, IBM now derives a lot of its revenues from nations that are building up their technology infrastructures. In the September quarter,

revenue in growth markets, like China, rose 12 percentage points faster than in IBM's more established markets, like the U.S. and Europe. Another potential problem may be the impact of recent flooding in Thailand on hard drive supplies. IBM has an extensive supplier network, but hard drive costs could rise.

The balance sheet remains healthy. Excluding its financing business, debt-to-capital was only 28% on September 30th.

IBM expects to earn $20 a share by 2015. It envisions further rapid revenue growth in developing nations, cloud computing, analytics, and IBM's Smarter Planet initiative, which seeks to apply technology to industry problems. Margin improvement, including raising the contribution of high-margin software to the mix, and share repurchases also figure in the plan. IBM reached the earnings target of its 2006-2010 plan sooner than it expected. Its 2015 goals are probably achievable.

The stock is timely, and is a solid selection for conservative investors. But the issue's continued strength discounts much of its 3- to 5-year potential.

Theresa Brophy *January 6, 2012*

(A) Based on average shares until '97, then diluted. Excludes nonrecurring gains (losses): '95, ($0.94); '96, ($0.20); '99, $0.40; '02, ($1.89); '04, ($1.13); '05, ($0.30); and losses from discontinued operations: '03, ($0.02); '04, ($0.01); '05, ($0.02); '06, $0.05. Quarters may not sum due to change in shares. Next earnings report mid-January.

(B) Dividends historically paid in early March, June, September, and December. ■ Dividend reinvestment plan available. (C) In mill., adj. for split. (D) Incl. Intang. In '10, $23.30/sh.

Company's Financial Strength	A++
Stock's Price Stability	95
Price Growth Persistence	55
Earnings Predictability	100

To subscribe call 1-800-833-0046.

Glancing at IBM's price chart, you see that after the 2002 crash it trended up a little, then down a little, rose 80 percent from its 2006 low to its 2008 high before crashing with the rest of the market at the end of 2008, then embarked on a long recovery that seemed to have momentum in early 2012. A green light for holding on.

The earnings trend looked solid. From when you bought in 1997, earnings per share rose steadily to 4.44 in 2000, slid down to 3.95 in 2002 when all of technology was hurting in the post-crash economy, but turned up again in the recovery. In years following 2002, IBM's EPS came in at 4.34, 5.05, 5.22, 6.06, 7.18, 8.93, 10.01, 11.52, and were expected to be 12.95 in 2011 and 14.25 in 2012. That trend line is a beauty. Another green light.

IBM looked good by the numbers, and Ms. Brophy agreed in words. She wrote that IBM probably ended 2011 "on a decent note" as demand in its "growth markets probably remained strong." Business momentum was favorable but she worried that it might moderate due to trouble in the euro zone and the lingering impact of flooding in Thailand, which damaged hard-drive supplies. The balance sheet was healthy and management expected to hit $20 EPS by 2015, aided by a focus on developing nations. Her main concern was that IBM's "continued strength discounts much of its 3- to 5-year potential."

How about a real-life test? Decide now whether you would have held your position or sold it. Then, check IBM's current price to see how you would have done. To help with your calculations, write down that IBM was $193 and the S&P 500 was 1,361 on February 17, 2012. Since then, which performed better?

Where to Find *Value Line*

You could find Value Line reports in your mailbox every week if your don't mind paying a lot. You receive a large binder containing all 1,700 reports in 13 sections. Each week, a new section arrives to replace one of the existing 13. As you can see, the entire binder is updated every 13 weeks, or four times a year.

Perhaps you don't want all 1,700 reports taking up space on your bookshelf. Instead, you just want reports for the companies that interest you at any given time. Then turn to your local library. Nearly every decent library I've been to has a copy of *Value Line* available. You can stop by with a list of companies that interest you, look them up, photocopy each page, and be on your way.

Finally, you could subscribe to the online edition. It provides the entire system in both HTML and PDF formats, enables you to search for profiles by entering company ticker symbols, and offers a stock screener with which you can create and save your own searches.

Contact Information: 800-833-0046, www.valueline.com. Price: very high

Limited Coverage in *Value Line*

One drawback to *The Value Line Investment Survey* is that it covers only 1,700 stocks. They're the big, well-established companies. Value Line does publish an expanded volume called the *Small & Mid-Cap Survey* that reports on 1,800 additional companies. The expanded reports lack analyst commentary and projections. Combined, the Value Line standard and expanded editions still cover only 3,500 stocks. That leaves about 17,000 companies without *Value Line* reports.

Thus, for small companies that you truly discover, you'll need to turn elsewhere for critical information. Such alternate sources include everything in this chapter, most notably information from the companies themselves. Financial statements tell you a lot of critical information about a company. Also, custom software packages and online screeners such as Yahoo! Finance Stock Screener (page 195) provide much of what's contained in Value Line's publications.

Companies Themselves

Before investing in any company, some people insist on seeing an investor packet from headquarters. In there, you'll find an annual report containing a happy look at the company's future and financial statements that may not be as happy, a recent 10-K and a recent 10-Q, press releases, analyst reports, and general information.

For many small companies that interest you, the company investment packet will form the bulk of your research. The whole idea of discovering small companies is, well, discovering them. If Value Line and everybody else already knows about them, they've been discovered.

This section shows how to request an investor packet and how to use it.

Request an Investor Packet

Get the company's phone number somewhere. You might get it from *Value Line*, a magazine article, the Internet, a custom software package, or directory assistance. The company website should contain investor information and might include a button to request a complete packet. At the very least, you should find the phone number.

Once you have the number, call it and ask to speak with the Investor Relations Department. The receptionist might ask if you need an investor packet and just take your address on the spot. Otherwise, you'll be transferred to Investor Relations. Tell the friendly voice that you want a kit that includes:

✔ The annual report

✔ The 10-K and 10-Q

✔ Analyst reports

✔ Recent press releases

✔ Any free product samples

While the free samples are a long shot—especially if you're investing in Ford or Boeing—the rest is pretty standard. A week to 10 days later, your very own investor packet will arrive free of charge. What a joy, capitalism!

If you can't find the company's phone number, contact the Public Register's Annual Report Service at www.prars.com to obtain a free current annual report for any public company. You won't get a packet as complete as the one from Investor Relations, but the annual report is better than nothing.

Tear open the envelope and . . .

Read the Investor Packet

Clear a space on your kitchen table or desk and spread the contents of the investor packet in front of you.

Annual Report

Start with the annual report. It's probably very attractive because it's as much marketing collateral as it is informative. Sometimes, if you're researching very young companies, the annual report will be little fancier than a student term paper. I personally like that. The money can be put toward something that will earn a profit. That's what we're all in this for, darn it!

Opening the report, you'll probably be greeted with a letter from the chief executive officer. Next, you'll page through photos of company headquarters, happy customers, select employees, and lots of product displays. Following the photo gallery is usually an article about the company's roots, its recent accomplishments, its mission statement, and how well equipped it is for the future. The easygoing stuff generally concludes with a reprinted advertisement or one that was created specifically for the annual report.

They're all a bit different, but that's the general idea. Read over the fun stuff, then move along to the financial statements. They're almost always contained in the back half of the annual report, but occasionally they're separate.

Let's learn about the financial statements by looking at real-life numbers from IBM's 2010 annual report. We also examined IBM on the Value Line report earlier.

Balance Sheet

A balance sheet is a quick look at what a company owns and what it owes, also known as assets and liabilities. The difference between the two is called stockholders' equity and is what causes the balance sheet to balance. Rather than drag you through Accounting 101, I'm going to highlight just the important parts of the sheet. Here's IBM's:

IBM 2010 Balance Sheet

(Dollars in millions)	2010	2009
Assets		
Cash and cash equivalents	$ 10,661	$ 12,183
Notes and accounts receivable	10,834	10,736
(a bunch of other stuff I won't list)	91,957	86,103
Total assets	113,452	109,022
Liabilities		
Current liabilities:		
Taxes	$ 4,216	$ 3,826
Short-term debt	6,778	4,168
Accounts payable	7,804	7,436
(other current liabilities)	21,764	20,572
Total current liabilities	40,562	36,002
Long-term debt	21,846	21,932
Retirement obligations	15,978	15,953
Other liabilities	11,893	12,380
Total liabilities	90,279	86,267
Equity		
IBM stockholders' equity	23,046	22,637
Noncontrolling interests	126	118
Total equity	23,172	22,755
Total liabilities and equity	113,452	109,022

Assets

Assets are divided into current and long term. Current assets are things like money in the bank and uncollected invoices. Long-term assets are things like buildings. I spared you the tedious divisions on my excerpt and just showed a couple important items along with the total.

Cash is exactly what you think it is. At the end of 2010, IBM had $10.7 billion in its bank account—nearly twice what I had at the time. You want a company to have plenty of cash so it can pay its debts and take advantage of opportunities, such as buying smaller companies.

Notes and accounts receivable is money that IBM was owed by customers for computer hardware, software, and services. Whereas your drinking buddy might owe you a ten spot for last Friday, IBM's buddies owed the company $10.8 billion at the end of 2010. On the one hand, it's good to see a lot of money coming to IBM in the future. On the other hand, you don't want receivables to grow faster than sales. You'll find sales on the income statement.

The rest of the asset section shows things like marketable securities, inventory, plant and property, and other things that IBM owned. I've added it all together as "a bunch of other stuff I won't list."

Liabilities

Liabilities are also divided into current and long term. Current liabilities are due within a year while long-term liabilities are due further in the future.

The liabilities section is pretty straightforward. Taxes are what the company owes to the IRS just like you need to pay every year.

Debt is bad. You would like to see as little debt on the balance sheet as possible, both current and long term. You'd love to invest in companies that don't have any debt. As Peter Lynch points out, a company can't go bankrupt if it doesn't owe any money. IBM owed a staggering $28.6 billion at the end of 2010.

The last item is accounts payable. That's the money IBM needed to pay its suppliers for items purchased on credit.

Equity

Equity is the difference between assets and liabilities. It consists of outstanding shares of stock and other things like retained earnings and unrealized gains. Added to liabilities, stockholders' equity causes the balance sheet to balance.

Income Statement

An income statement shows the company's earnings and expenses. It's where you can figure the all-important gross profit margin, the difference between what a company earns and what it spends. Here's an abbreviated version of IBM's income statement:

IBM 2010 Income Statement

(Dollars in millions except per share amounts)	2010	2009
Revenue		
Services	$ 56,868	$ 55,128
Sales	40,736	38,300
Financing	2,267	2,331
Total revenue	99,870	95,758
Cost		
Services	$ 38,383	$ 37,146
Sales	14,374	13,606
Financing	1,100	1,220
Total cost	53,857	51,973
Gross profit	46,014	43,785
Expense and other income, income taxes	31,181	30,360
Net income	14,833	13,425
Earnings per share of common stock	$11.69	$10.12
Weighted-average number of common shares outstanding:	1,268,789,202	1,327,157,410

There's not a lot to it, really. Revenue shows you what IBM sold in each division of its business. Cost shows you what it cost IBM to achieve those sales in each division. Then the statement breaks the numbers down into investor-centric stuff like gross profit and earnings per share.

You can see that IBM increased revenue more than it increased cost from 2009 to 2010, thereby adding an extra $2.2 billion of gross profit. That's a good sign. You want gross profit to grow from year to year.

Gross profit grew a lot, and so did earnings per share. Each share of stock earned only $10.12 in 2009, but earned $11.69 in 2010. That's a 15.5 percent increase! Current shareholders love to see that. The bottom of the income statement provides an additional explanation for the jump in earnings per share: There were 58 million fewer shares in 2010 than in 2009. IBM bought back a lot of its stock, another plus for current investors.

Want to check IBM's math? On your calculator, divide the 2010 net income (14,833,000,000) by the number of shares outstanding in 2010 (1,268,789,202) and see if you get the same earnings per share figure that they got. If you don't, call the Securities & Exchange Commission . . . or your calculator manufacturer.

10-K and 10-Q

If you want hard numbers without all the fancy marketing copy in the annual report, you're going to love the 10-K and 10-Q. Each is a meatier version of the financial information found in the annual report. 10-Ks come out yearly while 10-Qs come out quarterly. 10-Qs include management discussion of current issues facing the company. 10-Ks are audited, 10-Qs are not. As for the numbers on these sheets, you'll find revenues, costs, expenses, operating profits, net income or loss, and other items.

Stock Screeners

Since the earlier editions of this book, it's become easier and cheaper to find good stocks. As recently as a few years ago, stock databases came on CDs. You had to install the programs, then get data updates by downloading files from websites or receiving new CDs every month. The programs were expensive, too. Some cost more than $500 per year.

Free online stock screeners have changed the rules. Pros used to scoff at pared-down tools from places like Yahoo! Finance, and some still do. The thing is, free tools are no longer pared down. They do everything an individual investor needs them to do. Much as I've looked—and I've looked a lot—I can't see any compelling reason to pay for stock software anymore.

All you want from a stock screener is quick, easy research that allows you to make your own best decisions. With that directive in mind, let's look at three screeners.

Yahoo! Finance Stock Screener

Yahoo! is the place to start for fast results that you can sort by any criterion. If you get too many companies, just add more criteria to whittle the list down, or make your parameters stricter.

For instance, in February 2012 I was interested in companies that had a price-to-sales ratio (P/S) below 5, a price-to-earnings ratio (P/E) below 10, and projected earnings-per-share (EPS) growth in the five years ahead of more than 30 percent. I typed those criteria into the screener, and received 135 results.

That was too many, so I dropped the P/E to 5 and slapped on a minimum profit margin requirement of 20 percent and got a tidy list of 17 companies. I clicked the "5 yr Growth" criterion header in the results table twice to re-sort the list in descending order from highest growth rate to lowest. The whole process took less than two minutes.

The list included Cumulus Media (CMLS $4), Leucadia National (LUK $29), and SkyPeople Fruit Juice (SPU $2). Whether or not they did well (see for yourself by typing their symbols into Yahoo! Finance and checking their current prices) is not our concern here. What I want you to appreciate is how quickly I was able to find these potentially profitable recovery stories using Yahoo! Finance Stock Screener, and how easy it was for me to conduct additional research with just a few mouse clicks.

The basic HTML screener is usually fine for me, but Yahoo! also offers a Java screener that's fancier. It has a regular desktop softwarelike interface instead of a webpage interface, and offers more screening criteria. It, too, is free.

Contact Information: screener.finance.yahoo.com/stocks.html

FINVIZ Stock Screener

The FINVIZ stock screener offers a wide range of criteria sorted into three groups: descriptive, fundamental, and technical. Its drop-down menus help you navigate typical ranges instead of specific data.

For example, the choices for P/E include "Low (<15)" and "High (>50)" before a long list of options such as "Under 30" and "Over 25." This is a time saver because you probably don't care specifically if the P/E is 9.7, but just that it's low. Using this approach across all criteria, you can quickly create a basic profile of the kind of companies you want. The screener's technical criteria offer a rare treat among free screeners. Using the same pull-down range technique, you could look for stocks up 20 percent in the past month, with their prices 10 percent above their 50-day simple moving average, but with their RSI still below 50 indicating not yet overbought. Pretty slick.

In February 2012, I searched for American stocks with a forward P/E that was "Low (<15)," EPS growth for the next five years that was "High (>25%)," insider transactions that were "Very Positive (>20%)," and a price that was within 10 percent above the 50-day simple moving average. That returned just six stocks, including Harman International (HAR $51), Real Goods Solar (RSOL $2), and Textron (TXT $28).

The screener provides helpful features such as a results list that refreshes on the fly every time you add or change a criterion, a short definition of each criterion that pops up when you hover your cursor over it, and a mini price chart that appears when you hover your cursor over any stock symbol.

Contact Information: finviz.com/screener.ashx

Morningstar Stock Screener

Morningstar's screener is another good alternative. It taps into the firm's helpful analysis tools like its stock types, equity style box, and grading system.

In February 2012, I screened for aggressive growth companies with "A" or "B" grades for growth, profitability, and financial health. That turned up 51 companies. I clicked the "Score These Results" button to specify the importance of each criterion by clicking a radio button between 1 and 10 beneath it and prioritized "high growth grade," "high profitability grade," and "below 52-week high."

The top three by that filter were Discovery Communications (DISCA $45), Ebix (EBIX $24), and Gilead Sciences (GILD $47).

Contact Information: screen.morningstar.com/StockSelector.html

The Internet

What started as a gathering of investors under a buttonwood tree in lower Manhattan turned into the New York Stock Exchange. To trade, you had to be there. Then the telephone came around and people could call their orders in. Now, a successful investor can go his or her entire life without ever seeing Wall Street. Nothing represents everyman's worldwide access to the markets better than the Internet.

For links to each resource below and others I've found, visit my site at www.jasonkelly.com/resources.

Investment Sites

This section contains summaries of the best investment sites I know.

Barron's Online

I've liked *Barron's* for years, and the newspaper's website brings all the benefits of its print publication to the Internet, with extra features to boot. The quality of writing leads the industry, with the wit of editor Alan Abelson bringing a smile to many a worn trader on the weekend. He's rarely right about where the market's heading, because he always thinks it's going to crash even though history shows that it usually rises, but you won't care because he's so entertaining. He had a field day in 2008, though! Elsewhere on the site you'll find plenty of data in the famous Market Lab, commentary, interviews with experts, highlighted charts, research tidbits from analysts, forecasts from publications both mainstream and eclectic, and even a portfolio tracking service.

Contact Information: www.barrons.com

Bigcharts

Bigcharts, a division of MarketWatch, which is a division of Dow Jones & Company, provides free investment charts. They're customizable by time frame, offer benchmarks for comparison, come in various styles, and are available in a printer-friendly format.

Contact Information: www.bigcharts.com

Bloomberg

The famous news company got its start in the world of finance, so it's little surprise that its website offers useful stories and data about economies and markets. The "Quick" tab shows top news in a hurry, the site offers short investment video clips from Bloomberg TV, and special reports are richly detailed. Bloomberg expanded its offerings when it bought *BusinessWeek* magazine (deserving a direct look at businessweek.com) from the McGraw-Hill Companies. Toss in *Bloomberg Markets* magazine for professional investors and you end up with a worthwhile collection of money ideas.

Contact Information: www.bloomberg.com

Briefing.com

You'll find a refreshingly hype-free collection of news, commentary, and analysis at Briefing.com. It's clear from the writing that the staff specializes in finance, not English, and sometimes that's just fine. They make their points with little regard for style. The free section of the site contains 30-minute market updates, breaking news, a look at story stocks, an active portfolio that has performed well, an after-hours report, and updates on the economy.

Contact Information: www.briefing.com

FINVIZ

The name stands for "financial visualizations," and the site excels at them. You read in the previous section about its well-designed screener. Other tools include an efficient news and blog feed that shows opening sentences when you hover your cursor over a link, "heat maps" of the market showing stocks in a grid of red losses and green gains, and stock group performance displays in unusual formats such as a color spectrum that you can sort by various factors.

Contact Information: www.finviz.com

Google Finance

As with most offerings from Google, the online giant's finance site is simple and fast. Its stock profiles provide the usual statistics, a nice interactive chart, and windows into commentary from both Google discussion boards and external blogs. Its company management section is particularly well done with thumbnail photos of most officers along with links to their biographies and recent trading activity. The site offers free portfolio tracking.

Contact Information: www.google.com/finance

Jason Kelly

On my site, I track the investment strategies you learned about in this book, along with others I discover, test, and refine. You'll find updates to information contained in my books, articles on current investment issues, free worksheets (including the ones in this book) that you can print out and use to manage your money, and lots of resource reviews like the ones in this chapter. If nothing else, get yourself on my free email list for periodic commentary and investment ideas. I promise not to send you any credit card ads.

Contact Information: www.jasonkelly.com

MarketWatch

MarketWatch, brought to you by Dow Jones & Company, collects the latest news headlines but also brings columnists who offer their take on developments. The roster is a revolving list that changes with each edition of this book.

Contact Information: www.marketwatch.com

Morningstar

Morningstar has been the definitive source of mutual fund information for years and has diversified its coverage to include stocks. That dual focus combined with the company's expertise in presenting research has produced a superb investment website. The usual discussion boards and portfolio tracking are in place along with features you won't find elsewhere such as Instant X-Ray, where you input your portfolio holdings and get a report showing where your money is allocated by asset class, market cap, interest rate sensitivity, industry sector, and region of the world. You'll be surprised at how much of Morningstar's premium research is available on the website for free.

Contact Information: www.morningstar.com

Seeking Alpha

This is one of the Internet's deepest collections of investment content. Lest the name confuse you, here's the site's explanation: "*Alpha* is a finance term referring to a stock's performance relative to the market; it's used more loosely by fund managers to describe beating their index, so every stock picker is *seeking alpha.*" The site features articles from blogs, investment firms, newsletters, and its own writers; company conference call transcripts; a human-edited summary of real-time news and commentary; and various ways for investors to exchange ideas, such as comment sections, a "StockTalk" chat board, and an "Instablog" platform for quick contributions.

Contact Information: www.seekingalpha.com

StockCharts.com

You may be able to guess from the name what this site focuses on. Its charts are easy to create, a joy to look at, packed with features, and powerfully customizable. The site's Chart School is helpful. In addition to free charting capabilities, it offers subscription plans for more powerful features and advice from veteran chartists.

Contact Information: www.stockcharts.com

Wikinvest

Wikipedia has probably familiarized you with the concept of allowing users to add, modify, and delete content. Wikinvest applies the same approach to investment research. It assembles basic data about a company, gathers input from bulls and bears, and offers a crowd-sourced rundown of trends and forces affecting the company's prospects. Its concept overviews provide clusters of investment ideas for further research, such as "China's Water Scarcity" suggesting that Archer-Daniels-Midland (ADM) and Monsanto (MON) could benefit. The site's portfolio monitor is first rate, connecting directly to your brokerage accounts for a real-time view of your overall balance, news affecting your money now, fees you're paying, and your performance.

Contact Information: www.wikinvest.com

Yahoo! Finance

Yahoo! Finance is the champion investment research site. I use it every day. It aggregates most of what you need to know about a stock or mutual fund into one free location. Company and fund profiles are complete with management information, contact numbers, price history, split history, recent announcements, recent and archived news stories, blog postings, and everything else you'd expect. Profit margin? It's there. Return on investment? It's there. An interactive chart with adjustable time frame parameters and the ability to add other stocks and indexes for comparison? It's there. From how a stock did in the last five years to how it did in the last hour, Yahoo! Finance has you covered. You can create as many portfolios and watch lists as you want. Everything is fast and free.

Contact Information: finance.yahoo.com

Zero Hedge

This site's unsentimental worldview is right in its header: "On a long enough timeline the survival rate for everyone drops to zero." Its anonymous writers post articles under the pseudonym "Tyler Durden," a forceful character in the Chuck Palahniuk novel *Fight Club*, about risks and shady developments in financial markets, news that impacts economies, and politics. It also runs guest posts by named contributors. Zero Hedge says its mission is "to widen the scope of financial, economic, and political information available to the professional investing public" and "to skeptically examine and, where necessary, attack the flaccid institution that financial journalism has become." It uses anonymity as "a shield from the tyranny of the majority." Whenever you need a little raw reality, swing by Zero Hedge.

Contact Information: www.zerohedge.com

Other Sites

Other investment sites that might appeal to you include Business Insider at www.businessinsider.com, CNN Money at money.cnn.com, the financial section of The Economist at www.economist.com, the Financial Times at www.ft.com, Minyan-ville at www.minyanville.com, MSN Money at money.msn.com, and Reuters at www.reuters.com/finance.

Worthy financial blogs include Bespoke Investment Group at bespokeinvest.typepad.com, The Big Picture at www.ritholtz.com/blog, Buttonwood's notebook at www.economist.com/blogs/buttonwood, Calculated Risk at www.calculatedriskblog.com, Dealbreaker at www.dealbreaker.com, Footnoted by Morningstar at www.footnoted.com, Free Exchange at www.economist.com/blogs/freeexchange, FT Alphaville at ftalphaville.ft.com, Macroblog by the Federal Reserve Bank of Atlanta at macroblog.typepad.com, MarketBeat at blogs.wsj.com/marketbeat, Naked Capitalism at www.nakedcapitalism.com, and Pragmatic Capitalism at www.pragcap.com.

For links to breaking investment articles, stop by Abnormal Returns at www.abnormalreturns.com and RealClearMarkets at www.realclearmarkets.com. You'll find plenty about exchange-traded funds like the ones available for Double the Dow and Maximum Midcap at www.alletf.com, www.etfchannel.com, and www.etftrends.com. You can buy and sell entire predetermined portfolios at www.foliofn.com. If you want more charts and technical analysis tools, visit www.decisionpoint.com. To monitor insider investment activity, try www.j3sg.com.

The Securities and Exchange Commission maintains a site at

www.sec.gov. Search for a company's EDGAR filings and other documents at www.secinfo.com. Get economic data at www.eco nomicindicators.gov.

The New York Stock Exchange is at www.nyse.com and the NASDAQ is at www.nasdaq.com.

Want more information about investing? Stop by the American Association of Individual Investors at www.aaii.com and the National Association of Investors Corporation at www .betterinvesting.org.

7

This Book's Strategy

You've come a long way, my friend. You speak the language of stocks, you've studied master investors and the lessons of history, you know how to use permanent portfolios, you're all set up with your discount broker, and you know both how and where to conduct research. After all that preparation, it's time to assemble a strategy of your own. That's the focus of this chapter.

The strategy has three parts. First you'll build a core portfolio with the methods you learned in Chapter 4, next you'll assemble and track a list of potential investments, then you'll manage a portfolio of individual stocks from your list to enhance the returns of your core portfolio.

I'm trembling as I write. Profits are near. Years from now you'll look back and scribble in your personal journal the words of John Keats: "Much have I travel'd in the realms of gold . . ."

Build a Core Portfolio

Before you travel the realms of gold in search of riches, you need a strong fortress from which to base your searches. You can retreat to the fortress when your search party turns up nothing or is attacked by marauding bears. Your fortress will probably start small, but will grow in size as your search party returns with riches.

You're going to combine growth and value in your fortress and your search party. Some of the best investors combine these two approaches and history shows that they coexist well. Often, when growth investing is struggling in the market, value investing is soaring and vice versa. By combining the two, you should come closer to steady superior returns.

You're going to rely on a proven team to build your fortress: permanent portfolios.

Use Double the Dow to put all 30 Dow companies to work on your fortress at twice their normal strength. I provide background for all the Dow strategies in Chapter 4 and explain Double the Dow specifically on page 132. For an approach with an even better record, use Maximum Midcap to put 400 medium-sized companies to work at twice their normal strength. I explain that approach on page 136.

No matter which permanent portfolio strategy you choose, you'll add considerable strength to your fortress. When the Hun attacks with his army of bears, you'll be glad to have Dow or midcap companies ready to scramble and repair the curtain walls.

Maintain Your Stocks to Watch Worksheet

Once you've built a core portfolio, you've got a strong fortress from which to base your searches for wealth. The fortress should stand through good times and bad, strengthened by proven permanent portfolios. Now it's time to enter the wild world of individual stock picking. You'll rely on the advice you received from the six master investors in Chapter 2 and history's lessons in Chapter 3.

To shield yourself from the influence of rumors, great stories from your neighbors, catchy headlines, and cool-sounding company names, you're going to keep a personalized list of 20 companies to watch. That's right, just 20 companies. In order for a new company to get a space on the list, it must be better than one of the current 20. By structuring your list in this fashion, you force it to improve over time.

Continuing the Realm of Riches metaphor, this list is your roster of henchmen that you use to assemble search parties. When you actually invest in one or more of the stocks, you send them out of your fortress to find riches. When you sell, they return to the fortress, where you store the money either in your permanent portfolio or cash coffers. The Realm of Riches is a nasty place outside the fortress. Some of your henchmen may never return. In other words, some stocks might go to zero and you'll strike them from your list. Sometimes you'll sell a stock but still keep an eye on it. It stays on your list until something better comes along to bump it off.

I love this system. When I first started looking for good investments on my own, my life piled high with company reports, *Value Line* pages, *Standard & Poor's* profiles, magazine articles, and so on. It became so ridiculous that at one point I thought my portfolio was coming together based on which papers beat their way to the top of the pile that day. That's not a good way to invest.

So I stole a blank sheet of paper from my laser printer and scribbled across the top, "Stocks I Like." Then I went through every stack of paper, writing down the name of each company and a few measurements that were easily obtained from the paperwork. When the last piece of paper hit the floor, I had a list of 58 company profiles in front of me. Picture me looking at the sheet of paper as fairy dust sprinkled the air. What a revelation! Putting every company in the same place with the same measurements allowed me to instantly see which companies were most attractive. I scratched out the duds and gleefully whittled my list to a tidy group of 20 stocks. I've never looked back since. Now, whenever I encounter a stock tip in an article, a conversation, or on a bathroom wall, I simply find its worksheet measurements, compare it with the 20 stocks I'm watching, and see if it beats out any of the current 20. If not, I forget about it. If so, I strike the weakest of the 20 and replace it with the new stock. In the course of this simple process, I either save myself the hassle of reading a lot of material on a new company or I strengthen my list of potential investments.

Constant scrutiny of your list is healthy. Call it investment Darwinism or natural stock selection. I've evolved alongside my list since that first glorious day with the fairy dust. I now call the process Stockwatch and list my companies on the Stocks to Watch Worksheet. There's a copy for you in the back of this book. Let's explore how to use it.

Gather the Worksheet Criteria

You should be bursting with investment ideas after spending time with the resources explained in the previous chapter. If you're like me, there will be too many great investments and not enough money. The trick now is to pare your satchel of stocks down to the best 20 for placement on your Stocks to Watch worksheet. That's what this section is all about. It's the heart of our strategy. We've reached the point of your investment journey where it's time to discover specific measurements that capture the advice of our six master investors, reflect the lessons of history, and are easy enough for you to actually use. Too many books list hundreds of ideal measurements for your stocks to possess, but fail to note that it takes hours just to find them all—if you ever do. I don't have the patience for such approaches and assume that you don't, either.

For convenience, I group all measurements on the Stocks to Watch worksheet. To pack in all the information I like to know about a company, I needed to break the worksheet into two sets of column headings and put only 10 companies on a page. Thus, to track 20 companies, you'll have two Stocks to Watch worksheets. Your 20 stocks might contain 5 large cap value companies, 5 medium cap growth companies, and 10 small cap growth companies in one place. The combination will be unique to your interests, of course, but you don't need to juggle multiple criteria for different types of companies. I designed the worksheet to be flexible enough to follow any stock you like.

If you're scouring stocks for the first time, your goal is to build your initial list with the 20 best stocks you can find. Thereafter, you will scrutinize every stock you encounter against the 20 already on your list.

Your worksheet is in the back of the book. Follow along as I explain each measurement and where to find it. The worksheet looks like this:

Company Name	Current Price	52 wk Hi/Lo	Market Cap	Day Dol Volume	Sales	Net Prof Margin	Cash	Total Debt	Sales /Share	Cash Fl /Share	Earning /Share	Div Yield	ROE	Insider buy/own	Stock buyback
		/				↕			↑	↑	↑	↓			/

Company Name	EPS Rank	RPS Rank	5 yr Sales	5 yr Price	Proj Sales	Proj Hi/Lo	Time Safe	STARS Fair Val	Current P/E	Average P/E	P/S	P/B	Current Ratio	P/CF	SMA MACD RSI
						/	/	/							

For each measurement, I explain what it is, the requirement to make your list, the ideal direction of the measurement, and where to find it. In some cases, not all of the items apply, so I leave some out. Also, rather than reprint sample pages from information sources such as *Value Line*, I point you to the resources section where I reprint a sample page one time and identify each pertinent piece of information on it. You'll eventually know by heart where to look for the information you need.

Company Basics

These are the essential measurements of a company. They tell you who the company is, its stock price, and how big the company is.

Company Name, Symbol, and Phone

> Company Name,
> Symbol, and Phone

We'll start out easily enough. Simply fill in the name of companies that make your list, their ticker symbols, and their phone numbers. Make sure you get them right. That sounds silly, but a friend of mine bought a ton of MFS Communications (NASDAQ: MFST) back in June 1996 thinking he was buying Microsoft (NASDAQ: MSFT). Switching the F and S leads to a world of difference. Microsoft rose from a split-adjusted $7.50 in June 1996 to $31 in Feburary 2012. MFS Communications was acquired by WorldCom, which declared bankruptcy in July 2002. Luckily, my friend caught his error on his next monthly statement.

Where to Find It: If you encounter a stock in an article, its symbol is usually provided in parenthesis after the first appearance of the company name. You'll find abbreviated company names and ticker symbols in almost every newspaper's stock tables. You can also look up names and symbols at any online financial site.

Current Stock Price and 52-Week High/Low

> Current   52 wk
> Price   Hi/Lo

This is simply the stock's recent trading price along with its high and low over the past 52 weeks. It's always good to know the current price because that's what you'll be paying if you buy now. The high and low are good to know because they'll give you an idea if the current price is near the top or bottom of the range. Lots of growth investors prefer to buy near the top of the range, hoping that the stock will continue pushing the upper limit. Many value investors prefer to buy near the bottom of the range, hoping that the stock recovers to its previous highs. There is no such thing as an ideal stock price.

Where to Find It: Any newspaper's stock table lists yesterday's trading price and the 52-week high and low. The Internet is also a convenient place to find stock price information, with real-time quotes during the trading day. Stock quotes are one of the most common reasons people go online. Well, at least people like me.

Market Capitalization

This shows you how big the company is. To refresh your memory, determine market capitalization by multiplying the number of outstanding shares of stock by the current stock price. The number you get will reveal whether the company you're considering is large, medium, or small. Know the size of companies you're considering so you have an idea whether your portfolio is weighted too heavily toward one size or another.

You may already be investing in larger, established companies through the Dow. Remember that the 30 Dow stocks contain names like Boeing, Coca-Cola, Disney, IBM, Intel, 3M, McDonald's, Microsoft, Merck, and Wal-Mart. They're the hugest of the huge.

If you're already in larger companies through the Dow or other large cap index, consider focusing your individual stock-picking efforts on smaller companies. They'll add some spice to your portfolio and allow you to capture a truer picture of the marketplace. I'm not suggesting you ignore house-

Look for Smaller Companies

hold names just because they're big; I'm suggesting you make a concerted effort to find undiscovered companies that will be tomorrow's household names. Referring back to the Morningstar capitalization table on page 41, you'll see that small companies had a median market cap of $1.5 billion in early 2012.

I can't list an ideal market cap for a company because there is no such thing. I quadrupled my money in IBM while friends lost 60 percent in Diamond Multimedia, a small company. Opportunity and danger lurk everywhere.

Where to Find It: You can find the total number of shares outstanding listed in several places. The easiest is probably on the *Value Line* page you'll be using for gobs of other stock information. There you can see the number of shares over the past 15 years in addition to the current number. Shares outstanding is also printed with quarterly earnings in financial newspapers such as *Investor's Business Daily*. Finally, several Internet sites such as Yahoo! Finance list market cap itself, saving you the time of calculating it.

Daily Dollar Volume

While market cap tells you a company's size, dollar volume tells you how much money trades in the stock on a given day. That information determines how liquid the stock is, that is how easily it is bought and sold. It's easy to figure daily dollar volume: Multiply a stock's average daily trading volume by its share price. For example, on February 22, 2012, Exxon Mobil's daily trading volume was 11,983,901 and its price was $86.92. Multiplying the two, you see that on that day the stock traded a dollar volume of $1,041,640,675.

Small Caps Should Have Low Volume

Most mutual funds won't touch stocks with low dollar volumes because it might be difficult for them to sell the stock in the future. If nobody's buying, the price will drop and the spread will be big. If you try selling shares of Mister Magazine, people won't even know what the company does much less be interested in buying it. If you try selling shares of Exxon Mobil, there's a buyer at every turn. Mister Magazine is an illiquid stock, Exxon Mobil is very liquid.

Like market cap, there is no ideal number for daily dollar volume. The measure is of most interest to small cap investors. If you're a small cap investor, you'll look for low daily volume, say less than $3 million because that means mutual funds will stay away until the volume starts increasing. When it does, funds might buy in and drive the volume and price even higher. You will have been invested since the early days when you and 10 other people followed the stock. Handsome profits should come your way. Large cap investors don't pay much attention to daily volume because it's always big and everybody already knows about the company. You're not going to sneak up on the world with shares of Exxon Mobil.

By the way, don't get too illiquid no matter what your market cap preference is. A widely accepted bare minimum trading volume is $50,000 a day. Much below that and you're going to be selling your stock on the street corner along with cheap pencils and windshield cleanings.

Where to Find It: One place to locate volume information is *Investor's Business Daily*. Every day, it prints the number of shares traded in a stock and the percentage that the number differs from the stock's usual volume. In *IBD* listings, you'll find (along with other stuff) this information:

Exxon	852	-42	87.25

The number 852 is the previous day's trading volume shown in thousands. In this case, Exxon traded 852,000 shares; -42 shows you the percentage difference that 852,000 is from Exxon's usual volume. To arrive at the average daily volume, just divide 852,000 by .58 (the difference between 1, which represents 100 percent volume, and Exxon's dip of 42 percent. 1 minus .42 equals .58) to get an average daily share volume of 1,468,966. Multiply that by the share price of $87.25 to get, ta-da, an average daily dollar volume of $128,167,241. Every day $128 million of Exxon stock changes hands.

You'll also find volume information on the Internet.

Sales   Sales

It's helpful to know how much business your companies are doing. Sales reveals that number to you. Market cap, daily dollar volume, and sales usually follow the same trend. That is, small companies tend to trade in low dollar volumes and have modest sales. Large companies tend to trade in large dollar volumes and have a lot of sales. In early 2012, oil and gas explorer Quicksilver Resources had a $990 million market cap and previous one-year sales of $960 million, while Coca-Cola weighed in with a $153 billion market cap and previous one-year sales of $46 billion.

Once again, I can't tell you an ideal figure for this measure. Common sense screams *"Bigger, of course!"* However, that isn't always so. A lot of small cap investors prefer sales to be little because it indicates that the company is still undiscovered. Little sales can grow faster than big sales. Coke can't easily turn its $46 billion annual sales into $92 billion, but Mister Magazine can turn its $5 million annual sales into $10 million just by running a TV commercial. When sales and earnings grow quickly, share price tends to follow.

You won't pay too much attention to this figure for your large cap stocks. In the price-to-sales ratio discussed later, sales per share becomes important. But there are few times that I look at the overall sales of my large-company investments for anything other than curiosity: "$46 billion? Wow, that's a lot of Coke."

Where to Find It: The easiest place to get sales is on your handy *Value Line* sheet. It's right there along with nearly everything else you could ever want to know about a stock. By the time you're finished with this book, you'll want an I ♥ VALUE LINE bumper sticker on your car.

Financial websites also show sales for the trailing 12 months. Be aware that sales are sometimes called revenue.

Company Health

Now you know the basic information about your company. It's time to see how healthy it is. This section discusses measurements that will tell you.

Net Profit Margin

As you read in Chapter 2, a high net profit margin is one of Warren Buffett's requirements for investing in a company. On page 30, you learned that a company's net profit margin is determined by dividing the money left over after paying all its expenses by the amount of money it had before paying expenses. So, if a company makes $1 million and pays $900,000 in expenses, its net profit margin is 10 percent ($100,000 divided by $1,000,000).

Net profit margin is the first measurement on your sheet that looks beyond a company's size to the effectiveness of its operation. A management team that can maintain a high net profit margin in the midst of increasing competition is every investor's dream. This one number answers the question that gets to the heart of a company's capabilities: How much of its earnings does it keep?

On your worksheet, record the net profit margin and circle the up or down arrow based on the trend over the past five years. If the numbers aren't consistently increasing or decreasing, look at the change from five years ago and the projected figures for this year and next.

Required: Any company making your sheet should have a net profit margin in the top 20 percent of its industry. These are the leaders in their fields and where you want your money.

The reason I go with a relative value instead of an absolute value is that typical net profit margins change from industry to industry. Airlines generally have negative profit margins—I'm not kidding—and put in their business plans guidelines for declaring bankruptcy. Most commodity retailers such as supermarkets, auto parts stores, cheap clothing stores, and consumer electronics stores have net profit margins below 5 percent. I've seen some around 1 percent. For every dollar they sell, they keep a penny.

Companies with the highest net profit margins are those with exclusive rights to something, such as a brand-new database technology. If nobody else makes it, the company can charge whatever they want. Less competition, or no competition at all, allows prices to rise and profit margins to expand. As a consumer, you love *low* profit margins because they mean less money out of your pocket. As an investor, you love *high* profit margins because they mean more money out of customer pockets into company coffers. Sometimes it doesn't mean more money out of customer pockets. If the company is truly clever, the high net profit margin will come from cutting costs everywhere possible. That leads to a low price for the customer but more money kept by the company. Yes, you cynic, win-win situations are possible even in the business world.

I've met investors who insist on absolute minimum net profit margins, say 15 percent. That immediately keeps them from investing in Wal-Mart (3.8 percent), Nike (9.9 percent), and Ford (14.8 percent). But Apple passes with a net profit margin of 25.8 percent. Usually, people insisting on absolute profit margins are small cap investors, and the most common minimum is 10 percent.

If you decide in the course of your investment career that an absolute net profit margin makes sense among companies you consider, pencil it in above the column heading on your worksheet. There's nothing wrong with that. I've personally found that my portfolio holds companies of all stripes and I haven't been able to find a minimum net profit margin that fits them all. That's fine, too. There are lots of ways to make money in stocks.

Ideal: With net profit margin, bigger is always better. If you have a company on your sheet and encounter another in the same industry equal in all regards but net profit margin, strike the old company and add the new one. Sure, you'll want to look at how big the difference is and if the new company consistently boasts a higher margin, but you get the picture. Bigger is better, and a big net profit margin getting bigger every year is heaven.

Where to Find It: Both the Yahoo! Finance Stock Screener and the FINVIZ Stock Screener (page 195) enable you to group competitors by industry. You can then rank them by their net profit margins, seeing in seconds who's on top and who's not. Every financial site online shows net profit margin in single company profiles as well.

Look for a High Net Profit Margin

Cash and Total Debt

These two figures show you a company's health. The master investors in Chapter 3 teach that good companies have strong financial statements: high net profit margins, lots of cash, and little or no debt. You just finished reading about net profit margin. Now it's time to discuss cash and debt.

A company with a lot of cash can respond to business needs better than one with little cash. All a business does is buy things and sell them for more than they cost. It takes cash to buy things whether they're qualified employees, new equipment, supplies, marketing material, or even other companies. A business cannot have too much cash.

Debt, on the other hand, sucks a company dry. It eats up money that could otherwise go toward those employees, equipment, and supplies. If a business is forced to spend its money satisfying debt, then it can't spend as much strengthening its operation.

Ideal: We've already discussed cash and debt extensively, so I won't belabor the points here. Your companies should have a lot of cash, and little or no debt. We'll use ratios later in the worksheet to make sure the levels of cash and debt are acceptable.

Look for Lots of Cash and Little or No Debt

Where to Find It: Cash and debt are reported on a company's balance sheet. As with net profit margin, however, you can get what you need from *Value Line* as well. It lists cash assets and total debt.

You can also find the figures in stock databases and on the Internet.

Stock Health

You've got a pretty good picture of the company's health at this point. Let's take a closer look at the stock's health specifically. This section looks at seven great vital signs for every stock.

Sales per Share

You already know the importance of a company's sales. Now it's time to see that figure per share to understand how much you're paying for a piece of those sales.

In the sales discussion on page 212, I said there is no ideal sales figure. Because sales per share is simply sales divided by shares outstanding, there is still no ideal figure for sales per share. Small cap investors often prefer it small while large cap investors usually don't care except as it relates to price. We'll discuss that later in the price-to-sales ratio. For comparison's sake, let's break down the sales figures for the two companies in the sales discussion on page 212.

In 2012, Quicksilver Resources had sales of $960 million, while Coca-Cola had sales of $46 billion. Each company had shares outstanding of 169 million and 2.3 billion, respectively. Dividing the sales by the number of shares outstanding gives us a sales per share of $5.68 for Quicksilver and $20 for Coca-Cola.

On your worksheet, fill in the sales per share number and circle either the up or down arrow based on the trend over the past five years. If some years are up and others are down, you'll need to exercise judgment to decide whether it's an up or down trend. Compare the current number to five years ago. Is it bigger or smaller? Finally, look at projections. Is the company expected to report higher sales per share next year?

Required: For growth companies, list only those that have increased sales per share in each of the past five years and are projected to increase them again this year and next.

Ideal: While you will insist on five years of increasing sales per share in your growth companies, you want this number to have increased in each of the past five years for all companies. Even stocks that have been

Look for Increasing Sales per Share

hammered in price will occasionally show a history of increasing sales. Those are great bargains.

Where to Find It: *Value Line* prints sales per share for the past 15 years and projects the figure for this year and next. If you enjoy using your calculator, you could figure the number yourself by dividing sales by the number of shares outstanding.

Sales per share is also available on the Internet and in stock databases.

Cash Flow per Share	Cash Fl/ Share

As its name suggests, cash flow is the stream of money through a company. You want it to be positive and you'd love it to be big. A positive cash flow means the company is receiving in a timely fashion the profits that it's owed. It may come as a surprise to you that not every profitable company can boast a positive cash flow. Why? Because some companies sell their goods on credit. Let's say Mister Magazine, my stalwart subscription-selling company, came up with a promo that allowed people to try their new magazine subscriptions for six months before paying. That's great for business. Thousands of people would pile onto the Mister Magazine bandwagon and the company's accountants could put those promised subscription dollars on the books under "accounts receivable." At first glance, Mister Magazine appears to be flush with new profits.

And it will be—eventually. During the six-month lag time, lots of expenses need to be paid. There are the prizes to buy for the company's best sales reps, fliers to be printed, electricity bills, energy bars for the bicycle-based sales force, and so on. Where's the money going to come from? Not from the newly signed thousands of subscribers. They don't owe a dime for six months. If times get too tight, Mr. Mag might be swaggering its way to the local bank for a short-term loan. I won't even waste ink on how much you and I hate debt by now. The situation at Mister Magazine would be grim.

That's why you want to invest in companies with positive cash flow. They get paid as they sell. When the electric bill comes in, they cut a check from their profits. They don't need no darned bank because their businesses generate cash.

I like to see cash flow per share as opposed to cash flow for the whole company. Breaking this and other measures into their per share figures makes for easy comparisons and easily computed ratios. In this case, we'll eventually record the price-to-cash-flow ratio.

Let's look at some real-world figures for companies you know. In 1993, General Motors' cash flow per share was $12.06, Microsoft's was $0.12, and Nike's was $1.40. In 2008, GM's cash flow per share was -$7.05, down from a high of $32.32 in 1997 and $31.49 in 2004. The company's well-advertised business trouble in the recession was reflected in its cash flow per share. Little wonder the company sought a government bailout to survive. At least it worked. By early 2012, GM's cash flow per share had rebounded to $3.32.

Meanwhile, in 2008, Microsoft's cash flow per share was $2.16 but projected to be $2.05 in 2009 as it suffered lower demand for its products during the recession. Nike, too, hit hard times as its cash flow per share declined from $6.39 in 2006 to $4.53 in 2008. Microsoft rebounded to $3.45 in early 2012, but Nike languished at $3.84.

On your worksheet, fill in the cash flow per share and circle the up or down arrow based on the trend over the past five years. As with sales per share, use your own judgment to determine whether a company whose cash flow per share fluctuates up and down over the years is in an uptrend or a downtrend. Don't forget to look at projected cash flow per share when deciding on an arrow to circle.

Required: To make your list, a company must have a positive cash flow per share. For growth companies, list only those that have increased cash flow per share in each of the past five years and are projected to increase it again this year and next.

Ideal: For all companies, bigger is better and you prefer it to have increased over each of the past five years.

Look for Increasing
Cash Flow per
Share

Where to Find It: Cash flow is reported on, surprise of surprises, a company's statement of cash flows. It's one of the financial forms sent to you along with the balance sheet and income statement.

What we're searching for is cash flow per share. While you could figure it yourself by dividing the company's cash flow by the number of shares outstanding, it's easier to just get it from *Value Line*. Just below sales per share you'll find cash flow per share for the past 15 years along with projections for this year and next.

You'll also find the information in stock databases and on the Internet.

Earnings per Share

This is the most commonly cited per share measurement. It's the "E" part of the P/E ratio, the first yardstick almost every value investor examines to determine whether a stock is expensive or cheap. Before you can know the P/E ratio, you need to see the earnings per share. Also, you want to know whether earnings per share have been increasing or decreasing over time. Growth investors insist on an increasing earnings per share.

On your worksheet, fill in the earnings per share and circle the up or down arrow based on the past five years. For growth stocks, circle the up arrow only if earnings have increased in each of the past five years and are projected to increase this year and next. For value stocks, a super discount is often accompanied by a dip in earnings. Occasionally, however, something else hammers a stock's price and earnings remain constant or increase. In that case, you're really getting a bargain. With value stocks, use your judgment to decide on an up or down arrow based on whether the current number is an overall increase from five years ago, whether the increase is large or small, and by the projected earnings per share for this year and next.

Required: For growth companies, list only those that have increased earnings per share in each of the past five years and are projected to increase them again this year and next. This requirement is by definition. A growth company *is* a company that has been increasing earnings and should continue doing so. Just to be safe, though, I wanted to spell it out. If you are a growth investor, you'll invest only in companies that have the up arrow circled on your worksheet. In fact, the only companies that ever make it to your worksheet are ones with up arrows. It's a basic requirement for growth investors.

Ideal: While earnings increases are required for growth stocks, they're still nice among value stocks. For every stock, you prefer to see five years of earnings increases with projections for further increases this year and next.

Look for Increasing Earnings per Share

Where to Find It: Below cash flow per share and sales per share, *Value Line* prints earnings per share for the past 15 years along with projections for this year and next. In two seconds, you can get all three of these measurements from one place. That's the kind of research I like.

Once again, you can find this information in stock databases and on the Internet.

Dividend Yield

You read a lot about this measure in Chapters 3 and 4. A high dividend yield is the deciding factor used in the Dow dividend strategies and was proven to work among large companies in James O'Shaughnessy's study of stock market history. It's a very important figure to large-company investors.

Small-company investors ignore dividend yield because small companies don't usually declare dividends and therefore have yields of zero. The measure is neither a thumbs up nor thumbs down on a company that declares no dividend. It's a solid thumbs sideways, totally meaningless. Thus, if you're a small-company investor, you'll leave this column blank on your worksheet.

On your worksheet, record the dividend yield. You'll notice there are two sets of arrows in this column. Circle the up or down arrow on the left based on the past five years. As with the other measures in this section, use your judgment to decide on an arrow. If the current dividend yield is substantially larger than it was five years ago and is larger than it was last year, that's an uptrend. Dips along the way are common. Circle the up or down arrow on the right based only on whether the current dividend yield is larger or smaller than last year.

Ideal: In general, you want to buy large companies with high dividend yields.

To split hairs over this, you prefer to invest when the overall dividend yield has been decreasing but the change from last year to now has shown a remarkable increase. On your worksheet, this translates to the left down arrow circled and the right up arrow circled. Such a situation could indicate a stock that has been growing in price over the past few years, but took a quick fall recently. Notice that this is ideal, not required. I haven't tested this or confirmed it with anybody else. I merely read James O'Shaughnessy's findings in Chapter 3 and looked at how the Dow dividend strategies work. Judging from those two sources,

Large Companies Should Have High Dividend Yields

this treatment of dividend yield among large companies makes sense. Keep it in mind, but don't let it cloud the tried-and-true technique of choosing large companies with high dividend yields.

Remember, ignore dividend yield among small companies.

Where to Find It: *Value Line* prints the average annual dividend yield for the past 16 years along with projections for this year and next. The measure is of such importance to investors that *Value Line* prints the current dividend yield at the top of the page.

You will also find current dividend yield listed in the stock tables of most newspapers, in stock databases, and on the Internet.

Return on Equity

As you read on page 34, return on equity shows you what a company has earned with the money people have invested in it. You simply divide net income by total shareholders' equity to come up with a percentage. For example, if a company reports net income of $8 million and total shareholders' equity of $40 million, its return on equity is 20 percent. For those who are very tired right now, 8 divided by 40 equals .20, or 20 percent. Warren Buffett likes this measurement because it gives a clear picture of what a company does with its profits. If a company gets bigger every year, it will probably earn more money. But investors should ask, does it earn enough additional money to support its larger size? Return on equity answers that. If a company can maintain a high return on equity as it grows, you know that management is directing profits wisely.

Although there is no requirement for ROE, I like to see ROEs of at least 20 percent maintained or improved over the years. Occasionally, value investors will accept low or negative ROEs in companies they think are about to make a change for the better.

Look for a High Return on Equity

Ideal: Twenty percent is a solid return on equity. Of course, bigger is better. If you're bargain hunting, you might accept a low or even negative ROE from time to time. That should be quite rare, however. For the most part, you want a company that continues returning substantial profits to investors. A steady ROE will reveal that.

Where to Find It: Net income is reported on a company's income statement; total shareholders' equity is reported on a company's balance sheet. You'll receive both of these financial statements in the investor kit mailed to you from the company. You would never invest in a company without seeing these statements first. Remember, you're a professional now.

Also, ROE is in most stock databases and on the Internet.

**Insider
Buys/Ownership**

Remember that our master investors like to see insider owner-ship of a company. If the people who run the place have a mate-rial interest in its success, they're more likely to do a better job. To that end, you want to own companies that are owned by insiders.

It's worth repeating that you shouldn't pay attention to in-sider sells. People raise money all the time for needs ranging from housing down payments to exotic vacations. Sale of stock is not necessarily a comment on the seller's belief in the stock's future. It might just be a need for cash.

A key insider buy is what lead me to watch Sun Microsystems for a good opportunity in 2002. Bill Joy, one of Sun's cofounders, sold more than one million shares of Sun at prices between $74 and $87 in the year 2000. The technology bubble popped and Sun plummeted to earth. He waited a couple years and then bought one million shares on July 29, 2002, at prices between $3.93 and $4.01 per share. The only reason he bought shares of his com-pany's stock is that he thought it was undervalued and would eventually go up. When Bill Joy bought again, I researched Sun and concluded that it faced serious challenges, mainly from Microsoft, but that it was a survivor and would be able to parlay its $3 billion in cash to a good recovery. I monitored the stock. It dropped below Joy's buy price, eventually reaching $2.34 in October 2002. I bought one lot at $2.56, another at $2.96, and a third at $3.23. The stock rose 168 percent to its 2007 high before crashing with everything else in 2008. It was acquired by Oracle in 2010.

On your worksheet, write the number of insider buys over the past year and the percentage of insider ownership.

Ideal: The more insider ownership, the better. You can't have too many insiders buying shares of their own company. For small cap investors, insider ownership is of particular importance because a lot of small companies are just starting out and management is a crucial factor in their success. The founder and president probably knows how to run the machines, answer the phones, and respond to customer complaints. You want that person to own a stake in the company. I like small companies to have at least 20 percent insider ownership.

Where to Find It: *Value Line* prints a chart of insider decisions to buy and sell. It lists the numbers for each month over the past year. Simply add up the buy decisions and write the number on your worksheet. In a business overview box in the middle of each company's page, *Value Line* often prints the percentage of the company that officers and directors own.

Insider ownership is also reported in *The Wall Street Journal*, *Investor's Business Daily*, and *Barron's*. However, it's rare for one of the publications to be covering a company you just happen to be interested in. To find insider ownership for a company you're researching, the quickest path is a call to the company itself. You'll be calling to request an investor packet anyway and can ask the representative about insider ownership.

Websites such as J3SG focus on insider activity. FINVIZ provides a rundown of recent insider transactions on company profile pages. Finally, Yahoo! Finance keeps an insider page for every public company. It shows who's buying and selling, how many shares, when, and at what price. That's where I discovered that Bill Joy was buying shares of Sun Microsystems.

Stock Buyback

It's great to see a company buying its stock back. There will be fewer shares outstanding, which improves the supply-demand ratio and should increase the share price eventually. Also, as Peter Lynch wrote, "If a company buys back half its shares and its overall earnings stay the same, the earnings per share have just doubled. Few companies could get that kind of result by cutting costs or selling more widgets." You want to see your companies buying back shares of their stock.

Simply write the word *yes* or *no* in this column of your worksheet. Make sure if you write yes that it's a significant enough buyback program to earn a yes. If the company bought back a few token shares one time, that hardly qualifies as a stock buyback program. Use your judgment.

Ideal: You want a *yes* in this column.

Where to Find It: The best place to find out about a stock buy-back program is from the company itself. Contact the company by calling Investor Relations or browsing the company website.

Past Performance

After seeing the current health of the stock, it's a good idea to take a peek at how it's fared in the past. This section shows four measurements that tell you.

 EPS Rank

A company's earnings per share drives just about everything related to the stock. By now you know that. EPS rank looks at a company's earnings record and compares it to the earnings record of all other companies to see how the company stacks up. It's a quick way to see which companies are earnings machines and which are earnings accidents.

EPS rank is printed every day in *Investor's Business Daily*. The paper takes each company's earnings per share for the two most recent quarters and computes their percentage change from the same two quarters a year ago. That result is combined and averaged with each company's five-year earnings growth record. The final figures for every company are compared with each other, giving each company a rank from 1 to 99, with 99 being the best. Thus, a company with an EPS rank of 95 has earnings figures in the top 5 percent of all companies in the tables.

This measure is of most interest to growth investors because they look for consistently strong earnings and for the company to exceed expectations. Value investors like earnings, too, but they'll often buy a company with struggling earnings if it means the stock is enough of a bargain.

Required: Growth investors should insist on companies that have an EPS rank of 85 or better. Value investors have no requirement for this measure because they'll accept lower earnings if it means a bargain stock with a chance of recovery.

Ideal: For growth investors, bigger is better.

Growth Investors: Look for High EPS

Where to Find It: *Investor's Business Daily* prints every stock's EPS rank each day. How's that for convenient? Simply locate your stock in the tables and see its rank from 1 to 99 in the column titled EPS. A stock with a rank of 85 has earnings results in the top 15 percent of all companies.

Relative Price Strength Rank

This measure looks at the stock's price performance in the latest 12 months. That's it. It doesn't look at stories, earnings, or price ratios. It simply reports the hard numbers and answers the question, how did this stock perform compared with all others?

Investor's Business Daily updates the numbers daily, compares all stocks to each other, and ranks them from 1 to 99, with 99 being the best. That means a company with a relative price strength of 90 outperformed 90 percent of all other stocks in the past year.

As with EPS rank, relative price strength rank is of most interest to growth investors. Momentum investing, a strict growth discipline, requires investment in companies that have done well and should continue that momentum to do well in the future. So, a high EPS rank combined with a high relative strength rank could indicate a stock on a roll. Maybe even an ace in the hole.

Required: Growth investors should restrict themselves to stocks with a relative strength rank of at least 80. Value investors have no requirement for relative price strength because it would preclude bargain companies.

Ideal: For growth investors, bigger is better.

Where to Find It: *Investor's Business Daily* prints every stock's relative price strength each day. Just find your stock in the tables and record its rank from 1 to 99 on your worksheet. The column is titled "RelStr." A stock with a relative strength rank of 80 has outperformed 80 percent of all other stocks in the past year.

Growth Investors: Look for High RPS

Five-Year Sales and Earnings Gain

You've already found the company's sales per share in the Stock Health section of your worksheet. Now you're going to find its average annual gain for sales and earnings over the past five years. Our requirement for growth companies is to have increased sales and earnings in each of the past five years. Here we find out by how much.

With small companies especially, strong sales and earnings are essential. The typical requirement is for them to have grown at least 25 percent over the past year. We are looking at five-year history here. I like small companies to have five-year average annual sales and earnings increases of at least 15 percent. For larger companies, I accept nothing lower than 10 percent.

Want some real-world perspective? In 1999, General Motors' earnings per share were $9.18, Nike's were $0.79, and Microsoft's were $0.71. In 2004, GM's were $4.95, Nike's were $1.76, and Microsoft's were $0.75. In 2008, GM's were -$38.74 and had been negative since 2005, Nike's were $3.74, and Microsoft's were $1.87. In 2011, Nike and Microsoft earned $4.48 and $2.69, respectively, showing good recoveries from the recession.

About GM, *Value Line* analyst Jason A. Smith wrote in February 2009, "Amid languishing sales and record losses, the automaker is burning through cash at an alarming and clearly unsustainable pace. . . . These shares are too risky an investment at this juncture." He was right. GM declared bankruptcy in June 2009, which wiped out the investments of common shareholders. It emerged from Chapter 11 in July 2010 and was re-listed on the

New York Stock Exchange the following November. It earned
$4.58 per share in 2011.

Required: Look for companies that have grown both sales and
earnings an average of at least 10 percent a year over the past
five years. For small companies, require 15 percent.

**Look for Increasing
Sales and Earnings**

Ideal: For those who like to see a strong history of sales and earnings, bigger is better.
Count me and a lot of others in that camp.
There are some who look for weak sales and
earnings records in hopes of finding a turn-
around, but that approach makes me queasy.
It forces you to buy into an industry's worst
competitors instead of the best. I say stick
with strong sales and earnings even if you're a value investor.

Where to Find It: *Value Line* prints both sales and earnings growth
per share for the past 5 and 10 years in a small box titled
"Annual Rates" on the left side of each profile page.

You can also find the measure on the Internet and in stock
databases.

**Five-Year Price
Appreciation**

This one's simple enough. You just want to see how much the
stock price has changed over the past five years. I take the high
price from five years ago and compare it with the current price.
To compute the percentage change, you can use the "% CHG"
button on your handy business calculator or just do it manually.
For you manual types, divide the current price by the high price
from five years ago. Subtract 1 from the difference to get the percentage change. For example, say Mister Magazine traded at
a high of $22 five years ago and is trading at $95 today. Divide
95 by 22 to get 4.32. Subtract 1 to get 3.32, or a 332 percent
increase.

There's no rule for this number. A lot of value investors prefer
to see a decrease from five years ago. Growth investors won't

touch a stock that has lost money in the past five years. Regardless of your preference, it's good to know what happened to a stock in the past five years.

Where to Find It: *Value Line* prints the high and low stock price for the past 16 years at the top of each profile page. You can also get a recent trading price at the top of the *Value Line* page. For a stock's current trading price, check the stock tables in a newspaper or get a quote from the Internet. For historical quotes, see a stock's "Historical Prices" section at Yahoo! Finance.

Projected Performance

After seeing the stock's current health and how it has fared in the past, take a look at projected performance. This section uses two measurements from *Value Line*: projected sales and earnings, and projected stock high/low price.

Sales and Earnings

It's our old friends again. Sales and earnings comprise the lifeblood of a company and have more influence on a stock's price than any other measures. It makes sense to see how they're projected to grow in the next five years.

I look for companies that are expected to grow by double digits. I get stricter as company size gets smaller because small companies should be growing faster than large ones.

Required: Large companies should be expected to grow at least 10 percent a year, medium companies at least 15 percent, and small companies at least 20 percent.

Ideal: Bigger is better.

Where to Find It: *Value Line* prints the five-year projected rates of change for both sales and earnings in the same place you found results for the past five years. It's a box titled "Annual Rates" on the left side of the page.

Look for High Projected Sales

There are lots of other places to find earnings projections, including publications from Standard and Poor's, information from companies themselves, subscription newsletters, and the Internet. Because you're already using *Value Line* for so much of your other information, it's convenient to rely on its projections.

Projected Stock
High/Low

Want to see just how much money you stand to gain? This is the measure. It relies on projections, of course, and those are never guaranteed. But analysts spend their lives trying to be accurate and it never hurts to see what they expect to happen. This measure simply records the projected high and low stock price for the next three to five years.

Required: Both the high and low price projections must be bigger than the current price. Life-changing tip: Never invest in a stock that's expected to fall in price. Also, make sure the low projection represents a worthwhile gain. If the stock is currently trading at $50 and the three- to five-year projected low price is $55, why bother?

Ideal: Bigger is better for both the high and low.

Look for High Projected Prices

Where to Find It: I'm sure it'll come as a shock to learn that *Value Line* prints a company's three- to five-year projected high and low price. The numbers are in a box titled "(Years) Projections" on the upper left corner of the page, where "years" is the three to five range. For instance, in 2012 the title read "2014–16 Projections."

You'll also find projections on the Internet.

Rankings

Professional rankings are a quick way to see what others think of a company you're considering. The two Grand Pooh-Bah's of stock rankings are *Value Line* and Standard and Poor's. You'll record rankings from each of the two on your worksheet.

Value Line
Timeliness/Safety

The folks at *Value Line* are nice enough to provide three rankings for every stock, two of which we'll use. Each is on a scale from 1 to 5, with 1 being the best. Timeliness is a prediction of how well the stock should perform relative to all other stocks in the next 12 months. Safety is a measure of a stock's volatility as compared to its own long-term record. If a stock continually trades in a tiny range, it is considered safe and receives a better rating, say a 1 or 2. If the stock fluctuates widely from its historical average, it receives a rating of 4 or 5.

Required: I pay a lot more attention to the timeliness rank than the safety. In many cases, I actually prefer a wider trading history because it means there's a better chance the stock will rise. That translates into a poor safety rating, perhaps a 4 or 5. If a company is poised for tremendous things, I want it to break from its historical average. So take the safety rating with a grain of salt, unless you're looking for steady dividend payers and don't want much fluctuation in the stock value.

As for timeliness, limit yourself to stocks with ranks of 1 or 2. Nobody ever complains about a stock that rises in price.

Ideal: For timeliness, look for stocks ranked 1. There's no ideal for safety because some investors want volatility while others do not.

**Look for a
Timeliness of 1 or 2**

Where to Find It: *Value Line* prints timeliness and safety in a box at the upper left corner of each profile page. You can't miss them.

S&P STARS/
Fair Value

The Standard & Poor's STARS and fair value rankings are used to select stocks for the S&P platinum portfolio, which consists of S&P's favorite stocks. Now you'll gather both measurements for individual stocks you select.

Standard & Poor's uses its STARS system to predict a stock's potential over the next 12 months. STARS stands for Stock Appreciation Ranking System, and classifies stocks from 1 to 5, with 5 being the best. I know, it's a bummer that *Value Line* makes 1 the best and S&P makes 5 the best. Try this: Stars are in the sky and 5 is the highest number. Both are upward. That's a quick association to remember what S&P STARS strives for.

Fair value is a rank of the stock's recent trading price compared to what S&P considers its fair value. We'd all prefer to buy stocks at a price way below their fair value. Therefore, S&P ranks all stocks on the handy 1 to 5 scale, with 5 again being the best. That means stocks with a fair value rank of 5 are the most undervalued—bargains—and stocks with a fair value rank of 1 are overvalued—rip-offs. Well, they might not be rip-offs but they are selling at a price considerably higher than S&P thinks they're worth. In politically correct terms, they're value challenged.

Required: Limit yourself to stocks that are ranked 4 or 5 in each S&P ranking. That keeps you in stocks expected to be among the best performers and reduces your risk because you're buying in at a price below their estimated value. That's Graham's old margin of safety again. If the stock's already below its value, then it probably won't go much lower. That's the idea at least.

Ideal: Best of all is a stock ranked 5 STARS and with a fair value rank of 5. That combination, by the way, is what the platinum portfolio requires for a stock to enter. So, for a quick list of stocks that are ranked high in both categories, take a look at the S&P platinum portfolio list.

Look for S&P Rankings of 4 or 5

Where to Find It: The easiest place to find periodic lists of companies that are ranked high in both STARS and fair value is *The Outlook*, a weekly newsletter from Standard & Poor's. You can find it in most libraries, and some brokers supply it free to clients.

Stock Ratios

Only now are we getting to the stuff you'll hear most often on a public bus, or at a lunch meeting, or in the bleachers at Little League. Here are seven stock ratios to give you all the ammunition you need to defend your stock portfolio.

Current Price-to-Earnings Current P/E

Here it is at last—the granddaddy of valuation measures. Your reading in Chapter 3 should have convinced you that P/E is not the be-all and end-all of stock measures. In fact, P/S has proven itself more telling of a company's prospects. Nonetheless, P/E is so widely followed that you should know it for each of your stocks. It's the easiest measure in the world to find, second only to the stock price itself.

To recap from page 31, P/E is simply the stock price divided by the earnings per share. It shows you how much you're paying for each dollar of the company's earnings. Value investors want to pay as little as they can for each dollar of earnings; growth investors don't care very much. William O'Neil doesn't even look at P/E in his portfolio. Peter Lynch does, however. In *One Up on Wall Street* he writes:

> The P/E ratio of any company that's fairly priced will equal its growth rate. I'm talking about growth rate of earnings here. . . . If the P/E of Coca-Cola is 15, you'd expect the company to be growing at about 15 percent a year, etc. But if the P/E ratio is less than the growth rate, you may have found yourself a bargain. A company, say, with a growth rate of 12 percent a year and a P/E ratio of 6 is a very attractive prospect. On the other hand, a company with a growth rate of 6 percent a year and a P/E ratio of 12 is an unattractive prospect and headed for a comedown.
>
> In general, a P/E ratio that's half the growth rate is very positive, and one that's twice the growth rate is very negative. We use this measure all the time in analyzing stocks for the mutual funds.

I'd like to toss in another popular filter for value companies. The current P/E should be at or below the five-year average P/E. That keeps you from buying in just after the company has broken into higher trading territory. Sometimes a company will steadily improve its position, however, and its P/E will rise along with its growth rate. That's a positive sign for the company and you wouldn't want to overlook it simply because its current P/E is higher than its average. Therefore, we'll make this an ideal P/E condition instead of a required one.

For your value companies, keep a close eye on P/E. For your growth companies, write the P/E on your worksheet but don't let it affect your decision very much. There are more important measures for growth investing.

Value Investors: Look for a Low P/E

Required: For value companies, P/E must equal the earnings growth rate.

Ideal: For value companies, the lower the P/E, the better. As Lynch points out, a P/E that's half the earnings growth is a very positive sign. A P/E that's below the five-year average P/E is another positive sign.

Where to Find It: P/E is listed in the stock tables of most newspapers. *Value Line* considers P/E important enough to print it at the top of each company page. You can also find P/E ratios all over the Internet and in stock databases.

Both the numbers you'll compare to P/E are on your worksheet. Projected earnings is listed in the Projected Performance section. Average P/E is listed next.

Average Price-to-Earnings

Just after you pencil in the current P/E, take a moment to compute the average P/E for the past five years. Simply add up the five average annual P/E ratios and divide by five. Write the figure on your worksheet.

Knowing this number will let you see how the current P/E measures up to the stock's recent trading levels. As I just mentioned in the discussion on P/E, it's nice to have a current P/E that's less than the average for the past five years.

Ideal: You'd like the average P/E to be higher than the current P/E.

Where to Find It: *Value Line* lists the average annual P/E ratio for the past 16 years. You'll also find it in most stock databases.

Price-to-Sales   P/S

The price-to-sales ratio is catching on as investors recognize its superiority over P/E for valuing stocks. P/S is often a more accurate measure of a company's value because sales can't be manipulated as easily as earnings. Also, the measure helps even growth investors identify companies that are selling below their potential. Even growth companies are best purchased cheap.

At this point, you have the information you need to compute P/S from your worksheet. Simply divide the current stock price by the sales per share. That's it. Write the figure on your worksheet. If one of your stocks is selling for $72 per share and is expected to report sales per share of $47.65 this year, its P/S ratio is 1.51 ($72 divided by $47.65).

Ideal: For all companies except utilities, smaller is better. You want to pay as little as possible for the sales the company generates. I like to stay with a ratio below 2 but this is an ideal, not a requirement. Sometimes companies that are growing quickly show high P/S ratios but their share prices keep rising. History suggests, however, that a low P/S is a good sign.

Where to Find It: Because you have share price and sales per share on your worksheet, you can figure P/S yourself with a calculator. Simply divide share price by sales per share.

The Internet is another source of share price and sales per share. Some sites even list a company's P/S ratio for you. You'll also find P/S in most stock databases.

Popular magazines, such as *SmartMoney*

**Look for Low
Price-to-Sales**

and *Kiplinger's*, sometimes list P/S in tables summarizing potential stocks.

Price-to-Book P/B

As you read on page 30, price-to-book compares a stock's price to how much the stock is worth right now if somebody liquidated the company. It's the second most common valuation measure following price-to-earnings. It tells how much you're paying for the actual assets of the company.

In truth, P/B isn't worth much to me. I care a lot more about a company's use of its equipment to earn money than I do about the auction value of that equipment. If I really wanted to get the most equipment for my money, I'd go to the auction myself. I want the skill of human beings to turn the output of equipment into profit. That's the point of investing.

However, it is nice to see that if everything crumbles at the company you'll still get your money back. Growth investors don't care at all about P/B, but value investors like to see it less than 1. That means they're paying less for the company than it would fetch at auction.

Ideal: Smaller is better. A P/B of 1 means you're paying the auction price for a company. A P/B less than 1 means you're paying less than auction price. Benjamin Graham recommended investing in companies with a P/B less than .66. They were almost impossible to find during the bull market of the 1990s but became plentiful in the 2008 crash. I found 3,099 of them with a stock scan run in February 2009. In February 2012, I found just 1,805. That's what recoveries do to stock valuations.

Look for Low Price-to-Book

Where to Find It: Book value per share is computed from numbers on a company's balance sheet. Simply divide common stockholders' equity by the number of outstanding shares. Then, divide the stock's current price by its book value.

If you'd rather pluck out all your eyelashes than compute P/B on your own, you're not alone. Luckily *Value Line* prints book value per share for the past 16 years. You can also find P/B in stock databases and on the Internet.

Current Ratio

As you read on page 26, the current ratio is the most popular gauge of a company's short-term liquidity. It's the current assets divided by the current liabilities. That's it. It's usually expressed in the number of "times," as in the current ratio is three times. That would mean the company has three times as many assets as liabilities, which is good news. Perhaps the company has $300,000 in assets and only $100,000 in liabilities. The more assets a company has in relation to its liabilities, the better it's able to handle ugly surprises. Why? Simply because it owns more than it owes—a situation everybody prefers. Run the numbers, then write the current ratio on your worksheet.

Required: Every company on your sheet should have a current ratio of at least 2 (two times and 2-to-1 are other ways of saying the same measure).

Ideal: Bigger is better.

Where to Find It: Assets and liabilities are on a company's balance sheet. However, because we love *Value Line* so much by now, we'll just use the numbers printed there. Halfway down each profile on the left side of the page is a box called "Current Position." In there you'll find current assets and current liabilities. As usual, the current ratio is on the Internet and in most stock databases.

Look for High Current Ratios

Price-to-Cash-Flow

As you read on page 33, this measurement shows how much you're paying for a share of the company's cash flow, the stream of cash left over after it pays expenses. Back in Chapter 2, Bill Miller called this "the single best predictor of excess return." It's easy to see why. Healthy businesses generate cash, and cold hard cash requires no explanation. It's ready for spending without sales or conversions or convincing people of its worth. Remember that another way of saying low P/CF is high cash flow yield.

Ideal: Smaller is better because it means you're paying less for a share of the company's cash flow. I like to see a P/CF of less than 5, but that's just a rough guideline because the typical figure varies widely for different types of companies. One way to get around that is to look for companies with a current P/CF below their three- or five-year average P/CF.

Where to Find It: You already show cash flow per share on your worksheet. Just divide the current price by it to get P/CF. For three- and five-year averages, turn to *Value Line*. It shows past prices along with cash flow per share. You'll also find the figures on the Internet and in stock databases, and even the current and past P/CF ratios calculated for you. The FINVIZ and Morningstar stock screeners in the last chapter offer P/CF as a searchable criterion.

Look for Low Price-to-Cash-Flow

SMA, MACD, and RSI

These three technical measures are explained on pages 142 to 147. There, we looked at how to use them to limit or avoid the downside of our permanent portfolios, but they are available on charts of any stock you're considering and will help you understand its price trend.

You'll need to look at a chart with all three measures and decide for yourself what their combined message tells you. This is subjective, of course. For my worksheet, I use five labels to describe a clear trend: "Strong Up," "Up," "Sideways," "Down," and "Strong Down." Sometimes there's a trend change under way. If the chart shows the stock turning down, I write "Breakdown." If it shows the stock turning up, I write "Breakout." Use whatever words work for you. The point of the column on the worksheet is to characterize the technical picture of the stock so you can see how it stacks up to others on your sheet.

Required: Buy stocks in a strong uptrend or a breakout.

Ideal: The stronger the uptrend or the clearer the breakout, the better.

Where to Find It: Most financial websites provide charts that can add SMA, MACD, and RSI. I like the ones at Yahoo! Finance and StockCharts.com.

Track Your List

Now you know how to use the Stocks to Watch worksheet. It's your built-in filter that keeps your money away from hot tips and cold losses. Quite simply, whenever you encounter an investment idea, compare it with the companies on your list. If the new idea is better, strike one of the existing companies and add the new one. This process keeps your list of ideas streamlined and ready for action when opportunity presents itself.

Now let's look at four techniques you should use to track your list. Always compare competitors, ask why, store company information in folders, and keep the information current.

Compare Competitors

There's no better way to judge a company than by looking at its closest competitors. When a friend of mine decided to buy Dell in 1994, she did so because she thought it was competing well against IBM, Compaq, and Gateway. Later, she sold at a hefty profit, then watched the industry change. She saw Hewlett-Packard buy Compaq, IBM sell its PC business to Lenovo, and then Dell lose ground to Hewlett-Packard. Dell's shares hit $42 in December 2004, then fell dramatically to less than $20 by July 2006, when my friend began buying for the 50 percent rise to $30 in October 2007, before the stock fell 74 percent to its March 2009 low at $8. It bounced 125 percent to $18 in Feburary 2012. Notice that through this long history, she didn't compare Dell with Ford or MCI and she didn't choose it in a vacuum. It's critical to know where your investments stack up in their industries.

When you invest in a company, you want it to be either the best of breed or the best poised for recovery. You don't want just any computer company, you want IBM in the 1970s and Microsoft in the 1990s. You don't want just any milkshake stand, you want McDonald's in the 1960s. You don't want just any retail shop, you want the beaten-down RadioShack in June 2006 when its shares were less than $15 and it began a brilliant turnaround plan that doubled the stock in a year. The way you find the best of breed or the best recovery story is by looking among competitors.

If you're interested in McDonald's, conduct research on Jack in the Box, Wendy's, and Yum! Brands, owner of KFC, Pizza Hut, and Taco Bell. In the five years ended early 2012, both McDonald's and Yum! gained more than 130 percent, Jack in the Box lost 33 percent, and Wendy's lost 74 percent. If you want Wal-Mart, don't forget to look at Costco, Kohl's, and Target. Your favorite breakfast cereal might be from Kellogg, but don't invest in the company until you've read up on General Mills. If everybody's raving about Barnes & Noble, take a peek at Amazon. Compare profit margins. Who keeps more of every dollar they sell? If the winner has been consistent, that's a good sign. If one company keeps its head above the rest year after year, that's the one you want to buy. If one has been dominated by rivals for a long time but looks poised for a comeback, make sure it has what it takes to succeed.

How do the ratios compare? You might pay a lot more for each dollar of sales at one company than at another. You might find that one company's management owns half of all the stock while another company's management doesn't invest a dime in their own company. Maybe one company's return on equity is twice that of its nearest competitor. Perhaps every company in an industry carries a lot of debt, except for one little gem. Does that little gem shine in other areas as well? If so, you might have found a new entry for your worksheet.

Sometimes you'll find a better option than the company first grabbing your attention.

Occasionally, you'll reach a stalemate and decide to split your money between two companies. Owning more than one company from the same industry is an especially good technique if it means you own the entire industry. For instance, investors buying shares of both Advanced Micro Devices and Intel will benefit no matter which computer chip is in their next PC. In 2008 and 2009, shares in both companies became cheap. In the next few years, AMD gained 320 percent and Intel gained 120 percent.

If you don't already know a company's prime competitors, you'll find them quickly as you conduct research. Check the Industry Center on Yahoo! Finance. Articles will mention them. Sometimes you'll find competitors mentioned in annual reports or quarterly statements. If worse comes to worst, you can always call a company's Investor Relations Department and ask who the competitors are. If they hesitate, tell them you're organizing a boycott against all industry players except them and that you need a list of targets. That should get you some info.

Ask Why

As an investor, always question why a company's numbers are the way they are. Why is cash flow so low right now when it's been high in prior years? Perhaps you'll find in reading further into the annual report that the company is expanding overseas and has decided to create very flexible payment terms to attract new customers. If there's enough cash on hand to stay afloat while the new customers discover the company, the low cash flow is fine for a while.

Asking why is central to every investment decision. Growth investors want to know why a company is growing so quickly. They use that information to decide if the reason will maintain that growth in the future. Value investors always want to know why a company's price is depressed. If it's for a reason that won't go away any time soon, nobody should invest. If it's for a reason that is disappearing, now might be the time to get in before the price rebounds to its former glory.

Beyond a general understanding of your companies—which you should always possess—you need to exercise a lot of personal judgment when investing. If a company appears good in every regard on your worksheet except for one, say five-year earnings gain, you need to know why that earnings gain has lagged and whether it's an acceptable explanation. Only you can answer such questions for your portfolio. These measurements aren't fool-proof. There are millions of children with poor grades who achieve spectacular success in life. There is probably a better chance of finding successful people among the high grade earners, but that doesn't mean we should brush off the low grade earners. It works the same with stocks. For the most part, you should stick with those that shine on your worksheet. However, in some cases your better judgment will lead you to overrule the worksheet's verdict. Every investment rule gets broken from time to time.

For instance, I read several hand-wringing articles about Mc-Donald's in early 2003. The company's stock had fallen steadily from $45 three years earlier to $15 at the beginning of 2003, then kept falling to less than $13 in March of that year. An article in the March 3, 2003, *Business Week* titled "McDonald's Ham-burger Hell" described the company as "a reeling giant that tee-ters from one mess to another" with a system that was "losing traction," and claimed that "investors have already accepted that the growth days are over." The measurement most worrisome to analysts was a declining profit margin that produced the com-pany's first quarterly loss ever. As you know by now, profit margin shows how skillful management is at turning as much revenue into profit as possible. Bigger is better, but Mickey D's margin was ramping down, not up, due to its "addiction to dis-counting," according to *Business Week*. The margin fell from 11.9 percent in 2001 to 11 percent in 2002, and was projected to keep falling in 2003.

A red flag? Sure, but there was more information to consider. A successful former McDonald's executive came out of retire-ment to lead a recovery by focusing on the founding principles of service and quality rather than just cheapness. Sales were rising even as earnings declined, and the P/E was down from 30 in 1999 to less than 14 in early 2003. Would you have given McDonald's the benefit of the doubt that management could get its profit margin back on track to keep more of its growing sales as profit? You'd have been glad if you had. It traded above $100 in early 2012, sported a 3 percent dividend yield, and achieved a profit margin greater than 20 percent. CEO Jim Skinner said on the January 2012 conference call with investors that "with a 35 percent total return for investors, McDonald's was the number one performing company on the Dow for the one- and five-year periods ending in 2011. . . . I'm confident in our business strategies and the opportunities for growth that lie ahead." Forgiving the poor trend back in 2003 was the right move.

Having written that, I must underscore the need to be prudent. Remember O'Shaughnessy's conclusions after studying the history of the stock market. Certain stories play out again and again and again. Your worksheet uses proven stock measurements. If you are going to overrule what they say about a company, you'd better have a darned good reason for doing so and be able to explain it in a heartbeat. That's why this section instructs you to ask why. In asking why, you'll find the answers you need to make wise decisions. There's a story behind all those numbers. Make sure you've read it.

Store Company Information in Folders

Once you've decided to add a company to your worksheet, start a folder for it. Place in the folder all the research material you used to convince yourself that the company is worthwhile. Your folders will contain annual reports, financial statements, photocopied pages from *Value Line* and Standard & Poor's, printouts from the Internet, notes to yourself, clipped magazine articles and newspaper stories, and maybe even a photo of you in front of corporate headquarters or using the company product.

Whenever you run across additional information about your companies, add it to their folders. Over time you'll build your own investment research center. By opening your file cabinet and flipping through the alphabetized folders, you can remind yourself of why you like the companies on your list.

Keep the Information Current

Always keep your worksheet current. Update the information on it at least every quarter. It doesn't take long to do so and the small effort will reveal valuable trends. There's a tendency to research a company one time and then rely on the results of that research for months, even years. Bad idea. Some of the best investments come about by finding good companies and then watching them for the right opportunity. If a company is perfect in all regard but stock price and that price drops by 50 percent just when sales are beginning to increase, you better start buying.

Similarly, good companies can go bad. Just because a company was good enough to make your list a year ago doesn't automatically mean it gets to stay there. This isn't a tenured membership. Your companies need to undergo constant scrutiny and comparison to eager wannabes. You can't make fair comparisons unless you have current information. Remember my friend who invested in Dell. She needed to watch it carefully over the years to understand that the company in 1995 was completely different from the company in 2005. Understanding that was crucial to her knowing when to sell after the amazing gains of the 1990s, when to buy again at bargain prices in 2006, when to sell in late 2007, ahead of the crash of 2008, and when to buy again in early 2009 for the smart recovery.

You found the information once and should have a file folder for every company on your worksheet. To refresh the info, make a quarterly trip back to your library or go online to gather the information again. Refreshing your worksheet goes faster than finding the information the first time.

Use Your Reasons and Limits Worksheet

Once you've got a list of solid companies to work with, it's time to begin homing in on the select few you'll actually invest in. Here's where you need to make value and growth distinctions. Chances are good that you'll have some companies on your list that are beaten down in price, others that are pushing new highs and record earnings. My list always breaks down that way. My experience has never produced a list of growth companies only or a list of value companies only. I suppose if I insisted on a pure list, I could set out to find companies of one type or the other, but the natural tendency produces a mix.

By now you know that it's important to treat value investments differently than how you treat growth investments. One of the most common differences is the way you should view the P/E ratio. In a high-flying growth stock, you'll pay less attention to P/E and more attention to earnings and relative strength.

In a recovering value stock, you'll pay a lot of attention to P/E and price-to-book while accepting poor earnings and—by definition—a weak relative strength because the stock price will be depressed.

The Stocks to Watch worksheet doesn't cater to one side over the other. It isn't a pure growth play or a pure value play and no strict investor from either discipline would find the sheet useful. It's a 30,000-foot view of the land, allowing you to see different-colored fields but few of the plants growing there. It's relatively simple to look at a company's major characteristics and decide whether it's a growth or value bet. Once we've determined that, it's another simple task to focus on key measures appropriate to that type of company.

That's what you're about to do with the Reasons and Limits worksheet, which I affectionately dub the R&L. It forces you to define reasons you're interested in a company and what would cause you to lose interest. The R&L worksheet is invaluable when emotions start kicking in and—surprise, surprise—the market really does begin fluctuating just like everybody said it would. It doesn't just happen to other people, it happens to you, too.

So the Stocks to Watch worksheet is your consistency. It records the same measurements for every company. You'll always look at those measurements to identify a company as either a growth or value investment. Once that's complete, you'll focus on certain measurements to select the best growth companies and the best value companies from your list.

In this section, I'll give a quick recap of discerning growth from value, then explain how to use your R&L worksheet.

Discerning Growth from Value

You should be familiar with these characterizations by now. Growth companies are those that are growing sales and earnings every year. Their stock prices are rising, their profit margins are big, and their expectations are high. Value companies are trading at low prices. The low prices are usually the result of tough times at the company but occasionally just because the market's a weird place. Preferably, you buy a value stock just when it has fixed its troubles and begins to profit again, or just before the market discovers its discount price.

Often, the best growth investments are smaller companies. Of particular importance in evaluating growth companies are high earnings record, high relative strength, and low price-to-sales ratios. Remember that O'Shaughnessy found price-to-sales a great measure to mix with traditional growth yardsticks because it keeps growth investors from getting too carried away with emotion and paying too much for a stock. Other growth investors, such as O'Neil, insist on ignoring measures of valuation completely.

The best value plays are usually large companies. Not always, but most of the time. Large companies don't change much and that makes them prime candidates for bargain pricing. They're not going anywhere, after all, so they have no choice but to recover from whatever trouble they're in. These are the Chevrons and Intels and Wal-Marts of the market. For such companies, traditional value measures will be your focus. Those are dividend yield, P/E, price-to-book, and price-to-sales.

It's simple to look at your Stocks to Watch worksheet and say, "Hmm, I see Chipotle Mexican Grill, Clorox, Goodyear Tire & Rubber, and Panera Bread on here. I'd call Clorox and Goodyear value investments because they're both down in price but seem to be working toward recovery. Chipotle and Panera are both growing like crazy, I guess they're growth investments." Yep, that's about as sophisticated as it gets.

Here's a cheat sheet of what measurements you should pay particular attention to for the different types of stocks:

All Stocks	Growth Stocks	Value Stocks
Net Profit Margin	Earnings	Price-to-Earnings
Debt	Relative Strength	Dividend Yield
Cash Flow	Sales	Price-to-Book
Price-to-Sales		Price-to-Cash-Flow

How to Use the Reasons and Limits Worksheet

It's time to specify exactly why you like the company you're about to invest in and what would cause you to stop liking it. I got the idea for this worksheet from Peter Lynch, who uses what he calls the two-minute drill to identify company strengths and weaknesses. You can review the drill on page 68.

The worksheet is a snap to use. Photocopy it dozens of times because you'll need a copy for each stock in your portfolio. I recommend starting a separate folder for your portfolio information. In it you'll keep statements from your broker and R&L worksheets for each company. Your worksheet is in the back of the book. I explain each section of it below.

Growth or Value

Simply circle which type of investment this is, growth or value. You'd be surprised at the number of people you just surpassed. Differentiating between growth and value investments is a major step in keeping your expectations reasonable. It also helps make decisions later when things start getting hairy.

Company Strengths

Here you write in what attracts you to this company. Does it own a patent that nobody else can touch? Is it opening 500 new stores in Japan? Perhaps it just signed service contracts with every Dow company.

Company Challenges

Write in what you perceive as the major challenges facing this company. By the way, I'm not trying to be politically correct by calling them company challenges instead of company weaknesses. Most of what faces a good company are outside pressures, things like fierce competitors, rising supply prices, and changing demographics. These are not weaknesses of the company, they're challenges for the company to meet. Hopefully, you won't be investing in companies that have excessive internal weaknesses. Your list is supposed to contain the industry-leading, best-of-breed profit machines, and companies with strength enough to recover from temporary setbacks. Thus, all namby-pamby political correctness aside, you should be dealing with companies that have challenges instead of weaknesses.

Even the best companies face hurdles in their paths. As an investor, you want to be well apprised of such hurdles so you can see if they get bigger or if the company clears them with ease.

Why to Buy

Summarize why you're buying this stock. Presumably it's because you think the strengths are powerful enough to meet the challenges. To help jog your thoughts, I've included some common buy reasons for you to circle. Also write in any special developments in the world that you think will favor the company's industry, or move the company's product, or otherwise help matters.

Occasionally, I'll write in a measurement target in this section of the R&L worksheet. For instance, if I really like everything about a company but I think it's selling a bit too high at the moment, I'll pencil in all the things I like and conclude this section with a price target. If the stock hits that price, I buy. You can do this with ratios, too, which can trigger a buy if either of the numbers involved moves in the right direction. If you want to invest in a company when it reaches a price-to-sales ratio of 1.5 instead of its current 2.0, a falling price or rising sales will bring you closer to your target.

Why to Sell

Certainly just as important as why you buy a stock is what will cause you to sell it. I've included some common sell reasons for you to circle. The most common reason to sell is that the stock reaches a price target. If you bought Mister Magazine at $8.50, you might decide in advance that it has potential to double. So you write in a sell point at $17. When it reaches $17, you might reevaluate. Perhaps it's an even better company than when you bought it or maybe it really has run its course. If in doubt, you could sell half your position and wait to see what happens.

Be careful of getting too price-centric in this section. Remember that all stock measurements, not just price, change constantly. If the price doubles but the earnings triple, why in the world would you sell? I like to set sell points with ratios, just as I discussed in the why to buy section. Instead of saying you'll sell Mister Magazine at $17, say you'll sell it when the price-to-sales reaches twice its current measure or its P/E exceeds its growth rate. Combining factors provides you with a more complete

picture. Remember, it's your company. You should know everything that's going on, not just the price of the stock.

Sometimes you'll want to write in reasons to sell that aren't
measured on your worksheet. For example, the failure of medical
upstarts to get approval for a new drug or piece of equipment, the
departure of key management, and a sudden spate of lawsuits.
You won't always know about these possibilities, but sometimes
you'll read about them in your research. Pencil them in. It's good
to be aware of such potholes in the path.

Buy Your Stocks

The big moment has arrived. First you learned to walk, then
drink from a cup with no safety top, then speak in complete sentences, then drive a car, then ditch classes, and now you're about
to buy your first shares of stock. Darwin would be so proud
of you. In our Realm of Riches metaphor, you're about to hire
your first henchman to send out of the fortress with money from
your coffers to find fabulous wealth. You've researched his cre-
dentials and are convinced of his merits. All that remains is
funding him and sending him on his way.

Choose a Market or Limit Order

You read about different types of stock orders on page 158. A
market order buys at the current price and a limit order buys at a
price you specify. I almost always use limit orders because stocks
bounce around so much that I can take advantage of that
volatility to save a few bucks. In many cases, you can figure out
the exact price at which you want to buy, place a good-till-
cancelled limit order, and forget about it. If and when the stock
hits your target, your broker will buy it and send you a statement. This technique has worked wonders for me. Limit orders
are a great way to circumvent your emotions.

Rather than get taken by the market's gyrations, you simply
decide in a calm state of mind the price at which you want to
invest. Then you instruct your discount broker to buy a certain
number of shares at that price. If the stock never reaches the
price, you don't buy. There are plenty of opportunities out there.

If one gets away, move on to the next one. A rather terse woman I know has this to say about life: "Never chase a man, a bus, or a stock. There will be another one along in five minutes." The man I don't know about, and bus availability varies from city to city, but she's right about the stock. There are so many good ones day after day that there's never a reason to be upset about an opportunity lost. It's better to lose an opportunity than to lose money. So decide in advance what price is attractive to you and spell it out on a limit order.

Should you ever use market orders? Sure. There are times when you stumble on something that you think is so hot that it's not coming down for years. A limit order specifying a lower price than the current one might miss the chance to buy this rising star. I would caution you about jumping on something instantaneously, though. I've discovered over the years that what's a good buy today is usually still a good buy next week. The market moves around, but not as quickly as you might think. Emotions move a lot faster than the market. They also move faster than intelligent thoughts. So give the rational part of your brain time to catch up to the excited, frothy part. Never forget the power of clear thinking, predetermined prices, and the limit order.

Make Gradual Purchases

From your reading of the master investors and the history of the stock market, you've come to see the importance of reacting intelligently to the market's moves. That means buying more of a good company on sale, and more of a good company that's on a roll. But you can never be absolutely sure you're investing in a company whose stock will perform well. That being the case, I recommend putting only a portion of your money into a stock you're considering. If it drops in price, you can reassess whether to move your remaining money in at the discount or steer clear until you're truly convinced that the stock has bottomed out and is on its way back up. O'Neil would shudder at that advice, but it has been a splendid technique for Bill Miller, and for me. Good stocks drop in price frequently and speculation bids the price of crummy stocks high on a regular basis. Because it's an unreasonable force causing such gyrations, you can't think your way through it. You can improve your odds by investing in the best companies out there, but you can't know what the unreasonable market will do.

So if Mister Magazine has you salivating over its awesome future and you've got $50,000 to invest, put only $25,000 in at first. If you have $5,000 to invest, put only $2,500 in at first. If you happened to time it just wrong and the stock drops 50 percent with no significant changes in the company's fundamentals, move your remaining capital in. Instead of just recouping your losses when the stock recovers, you'll double the value of your second purchase.

Putting the same amount of money into a declining stock as you invested in your initial position is called doubling down if it's your second purchase. I do it all the time in *The Kelly Letter*. I believed in some stocks enough to triple and even quadruple down, and it paid off.

On October 5, 2005, I bought footwear maker Deckers Outdoor stock at $23. It owns the brands Simple, Teva, and UGG. It looked undervalued to me, and I thought it would benefit from a strong holiday season. The stock dropped 26 percent after I bought, but I didn't see any changes in the reason behind my investing in the first place. It looked to be just a better bargain. I doubled down at $17 on October 28, putting my average price paid at $19.55. On December 8, only six weeks after my second buy, the stock closed at $30 for a 53 percent gain. Two years later, it topped $160 for a 718 percent gain. Demonstrating yet again the value of stop-loss orders, it fell 77 percent to less than $38 in March 2009 and offered up a wonderful buying opportunity. In 2010, the stock split 3-for-1 and reached almost $119 in October 2011. At that high it had gained 1,725 percent from my split-adjusted average price paid in 2005 of $6.52, and 859 percent from its split-adjusted March 2009 low of $12.41.

Now, to review something you learned earlier, it's important that you believe in a stock's strength before you invest more money when the price is falling. I believed in Deckers Outdoor. It's a solid, well-managed company. I knew it would recover. The same can't be said for all stocks. Doubling and tripling down on a falling stock backed by a crummy company on the far-fetched hope that it will make a comeback is called putting good money after bad. Don't do it or you'll find yourself in a value trap. Investing in a falling price requires thorough research and a strong belief in the positive signs you turn up in that research.

Buy That Baby!

You've decided on your killer stock—certainly a hundred-bagger by anyone's reckoning—and you've chosen either a market or limit order. All that remains is contacting your broker. Because you've read this book and perused all the fine brokerage choices in Chapter 5, you probably have an account with a discount broker. Good for you!

Contact your broker by phone, online, or in person. Specify your order and sit back a second. Soak it up. You've just become a business owner if you placed a market order, and you'll soon be a business owner if you placed a limit order and the stock hits your price. The next time you're in Omaha, stop by Berkshire Hathaway to swap a few stories with Warren Buffett. The two of you are in the same business now.

When the Market's Up, Down, and All Around

Flip forward a few pages in your calendar from that halcyon day of your first stock purchase. "Egads," you're thinking, "how did I ever let that Kelly guy talk me into this mess? My hundredbagger is a minus twobagger and the headlines are getting worse." Yes, friend, I know what it's like to see that happen. The Realm of Riches is a tough place. A lot of your henchmen will never come back. Those that do come back to the fortress are sometimes pretty beaten up.

Since this book's first edition in 1998, the U.S. has experienced two monster bear markets: the dot-com crash of 2000–2002 and the subprime mortgage crash of 2007–2009.

The bull market of 1990–2000 took the S&P 500 and the NASDAQ Composite up 426 percent and 1,490 percent, respectively. The dot-com crash that followed took them down 50 percent and 78 percent. The bull market of 2002–2007 took them up

105 percent and 158 percent. The subprime crash that followed took them down 58 percent and 56 percent.

Fortunes come, fortunes go.

That's what we'll explore in this section: volatility. The market rises and falls, your stocks rise and fall, your emotions rise and fall. It's time to get a handle on all of this.

Be Skeptical of Gurus

Beware the so-called market gurus. They're also called experts, analysts, forecasters, pundits, and soothsayers. By and large they don't know anything more than what you know. Always keep in mind the market forecast of J.P. Morgan, "It will fluctuate." That's about all there is to say and it's never wrong.

I'm keenly aware of the fallibility of gurus because I am one. My forecasts have been tracked by an independent auditor called CXO Advisory Group. The best I've ever achieved is an accuracy of 76 percent, but it eroded over time to my current 60 percent. In almost any other field, a score of 60 percent is terrible. In school, that's a D- in danger of becoming an F. In stock forecasting, however, it ranks in the top 5 percent—and that should tell you something.

In the ongoing CXO study, which in early 2012 had tracked 6,000 forecasts from more than 60 gurus, the average accuracy score is just 48 percent. A coin flip has performed better than the typical market expert. The gurus tracked in the CXO study include famous people who have their own TV and radio programs. Most of the other gurus regularly join those and other programs to dispense views on the market. Whenever you see or hear one of us, remember these five syllables: 48 percent. Those are the odds of the expert being right.

Which may explain why experts dither so much. Over the years, I've collected my favorite noncommittal market forecasts, including these gems:

"Markets may shift focus, but will it be toward upbeat evidence about growth or a more negative look at twin deficits?"

"The longer-term picture still lacks clarity."

"The NYSE and NASDAQ are saying different things."

"Stocks have more upside ahead. . . . A move up here pro-

bably won't have the power to move us out of the down channel
we're caught in."

"Traders must be decisive, but willing to change."

"The S&P is gearing up for an October showdown. Either the
downside of this year's trading range will be broken in October,
or the upside will be."

"I think it's going to be on balance a quiet week. But there is
the distinct possibility, depending on who says what, that it could
become a much more volatile and exciting week than anybody
predicted."

"Will the market consolidate or will it shake out—or will it do
something worse?"

"Based on trends in corporate operating earnings and the
inflation rate, one of our models projects a retreat for the S&P
500 index over the next four quarters, and the other projects an
advance."

"S&P thinks the key to whether the latest weakness turns into
a correction is simply the action of the major indexes."

"The odds are 50/50 as to which way the index will swing
next."

"If the pattern and tone of the market are indeed changing, it
would be positive for the short term."

"There is an opening for either the bulls or the bears to take
over."

Find more at www.jasonkelly.com/resources.

Now, to be fair, analyzing stocks and predicting the future
course of the market is exceedingly difficult. I like what Michael
Santoli wrote in the October 30, 2006, issue of *Barron's*: "The job
of a stock analyst isn't an easy one, never mind the facile ridicule
thrown at Wall Street's stock pickers. To confirm this, just let
your view on a couple of dozen stocks be a matter of public
record for a few months."

That's a good point, one to keep in mind when you hear
somebody using hindsight to criticize a public market voice. It's
easy to be right looking back. Try looking forward.

Nonetheless and with due respect to those trying to provide
market guidance, it's important to remember that nobody,
absolutely nobody knows for certain what the market will do.
You need to remain skeptical and make your own decision.

You Knew This Was Coming, So Why Worry?

From all your reading to this point, you should be well aware that the market fluctuates. Always, friend. It won't stop because your money has finally arrived there. In fact, from your vantage point it will start fluctuating more than ever. It won't of course, but somehow the numbers mean more when it's your money on the line.

Money you invest in stocks shouldn't be money you need for groceries next month or college tuition next year. If you define your goals clearly and invest by those goals, you're geared for whatever comes. The money you do need for groceries is safely deposited in a bank account. The money you do need for college tuition next year might also be in a bank account or perhaps a conservative mutual fund. The money you have earmarked for long-term goals such as retirement or a new home can withstand any short-term market fluctuations, and even profit from them if you react intelligently.

Review Your Reasons and Limits

At some point, you're going to want to reevaluate your holdings. The hardest time to do so is when something serious has happened. That's not always a huge drop, by the way. Sometimes it's a huge gain where your stock has pushed beyond your wildest dreams. It's hard to make rational decisions when you've tripled your money and want so badly to believe it'll happen several more times. It might, but as with every "might" statement, it might not.

That's where your R&L worksheet comes into play. You filled it out before you even owned the stock, so your emotions were at a fairly even level. You were interested in the stock, but you just completed thorough research and were making an objective decision. Now, you own the thing and it's up, down, and all around. What should you do?

Look at that R&L sheet. Pull out your portfolio folder and scrutinize your every scribble about this company. Did it reach your price target, or one of your ratio targets? If so, has anything changed to give you reason to believe the stock still has legs?

If the stock is falling, has anything fundamental changed at the company? It might be the same company you first invested in, but at a cheaper price. Sometimes that's all it means when a stock drops in price. After checking over your R&L, it's time to follow the advice in the next section.

Reverse Your Emotions

Remember that Benjamin Graham said nobody ever knows what the market will do, but we can react intelligently to what it does do. Aha. If you're at a point where your investment has fallen into the mud, the words of Ben Graham are much more than ink on paper. They're good guidance indeed. So are those powerful words of Warren Buffett that I mentioned in Chapter 2: "Be fearful when others are greedy, and be greedy when others are fearful."

In "Where the Masters Agree" (page 95), I summarize the major agreements of our six master investors. They say to buy more of what's working and to take advantage of price dips. That seems to mean that no matter what's happening, you should buy more. That's only true regarding price. Are you starting to get the picture? Price is not really the most important thing. It seems to be and it's eventually the bottom line, but in the course of stock ownership there are a lot of things more important. For instance, Warren Buffett keeps an eye on profit margins and return on equity. If the company remains strong and keeps doing everything right, the market will eventually catch on and the price will rise.

You're beginning to see why it's so important to thoroughly research your companies and to have a clear understanding on your R&L sheet for why you invested. Such grounding enables you to see if the company is still as good, perhaps better, or worse than when you first invested.

If the price is rising and everything you liked about the company still persists, such as strong earnings, high margins, low debt, and steady cash flow, then you might decide to invest more. The market is finally recognizing what a great company you're invested in and people are beginning to buy. As William O'Neil recommends, you should move more money into that winner. Business owners buy more of what's working.

If the price is falling and everything you liked about the company still persists, you just stumbled onto a great company at a bargain price. It's incidental that you happen to already own shares purchased at a higher price; you still have the chance to buy a great company on sale. Think of owning property. Say you bought a 10-acre parcel at $5,000 an acre because of its beautiful meadows and stream. You build your dream home there. Two years later, another 10-acre parcel adjacent to yours goes on sale for only $2,000 an acre. It contains different parts of the same beautiful meadows and a different section of the same stream. Would you react by selling the land and home you already own? Of course not! It's still beautiful. Instead, you'd snap up the adjacent lot because of its identical beauty and the fact that it's selling at 60 percent less than what you paid for the first parcel. That, in a sense, is exactly how you should react when a perfectly solid company drops in price without any fundamental reason for doing so.

React intelligently to the market. It freaks out from time to time, but you don't need to. If the market goes haywire and drops the price of your company for no reason, smile coolly and buy more shares. If the market goes haywire and drives the price of your stock through the clouds, buy more on the way up.

If you bought quality companies after conducting thorough research, you have little to fear in the markets. You will prosper over time. The market will rise and fall, gurus will claim to know where it's going and when, you will hold winners and losers, and by reacting intelligently to all this cacophony your profits will mount. Your henchmen will return to the fortress with more money than you spent to fund their excursions into the Realm of Riches.

After the Crash of 2008

The rest of this section appears exactly as I wrote it in March 2009. I'll show what happened afterward in the next section.

From what you've read so far, what do you think was the right reaction, in March 2009, to a stock market down 57 percent in the previous 17 months? If you said "buy," you may have a future in this business.

As I write these words in March 2009, I have no idea what

path the market will take. You will read these words after that, however, and can look back. Pull up a chart of the S&P 500 and see what happened.

I'm sure it fluctuated. It probably went up from its March lows, probably moved sideways for a while, and probably dipped back down at some point. Eventually, though, you know where it had to go? Higher. The market moves higher over time, and it does best from extreme lows where valuations are cheap. It doesn't matter if March 2009 was the low of the bear. The point is that a stock environment down that far presents a time to get in, not out.

In post-crash markets like we saw in 2009, I suggest using indexes to overcome your fear. It's natural after the world almost ends to swear off stocks forever. It's at just such times, however, that they make the most sense. There was a lot *less* risk after the 57 percent drop in March 2009 than there was before it in October 2007, but in which month do you think investors showed more confidence? October 2007, of course.

The leveraged strategies you read about in Chapter 4 would have been good ways to benefit from the recovery. If they had been too volatile for your tastes, a good compromise would have been plain vanilla index investments such as SPY for the S&P 500, MDY for the S&P MidCap 400, and IJR for the S&P SmallCap 600.

With a foothold in an index, you could have next used some of your capital to grab quality companies from the bargain bin. The measurements you read about earlier in the book turned up some incredible sales in the post-crash market. If some of them were stocks you already owned, the deep discounts still presented a chance to put more money to work. Doing so would have lowered your average cost and brought you back to break-even more quickly in the recovery.

Stocks occasionally go down, and sometimes a lot. Investing when they do is a good way to get ahead.

The Recovery

We know now as I write in February 2012 what happened after the situation described in the previous section: an extraordinary recovery ensued. Buying almost anything in March 2009 proved to be very profitable. From their lows that month to their 2011 or early 2012 highs, here's how a sampling of investments performed: +1,050 percent, Ford; +495 percent, Maximum Midcap via MVV (page 140); +377 percent, Advanced Micro Devices; and +105 percent, the S&P 500.

You could have played "Pin the Tail on the Ticker" to choose stocks at random that March, and shot the lights out. Let's try it. Blindfold, spin, pin . . . Dick's Sporting Goods, up 346 percent. Blindfold, spin, pin . . . Wolverine Worldwide, maker of Chaco and Hush Puppies and Merrell brand footwear, up 244 percent. Blindfold, spin, pin . . . Innospec, a specialty chemical company, up 1,365 percent. See what I mean?

In retrospect, it looks easy. At the time, it took great courage to buy stocks in the face of some of the worst financial news we've ever seen. From my book *Stock Market Contest*, the story of 10 top business students who competed to turn $100,000 into the most money they could through stock investing from 1995 to 2009, comes the following overview of the way smart investors needed to ignore popular sentiment to buy stocks in March 2009:

> When it became clear on the contest website during the second week after the bottom that all contestants were fully long and racing each other higher with the market, the site began short-handing weeks lapsed since the Friday, March 6 close as BW1, BW2, and so on to mean bull-market week one, bull-market week two, and further. The site ran a report every Saturday showing the bull-market week ended the day before, the performance of the S&P 500 from its March 6 closing low to the end of the current week, and contestant rankings. The contest made no bones about its disdain for popular market forecasters who warned investors away from easy profits. It was a bull market, period, every contestant knew it, and anybody offering exhaustive reasons for not owning stocks simply announced to the world that they knew nothing about the business of making money in the market.

That business is sometimes as simple as buying great bargains when they appear, regardless of the headlines that introduce them. This book has taught you how to identify strong stocks, a good way to watch them, and how to know when they've gone on sale. You have everything you need to be a smart person who buys at market bottoms, not a person who sells.

Sell Your Stocks

Alas, the day will come when it's time to part with your stocks. You'll receive reports from the Realm of Riches about the successes and hardships of your henchmen. One day, you'll decide to give one or two or all of them a rest. You'll sell your shares and place your profits in a tidy money market account until the next happy henchmen come along.

Let's go over a few rules of selling, shall we?

Ignore Rumors and Popular Opinion

I've probably convinced you of the need to rely on yourself for decisions. Just in case, however, I must reiterate this point. Only you fully understand your goals and tolerance for risk. Nobody cares more about your money than you do. You worked hard for it, you searched the world for companies that meet your requirements, you became an owner of those companies, and you should count on yourself alone for the right time to sell.

It's not always easy to stand alone. Imagine this common scenario. You go to work on an average day and there's big news in the hallway. Mark McGillicuddy in the mail room read that one of your companies missed earnings last night. "Well," McGillicuddy sighs, "it's a worn story in American business. You just can't stay at the top of your game forever. I sold all my shares this morning. You guys better do the same." The hallway clears and you hear keyboards come to life in every direction. There you stand, a previously proud owner of 3,000 shares of the stock. What do you do?

The first thing to do is confirm that McGillicuddy read the darned news accurately. You'd be surprised at the number of times this simple step takes care of the problem. In many cases, the information is nothing more than a rumor. In this case, it turns out McGillicuddy is correct. The company really did miss earnings.

Rather than join your colleagues in rushing to sell, you'd be a much happier investor if you paused to think back to that trusty R&L sheet. Can you remember what you wrote on it? Probably not. In that case, forget about it. That's right, just forget about the current situation all day long. When you go home that night, pull out your R&L and move on to the next section.

Rely on Your Reasons and Limits

With your R&L sheet in hand, you can arrive at a prudent decision. The McGillicuddys of the world won't be offering their opinions, and you'll be oblivious to the impression that everybody but you has flown the coop just before the fox breaks in. And it is just an impression, by the way. Rarely is the entire world following the path of your acquaintances, but because your acquaintances form your little view of the world, it often appears that way. React intelligently, friend. Read that R&L sheet.

What did you write in the "Why to Sell" section? If you researched thoroughly, you should be aware of most of the challenges and risks facing the company. If it was making an acquisition, maybe you wrote that if the price paid exceeds a certain amount, you would sell because that's too much to pay. If the company was breaking into a new market, maybe you wrote that you need to see a certain sales level by a certain date or you would consider selling because the payoff would not be commensurate with the expense. There's no end to what you might have written as possible reasons to sell, and you'll be surprised at how rarely you're surprised by events. Good research pays.

Maybe in this case the company missed earnings because of a onetime acquisition that used a lot of cash for the quarter. You were aware of the acquisition and think it will create higher earnings in the future. If so and the market misinterpreted the meaning of the miss—which happens all the time—there's little reason to sell.

If instead you wrote on your R&L, "Slowing sales momentum? Watch earnings trend closely," then the miss might be precisely the signal you need to get out of the stock. I doubt you would need McGillicuddy to tell you about the company's earnings report, though. You'd tell him!

So, there will be times when you pull out your handy R&L

and notice that one of your sell conditions has been met, or one of the company's key strengths has genuinely disappeared. If nothing has come along to balance out the change, sell. The R&L sheet is there to help you navigate difficult decisions in times of emotion. If it says your stock is fine, hold or buy more. If it says your stock is in trouble, sell. Unless new information changes the conclusions you drew on the R&L sheet, pay attention to what you wrote there.

Review Your Stocks to Watch

Your R&L sheet is a good way to keep an eye on individual stocks. But it's all relative. Don't forget your Stocks to Watch worksheet. It's called that for a reason, namely, because you should watch those stocks.

Before you decide to sell, glance over your stocks to watch. Is there a better company available than the one you're currently holding? Often, that quick question combined with clear signals from your R&L sheet make the decision a breeze. For instance, if two of your R&L sheet's reasons to sell have been met in a company you own *and* a company you've been wanting to own just dropped 20 percent in price, sell the current holding and buy the stock to watch at a 20 percent discount. Sometimes one of your stocks to watch will present such an outstanding opportunity that you'll sell the least attractive of your current holdings just to take advantage of the opportunity. That's a legitimate strategy. Just as the companies on your Stocks to Watch worksheet must withstand constant comparison to new stocks you encounter, so must your portfolio withstand constant comparison to your stocks to watch. It's survival of the fittest, and you want to own the best companies around.

Even if there are no outstanding candidates on your Stocks to Watch worksheet, you might still elect to sell one of your current holdings. Often, a money market account is a better place than certain stocks. But don't forget to take a look at your stocks to watch. Your decision might be made for you.

Remember you're managing a portfolio. Don't make decisions in a vacuum. After you sell something, you have to put the proceeds somewhere. Sell one of your current holdings if a better one

surfaces from your Stocks to Watch worksheet. Sell one of them
if it reaches a predetermined reason to sell. If a stock drops dramatically but it is still a quality company, buy more shares or at
least hold on to what you already own. That is, unless one of your
stocks to watch is more deserving. In that case, move the money
to the more deserving stock. See how it works? Everything is
interwoven.

Watch the Chart

Don't forget the charting techniques you learned in Chapter 4.
One reason to sell could be that SMA, MACD, and RSI say you
should. Those three are helpful advisors and worth an occasional
confab.

The best case is that you bought a stock at or near the beginning of an uptrend and are now keeping an eye out for the end of
the run. You would watch for it to start falling back to its simple
moving average, then below, then fail to move back above; for
MACD to show a trend change with a downward crossover; for
RSI to signal oversold conditions.

Ideally, the chart will hint before the news that trouble is brew-
ing. If the chart says to sell and then the news confirms by providing one of your R&L reasons to sell, you'll have good reason to
press the button.

Choose an Order Type

You can place a market order to sell at the current price, a
limit order to sell at a price you specify, or a trailing stop to limit
how much you're willing to lose from the high. I sometimes try
to anticipate the end of a move higher by placing a limit order to
sell at a price near where I think the stock will turn south. Even if
the market has driven your stock to tremendous highs, a limit
order placed just a little higher usually comes through. If I think
the stock is already out of steam, I'll usually go with a tight
trailing stop, such as 5 percent. I almost never use market orders,
but many people do. Sometimes the stock backs off for a few
days, but it usually creeps up to my target.

If you don't care about a few extra bucks and you just want to

sell right away, place a market order. The beauty of an immediate sell is that you're not in limbo for an unspecified time
period, unsure whether you've got cash in your account or will
be waiting three months.

Make Gradual Sells

As with buying stock, I prefer to make gradual sells. The
market is just as unpredictable when it comes to choosing the
right time to sell as it is when choosing the right time to buy.
If you move everything out because you're afraid of losing it
all, how will you feel if the stock recovers to your buy price and
then pushes beyond? If the stock doubles after you buy it and
you sell everything, how will you feel when it becomes one of the
legendary tenbaggers? In both cases, you'll feel terrible. I know
because I've been there. Gradual moves into and out of positions
take some of the pressure off because everything doesn't need to
happen just right for you to make money. Things can be a little
fuzzy on the buy and sell. As long as you're making gradual
moves, you'll be fine.

Combining gradual moves with limit orders is a good way to
reduce investment stress. Let's say you own 2,000 shares of Mister
Magazine. A couple of the R&L sheet's reasons to sell have been
met, but the company has just opened a new distribution center
that you didn't know about when you first bought. You're not
sure if that's enough reason to hold on. The stock is trading for
$30—three times what you paid for it. You feel comfortable
taking that kind of profit now, but something about that new distribution center has you thinking the stock will go higher still.

If you sell nothing, you're going to blow a vessel if Mister
Magazine drops to $12 a share. If you sell everything, you're
going to blow a vessel if it rises to $40 a share, or even $32. So
you compromise on both the sell price and the amount you're
going to sell. You place a good-till-cancelled limit order to sell
1,000 shares at $32. Then you go hiking, or golfing, or swim-
ming, or take a run. Three weeks later while you're not paying
any attention, Mister Magazine hits $32 and your broker sells
1,000 shares. Now, no matter where the stock goes you can take
comfort in your interim profits. If the price begins to drop, you
will consider selling the remaining shares or buying additional

shares with the money you just made at $32. If the price rises, you'll make even more profit on your remaining shares.

Sell That Baby!

You've decided to sell some of your stock. Simply pick up the phone, get online, or walk into your local brokerage branch and place the order. A market order will go through that day with a confirmation statement sent to you immediately. A limit order will go through whenever your target price is reached. You'll know about it when the confirmation statement shows up.

Track Your Performance

The Lord or Lady of every fortress expects reports from the field now and then. Most of your reports will be in the form of periodic market updates, stock quotes, and statements from your discount broker. In addition to those, however, you must track your performance to find areas to improve.

I like to keep tabs on every stock to watch. If you followed the advice from earlier in this chapter, that means you'll follow around 20 stocks. You can do that in your spare time. I track their prices from the time they make it on my Stocks to Watch worksheet until they exit. If they exit at the same time I sell them from my portfolio, I still track their prices for another month or two just to see what happened to their prices after I sold.

From there, you're going to look at two components of your performance. The first is your overall portfolio profits, losses, and commissions. This is what most people mean when they talk about performance, how they did last year, who's a great investor, and so on. But you're also going to drill a little further into your own performance by looking at "the fearsome foursome," a term describing four prices you'll use to gauge your individual stock record.

Portfolio Profits, Losses, and Commissions

Either in a software package or on a ledger page, record what you paid for your stocks and mutual funds, what you sold them for, and the commissions you paid. Periodically, say once a year, note how the market performed as judged by the S&P 500 and compare your own performance. Are you ahead or behind?

Statements from your broker will help a lot in your calculations—especially if you consolidate all your investments at the same place, such as Fidelity or TD Ameritrade. You can see on your statement how much you started the year with and how much you ended with. Such numbers take everything into account including commissions. If you didn't invest any additional money, simply compare your ending balance with your beginning balance to see how your investments performed. If you did invest additional money, refer to your notebook or financial software for specific buy and sell prices.

I use Yahoo! Finance. It's easy and free to track my portfolio, and I can check it from any Internet-connected computer in the world. Entering new transactions is simple. Then, I just look over my transaction history at tax time for any sales to hide, er, report.

The Fearsome Foursome

Once you've got a handle on your overall performance, it's time to investigate how you've done on individual investments. For that I use an easy but strict system called the fearsome foursome. It's fearsome because it shows in no uncertain terms how you did.

It's a foursome because you write down four prices for every stock you've bought and sold: the price three months before you bought, your buy price, your sell price, and the price three months after you sold. The only one of these numbers that might not be handy is the price three months before you bought. If the stock was on your watch list and you tracked the price before you bought, then you'll have the number. Otherwise, you can call a broker to find out what it traded at, find its price history on the Internet, or consult a stock database on your computer. Here's what you might write down for Mister Magazine:

Mister Magazine Fearsome Foursome	
Three months before buy	$4
Buy price	$6
Sell price	$18
Three months after sell	$36

Well, you did the right thing on the buy. The stock had been rising and you picked it up before it rose too much. The sell, on the other hand, could use a little work. The stock doubled in the three months after you sold. Of course, gradual moves would have eased some of your pain since you might have left a little money in the stock to grab some of that journey to $36. But it's spilt milk now and the best thing is to learn from it and move on. With this system, you're looking to improve your buy points and your sell points.

Good Buy Points

Did you buy at a good time? For most growth investors, the price three months before the buy should be lower than the buy price. Growth investors expect to buy stocks on an upward move. For value investors, the price three months before the buy should be higher than the buy price. Value investors expect to buy when stocks go on sale.

Try to get your buy prices right around the price of three months before. That means you'll be buying growth at the beginning of its rise or value right near its bottom. It's rare to catch a stock at the absolute beginning of an upward launch or the bottom of a fall, but that's the ideal you're striving toward.

Good Sell Points

Did you sell at a good time? Everybody wants the same thing here: to sell at the top just before the stock dives to lower prices. Growth and value investors can agree on this point.

As with buying at the exact perfect moment, it's nearly impossible to sell at a stock's peak. They almost always bounce a little bit higher. By pushing your tracking period out to three months, you avoid killing yourself over a small uptick the day after you sell. Such occurrences are up to the whims of the universe and no amount of studying prices will improve your odds of timing it right. That's why we look at three-month time frames. You're interested in trends, not flukes.

How to Improve Your Buy and Sell Points

I suppose the ultimate coup would be a sky-high price three months before the buy, a dirt cheap buy price, a sky-high sell price, and a dirt cheap price three months after the sell. You could brag about that one for years. To luxuriate in this dream a moment, pretend this is your very own fearsome foursome:

In Your Dreams Fearsome Foursome	
Three months before buy	$150
Buy price	$5
Sell price	$200
Three months after sell	$10

The Realm of Riches would whisper your name for eons: $10,000 became $400,000. You would have tricked them all by getting in just after a tremendous tumble and getting out just before another tremendous tumble. You could move that $400,000 back in at $10 for another recovery if your R&L sheet indicated that the company was still sound.

Now, back to reality. If there are drastic differences between the four numbers, go back to the file you keep on the company and see if you can re-create your thoughts at the buy and sell. Your folder should have clipped news stories, company mailings, updated research reports, and so on. Did you buy at the right time based on something you read? Perhaps you sold too soon because of a short-term scare that turned out fine in the end.

Look over several fearsome foursomes for different stocks you've owned. Watch for trends. If you're consistently buying or selling too soon or too late, make note of that tendency. In many cases, your fearsome foursome numbers will tell entirely different stories for different stocks. If so, there's little you can do because all the evidence is contradictory and that's par for this course. Every adage learned on the last stock will be reversed on the next.

That's why you're searching for trends. I discovered after looking over several fearsome foursome results from my own portfolio that I tend to sell too soon. My buy tendencies are too mixed to draw conclusions, but my sells almost invariably come early. That means I should trust my judgment in finding good companies and start letting them do their thing. I need to constantly read what Warren Buffett says: Time helps wonderful businesses but destroys mediocre ones. Since discovering this tendency of mine to sell too soon, I've improved my returns by a few percentage points on the stocks I've sold. Others I haven't sold at all and am still holding on as they continue mounting profits. Before the fearsome foursome analysis, I probably would have sold after they doubled.

You can do the same. Whenever you sell a stock, wait three months and write up the fearsome foursome results. Put the results in the company's folder when you're finished. Take a hard look at the numbers, compare them to your other results, and look for trends.

8
Bon Voyage

That's about it. This book should help you get going safely with a stock investment program. I like the fact that you won't run out and throw all your extra dollars into a $2 start-up because of something you read here. On the other hand, you won't languish for the next 20 years in Treasury bills for safety's sake. It's not safe to underperform inflation.

For you this book's strategy is going to be a lifelong friend. It's not the only way to make money in stocks, but it's a way that anybody can follow from their kitchen table. You start gradually, perhaps in a bank savings account, then work your way into a discount broker's core money market account, then into permanent portfolios, and finally into the open market itself, where you'll search for stocks that measure up to high standards. It's a safe, profitable progression that allows you to learn more as you go without paying big money to do so.

Now, I have to warn you that reading about succeeding in the market and actually succeeding in the market are two different things. This book demystifies stock jargon and simplifies the process of finding companies, analyzing them, and managing a portfolio of stocks for profit. However, in doing so it runs the risk of making stock investing look easy. I've received many notes from readers over the years that begin, "I'm so excited to get started. What do you think I should buy first?"

Notes like that have made me realize that this book does not show what the market can do to your life. Knowing the mechanics of placing a buy order is not the same as knowing how you're going to feel when it fills and you own shares of a stock, and then it falls 10 percent. Time to sell or time to buy more? You've explored the topic in this book and you know what to do in theory, but does that make it easy? No. There will be no Warren Buffett, Peter Lynch, or Bill Miller by your side.

You will have to make the call in real life with real money—and that's nerve-racking.

To help you better understand the emotional toll of the market, I wrote a companion to this book called *Stock Market Contest*. It tells the story of 10 top business students chosen from more than 900 applicants to compete in a 15-year contest to turn $100,000 into the most money they could by trading stocks. The 15-year period, 1995–2009, was one of the most tempestuous in stock market history—as you saw in many examples in this book. It included the dot-com rocket and crash, irrational exuberance, the subprime housing bubble and collapse, 9/11, giant swings in oil prices, the disappearance of "must own" companies, and unprecedented monetary stimulus. Into the eye of the turbulence marched the 10 highly skilled contestants, clawing out paths that reveal what stocks do to a person's life, how they get into our heads and don't get out, how they interfere with vacations and romantic dinners and intrude in other ways beyond the scope of this book.

There's more than money at risk in stocks. The emotions of the market are real, and they're relentless. Before you begin your investing journey, take the knowledge you gained in this book and see it at work in *Stock Market Contest*. It will show you what it's really like to get into stocks, and what happens when they get into you. To learn more, visit www.jasonkelly.com/books.

I'd like to part with some wise words from Charlie Michaels, my friend who is president of Sierra Global Management, LLC, a hedge fund company in New York City. Charlie helped me on the first edition of this book, and has provided a closing comment for each subsequent edition. He's worth reading. In 2008, when the S&P 500 lost 38 percent and the FT Europe index lost 41 percent, Charlie's Sierra Europe Fund *gained* 8 percent. At the end of 2011, the MSCI Europe Total Return index posted a cumulative 20 percent loss over the previous five years while Sierra Europe gained almost 34 percent. Charlie's approach to investing not only outperforms the market, it does so with less volatility. His annual returns in those five years ranged from roughly -3 percent to 15 percent while MSCI Europe ranged from -39 percent to 28 percent.

For the 2004 edition, he wrote, "Being patient and buying great business franchises with strong growing cash flows will never make one poor. Almost every other form of investing has the potential to destroy one's capital."

For the 2008 edition, he warned that "the stock market is being propped up by the hundreds of billions of dollars allocated to private equity funds. These funds are levering their capital and buying companies right and left. There will come a time when these funds become net sellers (the day of reckoning) as their performance fees are based on realized profits. Hence the private equity prop will turn into a private equity drag. It is vital to invest in high quality companies with strong business franchises that are most likely to be resilient in the next bear market. Timing is important in most walks of life including investing. Hence, I advocate being patient and buying shares when valuations are attractive (low/cheap) so that when price earnings multiples compress, the securities you have bought will be resilient and hold up."

For the 2010 edition, he wrote, "In 2007, which turned out to be the peak of the last bull market, I warned that the stock market was being propped up by private equity funds levering their capital. The key to my warning was leverage. Today, we are witnessing the most profound delevering of the world's financial markets, the unwinding of speculation that built up over past decades. We can clearly see the value of investing in 'high quality companies with strong business franchises' because they have indeed been resilient. The good news is that this very deep bear market is bringing the prices of stocks to the most attractive levels in our lifetime. For the foreseeable future, investors don't need to worry about investing in overvalued stocks. This is likely a great time to slowly build a portfolio of great businesses using the principles described in previous chapters of this book."

He was right. As you read in "The Recovery" on page 258, the S&P 500 more than doubled from its March 2009 low, when Charlie wrote the above paragraph. For this edition, he writes:

Unfortunately, many if not most investors held high cash balances earning nearly nothing since 2009. Why? Perhaps the investment public looked backward to the poor returns from the years 2000 to 2009, or they listened to the press and "talking heads" who spend too much time on the latest story du jour versus discussing the long-term merits of holding stocks. So how can investors capitalize on the fact that, over the long run, stocks are among the best instruments to own and have outperformed bonds and cash handsomely?

A good starting point is to carefully reread parts of this book, especially Chapter 2 about the masters. I admire all those described in it. As far as my investing style is concerned, I am a Phil Fisher/Peter Lynch growth stock investor combined with a deep appreciation for buying Warren Buffett quality companies with strong business franchises. I believe the best investments are in quality growth companies that can defend their sales momentum and defend their profitability armed with competitive advantages and strong management. I call such companies, "value-creating strong business franchises." However, as in most aspects of life and investing, there are many great ways to travel. And fortunately there are many useful investing "rules" highlighted in this book.

I would like to leave you with one thought. While the S&P has doubled off of its March 2009 lows, it is only roughly at the same level that it traded at in the year 1999! During the '90s, the S&P quadrupled. Looking forward over the next decade, which is vital in this business, the S&P will likely rise significantly—much more than bonds. The key to capitalizing on this likely trend will be to buy and hold "quality stocks" on reasonable valuations. Importantly, you will need to hold on and not panic during temporary periods when the market is weak and the press and "talking heads" highlight how negative the stock market's prospects are. Think long term, and remember from Chapter 1: "Stocks have been the best investments over time!" [my exclamation mark.]

Like our master investors in Chapter 2, Charlie looks for quality companies at good prices. Now you know how to find them, and you know how to determine if their current price is a bargain. All the research you need is sitting somewhere at this very moment, just waiting for you to take a look.

Drop me a line sometime. You can email me directly, jason@jasonkelly.com, or stop by www.jasonkelly.com to send me a message from there.

Reasons and Limits Worksheet

This investment is: GROWTH   VALUE   **Company Name:**   **Ticker:**

Company Strengths

Why to Buy

Industry Leader   Growing Industry   Strong Sales Growth   Decreasing Debt   Increasing Margins   Superior Technology   New Management

Company Challenges

Why to Sell

Reached Price Target   Increased Competition   Declining Industry   Weakening Sales   Increasing Debt   Decreasing Margins   Legal Trouble

Stocks to Watch Worksheet

Company Name, Symbol, and Phone	Current Price	52 wk Hi/Lo	Market Cap	Day Dol Volume	Sales	Net Prof Margin	Cash	Total Debt	Sales /Share	Cash Fl /Share	Earning /Share	Div Yield	ROE	Insider buy/own	Stock buyback
[Example] Excellent Co. EXCO, 800-YOU-GAIN	10	12/5	$2 Bil	$1 Mil	$8 Bil	25% ◆	$10 Mil	$12 Mil	$85 ◆	$4 ◆	$4 ◆	4.2% ◆◆	20%	10/30%	Yes
[Example] Terrible Co. TECO, 800-YOU-LOSE	150	150/142	$200 Bil	$85 Mil	$18 Bil	2% ◆	$100 Mil	$60 Bil	$4 ◆	-$1.25 ◆	$3 ◆	NA ◆◆	5%	0/3%	No
1)		/				◆▶			◆▶	◆▶	◆▶	◆◆		/	
2)		/				◆▶			◆▶	◆▶	◆▶	◆◆		/	
3)		/				◆▶			◆▶	◆▶	◆▶	◆◆		/	
4)		/				◆▶			◆▶	◆▶	◆▶	◆◆		/	
5)		/				◆▶			◆▶	◆▶	◆▶	◆◆		/	
6)		/				◆▶			◆▶	◆▶	◆▶	◆◆		/	
7)		/				◆▶			◆▶	◆▶	◆▶	◆◆		/	
8)		/				◆▶			◆▶	◆▶	◆▶	◆◆		/	
9)		/				◆▶			◆▶	◆▶	◆▶	◆◆		/	
10)		/				◆▶			◆▶	◆▶	◆▶	◆◆		/	

Company Name (cont. from above)	EPS Rank	RPS Rank	5 yr Sales	5 yr Price	Proj Sales	Proj Hi/Lo	Time Safe	STARS Fair Val	Current P/E	Average P/E	P/S	P/B	Current Ratio	P/CF	SMA MACD RSI
[Example] Excellent Co.	95	95	20%	900%	25%	100/60	1/2	5/5	10	12	0.5	1	10	3	strong up
[Example] Terrible Co.	25	25	2%	50%	3%	165/135	5/5	1/1	35	25	8	6	0.5	35	down
1)						~	~	~							
2)						~	~	~							
3)						~	~	~							
4)						~	~	~							
5)						~	~	~							
6)						~	~	~							
7)						~	~	~							
8)						~	~	~							
9)						~	~	~							
10)						~	~	~							

Appendix 1:
What You Should Retain from This Book

The principles of successful investing never change because the goal is always to put your money in the strongest companies. They eventually win. This book shows how to find them and that's why its advice works no matter what the market is doing. Here are the key points of that advice:

Chapter 1:
Speak the Language of Stocks

✔ You need to invest in stocks because they allow you to own successful companies. When a company prospers, so do its owners. Stocks have been the best investments over time.

✔ You make money from stocks through capital appreciation and dividends. Capital appreciation is the profit you keep after you buy a stock and sell it at a higher price. Dividends are shares in the company's earnings, which are paid to stock owners every quarter. Not all companies pay dividends.

✔ You should use a discount broker and make your own investment decisions. The advice you get from full-service brokers is worthless anyway, and they charge too much.

✔ The most basic division among investors is growth and value. Growth investors look for successful companies that are increasing earnings every quarter, and they are willing to pay a price for them. Value investors look for companies that are overlooked or struggling, and they want to buy their stocks on sale. These disciplines coexist nicely. For example, you don't want to pay too much for a growth stock, nor do you want to buy a value stock that has no prospect for future growth.

Chapter 2:
How the Masters Tells Us to Invest

✔ Your investment strategy should be clearly defined and measurable. This way, you avoid the common emotional traps of greed and fear. Rely on a set of specific criteria to find superior companies.

✔ Look for strong income statements and balance sheets. Every company is helped by high profit margins, lots of cash, and little or no debt.

✔ Look for insider stock ownership and company buybacks. Peter Lynch writes, "There's only one reason that insiders buy: They think the stock price is undervalued and will eventually go up."

✔ Conduct thorough research. Warren Buffett says to exercise the same scrutiny when buying shares in a company as you'd exercise when buying the company itself. Never act on tips. Always know what you're buying and precisely the reasons why.

✔ Know the reasons that led you to buy a stock, so you know the right time to sell. In two minutes, you should be able to run down the factors that made the stock attractive to you.

✔ Buy at a price below the company's potential. If it's an expensive growth stock, it had better be growing quickly enough to justify the high price. If it's a depressed value stock, it had better have some good plans for recovery and be executing them well.

✔ Buy more of what's working. If you identified a good company and its stock is rising, consider buying more if the company's strengths have improved as the price rose.

✔ Take advantage of price dips. If you own a quality company and its stock drops, verify that it remains a quality company. If it's just as strong as when you first invested, consider buying more at the discount price. As Bill Miller says, "Lowest average cost wins."

Chapter 3:
How History Tells Us to Invest

✔ The best all-purpose value measure is EBITDA/EV, which can be approximated with free-cash-flow/market-cap.

✔ EBITDA is earnings *before* interest, taxes, depreciation, and amortization. Those four expense categories can be misleading when trying to compare companies because finance and accounting methods vary widely from place to place. EBITDA strips out those vagaries to look at raw profitability.

✔ EV stands for enterprise value, which is market capitalization minus cash, but plus debt, minority interest, and preferred shares. It's more accurate than market cap alone because somebody buying the whole company would need to pay its enterprise value, not its market cap.

✔ Dividend yield is a great value measure against large, market-leading companies.

✔ The best growth measure is relative strength. Specifically:

- *Six-month relative strength is best.*

- *Do not buy relative strength winners in moments of extreme optimism.*

- *Relative strength losers perform well only during initial recoveries from extreme pessimism at bear market bottoms.*

✔ The winning value recipe finds the cheapest stocks by these measures:

- *Price-to-book*

- *Price-to-cash-flow*

- *Price-to-earnings*
- *Price-to-sales*
- *EBITDA/EV*
- *Shareholder yield*

✔ Shareholder yield combines the value of dividends with the benefits of company share buybacks. Companies with high shareholder yields outperform their low-yield peers.

✔ The simplest and one of the best value strategies is to buy large, market-leading companies with high dividend yields. A perfect example of this approach is the Dow dividend strategies explained in Chapter 4.

✔ Using six-month relative price strength to find upward movers among the cheapest stocks flagged by the winning value recipe produces the best risk-adjusted return. This super strategy combining value and growth is called Trending Value.

✔ It's essential to stick with proven strategies through complete market cycles, even though they'll underperform in some years.

Chapter 4:
Permanent Portfolios

✔ Value averaging is an automated way to buy low and sell high as the market fluctuates. You'll use it with the IJR small-company ETF to achieve steady 3 percent quarterly growth in your core portfolio.

✔ The Dow Jones Industrial Average comprises 30 of the most powerful companies in America including American Express, Coca-Cola, Disney, Exxon Mobil, Home Depot, Intel, IBM, McDonald's, Microsoft, and Wal-Mart. The defining characteristic of all 30 Dow companies is their gargantuan size. To give one example, Wal-Mart had sales of $450 billion in 2011, a full 3 percent of America's gross national product.

✔ Because Dow companies are so dominant, they usually rebound from depressed stock prices. That makes the Dow a prime hunting ground for bargain stocks. As you learned in Chapter 3, the best way to find undervalued large companies is by looking at their dividend yields.

✔ There are three Dow dividend strategies that have beaten the overall Dow's performance over time. Each involves screening out the 10 highest yielding of the 30 Dow stocks, then investing in all 10 of them, the five highest yielding of the 10, or the five lowest priced of the 10. The best of the bunch, the Dow Low 5, averaged 9.6 percent per year in the 40 years ended December 31, 2011. During that same time, the overall Dow averaged just 6.8 percent.

✔ As good as the Dow dividend strategies are, there's a simple way to beat all of them: leverage the entire Dow to twice its return. Leveraging is a technique that magnifies an investment's return with borrowed money and options. Both gains and losses are magnified.

✔ The simplest way to double the Dow is through the Pro-Funds Ultra Dow 30 mutual fund, symbol UDPIX. It returns roughly twice what the Dow returns on a daily basis.

✔ The S&P MidCap 400 index has outperformed the Dow. In the 10 years ending December 31, 2011, the Dow returned -22 percent, but the MidCap 400 returned 73 percent. Like the Dow, the MidCap 400 can be leveraged to twice its performance. This approach, what I call my Maximum Midcap strategy, has proven to be even better than doubling the Dow.

✔ The elephant in the china shop of these leveraged strategies is an extreme bear market. The magnified loss is devastating, and ruins long-term performance.

✔ Therefore, you should try to avoid the downside with timing signals created by SMA, MACD, and RSI. These three charting tools help identify price trends and will often warn you to get out of the strategies before big drops.

✔ Because the Dow and the S&P MidCap 400 are groups of stocks and not individual stocks, they eventually recoup losses. That provides confidence through the volatility. Extreme volatility coupled with assured recovery is a potent combination. Buying when these volatile strategies are down in price has led to tremendous gains.

Chapter 5:
Get Ready to Invest

✔ Choose one of the following discount brokers: E*Trade, Fidelity, Firstrade, Schwab, Scottrade, TD Ameritrade, or TradeKing. You might also consider a super discounter such as BuyandHold, ShareBuilder, or Zecco.

✔ Use limit orders to specify the price at which you want to buy and sell stocks, along with the time frame. Use market orders to execute your buys and sells immediately. The situation and your personal preference will guide you to choose the right type of order. I almost always use limit orders because they enable me to take advantage of the market's fluctuations without getting emotionally involved.

✔ Trailing stop orders enable you to own a stock as long as its uptrend continues, then get out when it reverses. They "trail" behind the price as it rises upward but lock into place when the price begins to fall. Limit orders and trailing stops are just about the only order types I use.

Chapter 6:
Research to Riches

✔ Pay attention to your personal experience and the investment grapevine for good ideas.

✔ I provide a selection of magazines, newspapers, newsletters, and specialty publications for you to consider. The most useful are *Investor's Business Daily* with its SmartSelect stock ratings and *The Value Line Investment Survey* which prints almost everything you need to know about a stock.

✔ Contact companies themselves to request an investor packet. It should include an annual report, balance sheet, and income statement. Reading them will show you the company's health in terms of what it owns, what it owes, and how much profit it keeps.

✔ Stock screeners are helpful for running criteria filters across all stocks to find just the ones you want. You'll find good screeners at Yahoo! Finance Stock Screener, FINVIZ, and Morningstar.

✔ There's a handful of investment websites that I recommend, the most useful being Yahoo! Finance. For a convenient click list of the sites listed in this book, visit www.jasonkelly .com/resources.

Chapter 7:
This Book's Strategy

✔ Build a core portfolio with one of the permanent portfolio strategies in Chapter 4. Choose either a Dow dividend strategy, my Double the Dow strategy, or my Maximum Midcap strategy. I use Maximum Midcap because it returns the most over the long term. Both Double the Dow and Maximum Midcap are twice as volatile as the market.

✔ Fill and maintain your Stocks to Watch worksheet using the investment resources you learned about in Chapter 6. The worksheet is provided on pages 276–277.

✔ Key measurements on the worksheet are:

  • **Net profit margin.** *Should be in the top 20 percent of its* *industry and bigger is better. Found in the investor packet,* Value Line, *and on the Internet.*

- **Sales per share.** *Should be increasing over the past five years. Found in* Value Line *and on the Internet.*

- **Cash flow per share.** *Should be positive and increasing each year. Found in* Value Line *and on the Internet.*

- **Earnings per share.** *Should be positive and increasing each year. Found in* Value Line *and on the Internet.*

- **Dividend Yield.** *Should be high for large companies. Found in most newspapers,* Value Line, *and on the Internet.*

- **Return on equity.** *Should be 20 percent or higher. Found in the investor packet and on the Internet.*

- **Insider buys/ownership.** *Should be high because insiders buy their stock only when they think it will go higher. Found in* Value Line, Investor's Business Daily, *and Yahoo! Finance.*

- **Stock buyback.** *You want a company buying back its stock. Found by calling the company.*

- **EPS rank.** *Growth investors should insist on 85 or higher. Found in* Investor's Business Daily.

- **Relative price strength rank.** *Growth investors should insist on 80 or higher. Found in* Investor's Business Daily.

- **Five-year sales and earnings gain.** *Should be at least 10 percent for all companies and 15 percent for small companies. Found in* Value Line *and on the Internet.*

- **Projected sales.** *Large companies should be expected to grow at least 10 percent a year, medium companies at least 15 percent, and small companies at least 20 percent. Found in* Value Line, *many other publications, and on the Internet.*

- **Projected stock high/low.** *Bigger is better for both the high and the low. Found in* Value Line *and on the Internet.*

- **Value Line timeliness/safety.** *Timeliness should be ranked 1 or 2; the safety rank is up to your volatility preference. Found in* Value Line.

- **S&P STARS fair value.** *Both STARS and fair value should be ranked 4 or 5. Found in S&P's weekly newsletter,* The Outlook.

- **Current price-to-earnings.** *For value companies, should be equal to or below the earnings growth rate. Found in* Value Line, *most newspapers, and on the Internet.*

- **Average price-to-earnings.** *Should be higher than the current P/E. Found in* Value Line.

- **Price-to-sales.** *For all companies except utilities, smaller is better. Found in investment magazines and on the Internet.*

- **Price-to-book.** *Smaller is better. Found in* Value Line *and on the Internet.*

- **Current ratio.** *Should be at least 2. Found in* Value Line, *the investor packet, and on the Internet.*

- **Price-to-cash-flow.** *Smaller is better. Found in* Value Line *and on the Internet.*

- **SMA, MACD, and RSI.** *Should show a strong uptrend or a breakout. Found on charts, such as the ones at Yahoo! Finance and StockCharts.com.*

✔ Constantly track and prune your Stocks to Watch worksheet. Compare the companies on it to competitors, maintain an information folder on each company, and keep all of your information current. In this way, you are prepared for opportunities that the market serves up by lowering the stock price of companies you know to be solid.

✔ Make gradual purchases. Everybody is wrong about a stock price now and then. Limit the damage by using only part of your money for the first buy. You can always buy more later.

✔ Avoid common emotional investment traps by filling out a Reasons and Limits worksheet, or R&L, for each of your stocks. The worksheet is provided on page 275. Circle whether the stock is growth or value, list the company's strengths and challenges, and write the reasons you're buying and what would cause you to sell.

✔ Be skeptical of so-called gurus or market experts. An ongoing study by CXO Advisory Group shows the average market expert's accuracy to be just 48 percent—less reliable than a coin flip. For a collection of noncommittal forecasts, see page 253.

✔ The market is volatile. Your money invested in stocks will fluctuate in value. Understand that before you invest so you are emotionally equipped to deal with the fluctuations.

✔ Reviewing your Reasons and Limits worksheet is a wonderful way to keep a cool head when things heat up. You wrote it when you were not under duress. Rely on those steadier times for guidance as you decide whether to sell. Your R&L will prove a more reliable investment companion than most coworkers, relatives, or analysts.

✔ Keep an eye on the chart. SMA, MACD, and RSI will often signal a changing trend. If they do so before or just as the news brings one of your R&L sheet's reasons to sell, you'll have good reason to press the button. To review the three, see pages 142–152.

✔ Make gradual sells for the same reasons you make gradual buys.

✔ Track your performance in a software package or ledger page. Use the fearsome foursome to follow four price points for each of your stock investments: the price three months before you bought, your buy price, your sell price, and the price three months after you sold. Learn from your mistakes and improve your abilities over time.

Chapter 8:
Bon Voyage

✔ This book's strategy takes you on a safe, profitable progression that allows you to learn more as you go without paying big money to do so. You start gradually, perhaps in a bank savings account, then work your way into a discount broker's core money market account, then into permanent portfolios, and finally into the open market itself, where you'll search for stocks that measure up to high standards.

✔ Read *Stock Market Contest* to feel the emotional stress of investing by following 10 excellent investors through two bull markets and two bear markets from 1995 to 2009.

✔ Follow Charlie Michaels's lead in buying high-quality companies with strong business franchises—on sale.

✔ I wish you all the best. You can email me directly, jason@jasonkelly.com, or stop by www.jasonkelly.com to send me a message from there.

Appendix 2:

A Sampling of Exchange-Traded Funds

The following are ETF trading clusters that I follow. You can get them on a printable sheet at my website, www.jasonkelly.com/resources.

U.S. LARGE-COMPANY STOCKS

DDM | 200% the Dow (2x)

DIA | Same as the Dow (1x)

DOG | Inverse of the Dow (-1x)

DXD | 200% inverse of the Dow (-2x)

SSO | 200% the S&P 500 (2x)

SPY | Same as the S&P 500 (1x)

SH | Inverse of the S&P 500 (-1x)

SDS | 200% inverse of the S&P 500 (-2x)

BGU | 300% the Russell 1000 (3x)

IWB | Same as the Russell 1000 (1x)

BGZ | 300% inverse of the Russell 1000 (-3x)

U.S. MEDIUM-COMPANY STOCKS

MVV | 200% the S&P MidCap 400 (2x)

MDY | Same as the S&P MidCap 400 (1x)

MYY | Inverse of the S&P MidCap 400 (-1x)

MZZ | 200% inverse of the S&P MidCap 400 (-2x)

U.S. SMALL-COMPANY STOCKS

TNA | 300% the Russell 2000 (3x)

UWM | 200% the Russell 2000 (2x)

IWM | Same as the Russell 2000 (1x)

RWM | Inverse of the Russell 2000 (-1x)

TWM | 200% inverse of the Russell 2000 (-2x)

TZA | 300% inverse of the Russell 2000 (-3x)

SAA | 200% the S&P SmallCap 600 (2x)

IJR | Same as the S&P SmallCap 600 (1x)

SBB | Inverse of the S&P SmallCap 600 (-1x)

SDD | 200% inverse of the S&P SmallCap 600 (-2x)

U.S. NASDAQ STOCKS

QLD | 200% the NASDAQ 100 (2x)

QQQQ | Same as the NASDAQ 100 (1x)

PSQ | Inverse of the NASDAQ 100 (-1x)

QID | 200% inverse of the NASDAQ 100 (-2x)

U.S. SECTOR STOCKS

UGE | 200% the DJ U.S. Consumer Goods (2x)

IYK | Same as the DJ U.S. Consumer Goods (1x)

SZK | 200% inverse of the DJ U.S. Consumer Goods (-2x)

UCC | 200% the DJ U.S. Consumer Services (2x)

IYC | Same as the DJ U.S. Consumer Services (1x)

SCC | 200% inverse of the DJ U.S. Consumer Services (-2x)

FAS | 300% the Russell 1000 Financial Serv. (3x)

UYG | 200% the DJ U.S. Financials (2x)

IYF | Same as the DJ U.S. Financials (1x)

SEF | Inverse of the DJ U.S. Financials (-1x)

SKF | 200% inverse of the DJ U.S. Financials (-2x)

FAZ | 300% inverse of the Russell 1000 Financial Serv. (-3x)

RXL | 200% the DJ U.S. Health Care (2x)

IYH | Same as the DJ U.S. Health Care (1x)

RXD | 200% inverse of the DJ U.S. Health Care (-2x)

UYM | 200% the DJ U.S. Materials (2x)

XLB | Same as the S&P Materials (1x)

SMN | 200% inverse of the DJ U.S. Materials (-2x)

ERX | 300% the Russell 1000 Energy (3x)

DIG | 200% the DJ U.S. Oil & Gas (2x)

IEO | Same as the DJ U.S. Oil & Gas (1x)

DDG | Inverse of the DJ U.S. Oil & Gas (-1x)

DUG | 200% inverse of the DJ U.S. Oil & Gas (-2x)

ERY | 300% inverse of the Russell 1000 Energy (-3x)

URE | 200% the DJ U.S. Real Estate (2x)

IYR | Same as the DJ U.S. Real Estate (1x)

SRS | 200% inverse of the DJ U.S. Real Estate (-2x)

USD | 200% the DJ U.S. Semiconductors (2x)

IGW | Same as the S&P N. American Semiconductors (1x)

SSG | 200% inverse of the DJ U.S. Semiconductors (-2x)

ROM | 200% the DJ U.S. Technology (2x)
IYW | Same as the DJ U.S. Technology (1x)
REW | 200% inverse of the DJ U.S. Technology (-2x)

LTL | 200% the DJ U.S. Telecom (2x)
IYZ | Same as the DJ U.S. Telecom (1x)
TLL | 200% inverse of the DJ U.S. Telecom (-2x)

UPW | 200% the DJ U.S. Utilities (2x)
IDU | Same as the DJ U.S. Utilities (1x)
SDP | 200% inverse of the DJ U.S. Utilities (-2x)

INTERNATIONAL STOCKS

FXI | Same as the FTSE/Xinhua China 25 (1x)
FXP | 200% inverse of the FTSE/Xinhua China 25 (-2x)

EFA | Same as the MSCI EAFE (1x)
EFZ | Inverse of the MSCI EAFE (-1x)
EFU | 200% inverse of the MSCI EAFE (-2x)

EEM | Same as the MSCI Emerging Markets (1x)
EUM | Inverse of the MSCI Emerging Markets (-1x)
EEV | 200% inverse of the MSCI Emerging Markets (-2x)

EWJ | Same as the MSCI Japan (1x)
EWV | 200% inverse of the MSCI Japan (-2x)

CURRENCY

UUP | Same as US Dollar vs. Euro, Pound, Yen, etc. (1x)
UDN | Inverse of US Dollar vs. Euro, Pound, Yen, etc. (-1x)

Appendix 3:
Value Averaging the S&P SmallCap 600

In Chapter 4, you read about using the iShares S&P SmallCap 600 ETF, symbol IJR, with value averaging. The table on the next page shows the plan used to achieve 3 percent quarterly growth from December 2005 to December 2011, a period that saw the ETF rise from $57.80 to $71.10, fall to $36.39, then rebound to $73.56.

Share quantities are rounded to the nearest whole and balances to the nearest dollar. New Cash Balance shows the plan's cash account. If a buy signal requires more cash than the balance can afford, the balance hits $0 and the plan needs a cash injection. If you don't fund it, the plan will stand pat to at least avoid the worst course of action in extreme down times, which is selling.

Notice the clear timing signals issued in the Action to Take column, and how their urgency is communicated in the Cash Flow column. When the market began its slide into December 2008 and March 2009, the plan said to buy. When the market bottomed out in those quarters, the plan said to buy big. Doing so paid off quickly. Following the plan would have put you far ahead of the people Charlie Michaels described on page 272 as holding "high cash balances earning nearly nothing since 2009."

After the initial $10,000, the plan required another $10,396 over this history to stay on track. If you'd put the whole $20,396 into IJR in December 2005 and held it, you might have panicked when it fell to $12,846 in March 2009. If you'd held it, it would have rebounded to $24,110 by December 2011. Running this plan instead grew your balance to $26,127 without the emotional risk of selling at the bottom. To see the plan in action today, visit www.jasonkelly.com/resources.

Quarter Ending	IJR Price	Shares Held	Current Value	Shares Needed for 3% Growth	Action to Take	Cash Flow	New Cash Balanace	New IJR Balanace
Dec 2005	$57.80	0	$0.00	NA	Buy 173 shrs	-$9,999	$0	$9,999
Mar 2006	$65.23	173	$11,285	158	Sell 15 shrs	+$978	$978	$10,306
Jun 2006	$62.10	158	$9,812	171	Buy 13 shrs	-$807	$171	$10,619
Sep 2006	$61.29	171	$10,481	178	Buy 7 shrs	-$429	$0	$10,910
Dec 2006	$65.99	178	$11,746	170	Sell 8 shrs	+$528	$528	$11,218
Mar 2007	$67.91	170	$11,545	170	Hold	$0	$528	$11,545
Jun 2007	$71.10	170	$12,087	167	Sell 3 shrs	+$213	$741	$11,874
Sep 2007	$69.75	167	$11,648	175	Buy 8 shrs	-$558	$183	$12,206
Dec 2007	$65.02	175	$11,379	193	Buy 18 shrs	-$1,170	$0	$12,549
Mar 2008	$59.93	193	$11,566	216	Buy 23 shrs	-$1,378	$0	$12,945
Jun 2008	$60.17	216	$12,997	222	Buy 6 shrs	-$361	$0	$13,358
Sep 2008	$59.51	222	$13,211	231	Buy 9 shrs	-$536	$0	$13,747
Dec 2008	$43.97	231	$10,157	322	Buy 91 shrs	-$4,001	$0	$14,158
Mar 2009	$36.39	322	$11,718	401	Buy 79 shrs	-$2,875	$0	$14,592
Jun 2009	$44.43	401	$17,816	338	Sell 63 shrs	+$2,799	$2,799	$15,017
Sep 2009	$52.34	338	$17,691	296	Sell 42 shrs	+$2,198	$4,997	$15,493
Dec 2009	$54.72	296	$16,197	292	Sell 4 shrs	+$219	$5,216	$15,978
Mar 2010	$59.45	292	$17,359	277	Sell 15 shrs	+$892	$6,108	$16,468
Jun 2010	$54.14	277	$14,997	313	Buy 36 shrs	-$1,949	$4,159	$16,946
Sep 2010	$59.09	313	$18,495	295	Sell 18 shrs	+$1,064	$5,223	$17,432
Dec 2010	$68.47	295	$20,199	262	Sell 33 shrs	+$2,260	$7,483	$17,939
Mar 2011	$73.56	262	$19,273	251	Sell 11 shrs	+$809	$8,292	$18,464
Jun 2011	$73.32	251	$18,403	259	Buy 8 shrs	-$587	$7,705	$18,990
Sep 2011	$58.54	259	$15,162	334	Buy 75 shrs	-$4,391	$3,314	$19,552
Dec 2011	$68.30	334	$22,812	295	Sell 39 shrs	+$2,664	$5,978	$20,149

Index

Note: Page numbers in *italics* denote charts and tables.